THE DIAGNOSIS OF READING IN A SECOND OR FOREIGN LANGUAGE

The Diagnosis of Reading in a Second or Foreign Language explores the implications of language-assessment research on classroom-based assessment practices by providing an in-depth look at the little-examined field of diagnosis in second and foreign language reading. This volume examines the development of second and foreign language reading and how subsequent research findings, couched in this knowledge, can help facilitate a more-informed teaching approach in second and foreign language classrooms. By contextualizing the latest in classroom settings and presenting implications for future research in this developing area of linguistics, this book is an ideal resource for those studying and working in applied linguistics, second language acquisition, and language assessment and education.

J. Charles Alderson is Emeritus Professor of Linguistics and English Language Education at Lancaster University.

Eeva-Leena Haapakangas is Research Assistant in the DIALUKI project at the Centre for Applied Language Studies at the University of Jyväskylä.

Ari Huhta is Professor of Language Assessment at the Centre for Applied Language Studies, University of Jyväskylä.

Lea Nieminen is a Postdoctoral Researcher at the Centre for Applied Language Studies at the University of Jyväskylä.

Riikka Ullakonoja is a Postdoctoral Researcher at the Centre for Applied Language Studies at the University of Jyväskylä.

NEW PERSPECTIVES ON LANGUAGE ASSESSMENT

Series Editors: Antony John Kunnan,
California State University, Los Angeles, USA, and
James E. Purpura, Teachers College, Columbia University, USA.

Headed by two of its leading scholars, this exciting new series captures the burgeoning field of language assessment by offering comprehensive and state-of-the-art coverage of its contemporary questions, pressing issues, and technical advances. It is the only active series of its kind on the market, and includes volumes on basic and advanced topics in language assessment, public policy and language assessment, and the interfaces of language assessment with other disciplines in applied linguistics. Each text presents key theoretical approaches and research findings, along with concrete practical implications and suggestions for readers conducting their own research or developmental studies.

The Diagnosis of Reading in a Second or Foreign Language
*J. Charles Alderson, Eeva-Leena Haapakangas, Ari Huhta,
Lea Nieminen, and Riikka Ullakonoja*

THE DIAGNOSIS OF READING IN A SECOND OR FOREIGN LANGUAGE

J. Charles Alderson,
Eeva-Leena Haapakangas, Ari Huhta,
Lea Nieminen, and Riikka Ullakonoja

Routledge
Taylor & Francis Group

NEW YORK AND LONDON

First published 2015
by Routledge
711 Third Avenue, New York, NY 10017

and by Routledge
2 Park Square, Milton Park, Abingdon, Oxon, OX14 4RN

Routledge is an imprint of the Taylor & Francis Group, an informa business

Library of Congress Cataloging-in-Publication Data

The diagnosis of reading in a second or foreign language / J. Charles
   Alderson [and four others].
      pages cm. — (New perspectives on language assessment series)
   Includes bibliographical references and index.
   1. Second language acquisition.   2. Reading.   3. Language and
languages—Ability testing.   4. Language and languages—Study and
teaching. I. Alderson, J. Charles.
   P118.2.D53 2014
   418.0071—dc23
   2014010603

ISBN: 978-0-415-66289-5 (hbk)
ISBN: 978-0-415-66290-1 (pbk)
ISBN: 978-0-203-07183-0 (ebk)

Typeset in Bembo
by Apex CoVantage, LLC

MIX
Paper from
responsible sources
FSC   FSC® C013056
www.fsc.org

Printed and bound in Great Britain by
TJ International Ltd, Padstow, Cornwall

We dedicate this book to the memory of Professor Kari Sajavaara (1938–2006), who was instrumental in establishing applied linguistics as a field of study in Finland and who was the first coordinator of the project that developed DIALANG.

CONTENTS

SERIES PREFACE

Language assessment or testing started in the late 19th century with assessments in foreign languages (French, German, and Spanish mainly) in the U.S. and English as a second language at Oxford and Cambridge Universities in the U.K and language assessments in France (*le baccalauréat*) and Germany (the *Abitur*). But most scholars consider the birth of modern language testing as a field of study to be the year 1961 with the publications of Robert Lado's book *Language Testing* and John Carroll's chapter *Fundamental Considerations in Language Testing,* and the earliest efforts to organize one of the world's influential tests—what is known today as the *Test of English as a Foreign Language* or *iBT (internet-Based TOEFL)*. In the last 50 years, the field has developed into an interdisciplinary enterprise in part influenced by disciplines such as applied linguistics, language teaching, educational and psychological measurement, and more recently sociology and ethics and in part by carving out its unique identity through the development of its own theories and practices.

This series will capture this burgeoning field by offering a cogent and comprehensive state-of-the-art coverage in the following areas:

1. The use of quantitative and qualitative research methods for conducting validation research on various aspects of the assessment process (e.g., the use of multivariate methods for test validation, the use of conversational analysis for speaking assessment);
2. The development and use of language assessments to understand and promote learning and performance in diverse contexts such as classrooms or computer-mediated learning spaces (e.g., diagnostic assessment, placement assessment, learning-oriented assessment, young learners assessment; scenario-based assessment, task-based assessment);

3. The new areas of language assessment that are becoming critical to the field such as pragmatics, the use of corpora, translation, intercultural communication (for example, in contexts such as assessing aviation specialists, court interpreters and translators);
4. The modern use of technology in the construction and use of computer-delivered and computer-adaptive tests (e.g., speech recognition and automated scoring of speaking or writing; learner engagement and agency in computer-delivered assessments);
5. The development of language assessments for immigration, citizenship and asylum contexts;

The primary purpose of this series is to provide theory, research, and practice-informed academic texts for addressing some of the contemporary questions, issues, and concerns in the field that involve the use of assessment. The scope of the series is designed intentionally to be broad enough to include books that discuss methods for carrying out language assessment research as well as newer uses of language assessments and technologies in the field of applied linguistics.

This series will be of interest to students of language assessment in undergraduate, graduate and doctoral programs, faculty in applied linguistics, as well as officers in education, government, and military departments involved in language assessment. Researchers in other fields of applied linguistics (e.g., discourse analysis, L1 literacy, SLA, second and foreign language pedagogy and communications) and psychology, education, measurement, assessment, and research methods will also find the series valuable.

The series will experiment with different formats and will include authored and edited books featuring a particular area of interest (e.g., evaluating language assessments) or a single scholar's work (e.g., Lyle Bachman), interviews with language assessment experts, and debates and controversies.

Book Preface

In the current book, *The Diagnosis of Reading in a Second and Foreign Language,* Charles Alderson, Eeva-Leena Haapakangas, Ari Huhta, Lea Nieminen, and Riikka Ullakonoja address the often-neglected topic of the diagnostic assessment of reading in a second and foreign language. In problematizing what teachers ought to consider when diagnosing learners' strengths and weaknesses through tests, Alderson et al. argue that diagnostic tests need to be conceptualized and operationalized, from the onset, "as diagnostic tests", rather than "as diagnostic information" gleaned from tests that were originally designed for other purposes (e.g., achievement, placement, or proficiency).

Alderson et al. first discuss in some detail the notion of diagnosis and the research and theory associated with second and foreign language proficiency. This is followed by a discussion of how feedback from diagnosis can be used to provide meaningful information to close learning gaps. Then, drawing on the literature in language assessment, applied linguistics, reading theory, and educational psychology, they provide a thorough and insightful analysis of the reading construct followed by concrete examples of diagnostic tests. They then then turn to a state-of-the-art discussion of some of the critical components of diagnostic assessment, namely, the linguistic, cognitive and motivational bases of reading in a second and foreign language. These considerations are then examined in how they apply diagnostic assessment to classroom contexts. Alderson et al. end the discussion on diagnostic assessment by proposing a model of how these components fit together to provide a coherent framework to drive diagnostic assessment. They also have suggestions for how further research on the topic might be conceptualized and implemented. This volume makes a major contribution to the field of language assessment, not only in problematizing the topic, but also in examining how research and theory inform the conceptualization and implementation of diagnostic assessment for classroom and large-scale assessments in both second and foreign language contexts.

Antony John Kunnan and James E. Purpura
Bologna, Italy

ACKNOWLEDGMENTS

The idea for this book arose during our work on the project *DIALUKI—Diagnosing reading and writing in a second or foreign language* in 2010–2013. We had been interested in the fuzzy notion of diagnostic testing since the late 1990s, when some of us were involved in designing DIALANG, the first large-scale assessment system that aimed to diagnose learners' foreign-language skills.

One of the main lessons we learned during the development of DIALANG was how little anybody, ourselves included, knew about diagnosing second or foreign language (SFL) proficiency and its development. Clearly, much more work was needed and, indeed, the past decade has seen the emergence of diagnostic testing and assessment as an important field that intersects language testing and second language acquisition research as well as several other areas of applied linguistics. Other fields such as psychology, educational research, and first-language acquisition research, to name just a few, have also significantly contributed to SFL diagnostic testing, as will become clear to readers as they work their way through the book. It therefore seemed that the time might now be ripe for taking stock of where we are in diagnosing second or foreign language proficiency and its development.

Since language proficiency is such a broad phenomenon, we decided to focus on only one skill and chose SFL reading because it is an area in which diagnosis is much less researched than are writing and speaking, and because it was one of the two foci of the DIALUKI project.

Because diagnostic assessment cuts across several disciplines and fields of study, no one person (or even a group of researchers) could have accomplished the synthesis of information presented here, let alone carried out the research on reading in an SFL that forms the background to the book. We are therefore greatly indebted to a large number of people and institutions for their contribution.

The launch of the New Perspectives on Language Assessment series by Routledge provided us with an excellent venue for publishing this book. We would like to express our sincere gratitude to the series editors Antony Kunnan and James Purpura, to Leah Babb-Rosenfeld from the Routledge editorial team, as well as to the anonymous reviewers, for all their feedback and constructive criticism during the different stages of preparing the manuscript for publication.

The four-year DIALUKI project increased our understanding of SFL diagnosis significantly and without it the present book would not have been possible. Therefore, all those who contributed to the project deserve our warmest thanks. The following DIALUKI Advisory Board members generously shared their expertise with us throughout the project: Riikka Alanen, Kate Cain, John H.A.L. de Jong, Kenneth Eklund, John Field, Scott Jarvis, Judit Kormos, Paavo Leppänen, Heikki Lyytinen, Maisa Martin, Tarja Nikula, Ulla Richardson, and Sauli Takala. We are also grateful to the following individuals for their professional advice at specific points of the project: Mikko Aro, Gareth McCray, Karen Dunn, Esther Geva, Janina Iwaniec, Eunice Jang, Eun Hee Jeon, Glyn Jones, Vesa Rantanen, John Read, Norbert Schmitt, Alistair van Moere, Åsa Wengelin, and Ying Zheng.

Due to the extensive nature of the DIALUKI project, we depended on the contribution of a considerable number of students, teachers and other professionals who worked as research assistants, data collectors, data coders, raters, pilot test informants, computer specialists, and reviewers when the data collection instruments were designed and the data were collected, coded, rated, and analyzed. We would like to express our heartfelt gratitude to the following individuals without whom the project would not have been possible: Mari Aro, Dmitry Chernikov, Mia Halonen, Iina Herrala, Tuija Hirvelä, Reija Hirvonen, Riku Huhta, Satu Huumarkangas, Marita Härmälä, Katja Jääskeläinen, Maija Kaibijainen, Paula Kalaja, Asta Karjalainen, Kati Karvonen, Päivi Kokkonen, Pauliina Kylä-Utsuri-Ripatti, Liisa Lahtinen, Sinikka Lampinen, Maija Lappalainen, Pirjo Lehtonen, Sini Lemmetty, Dmitri Leontjev, Anna-Sisko Liimatainen, Alexei Lobski, Helena Mackay, Ari Maijanen, Laura McCambridge, Katja Mäntylä, Reeta Neittaanmäki, Jiri Nieminen, Annastiina Norppa, Marta Pejda, Riitta Pennala, Piia Porvali, Hanna Punkkinen, Marja Pylkäs, Maria Ruohotie-Lyhty, Tatjana Rynkänen, Viola de Silva, Sari Sulkunen, Veera Tomperi, Riikka Toivanen, Henna Tossavainen, Natalia Turunen, Paula Tyni, Jaana Vilkman, and Eeva-Liisa Väisänen.

A number of students have either completed or are in the progress of completing their bachelor's, master's, or doctoral theses based on the data gathered in our project. Some of them also participated in the data collection or in other project activities. We acknowledge their contribution with gratitude: Jaana Alila, Saara Kallioinen, Sanna Kyyhkynen, Meija Meuronen, Sanna Olkkonen, Matti

Parkkinen, Johanna Pensas, Irina Rautio, Lotta Saariaho, Inka Sopanen, Emma Takkinen, and Annemari Välipakka.

The biggest contribution to the DIALUKI study was made by the students and teachers who participated in it. Without them there would have been no study. All together, 1,015 students and almost as many parents contributed their answers to a range of different tasks, tests, and questionnaires. Thirty-eight language teachers agreed to be interviewed, and numerous teachers and rectors helped us organize the study in a total of 123 schools throughout Finland in the following municipalities: Espoo, Hamina, Hankasalmi, Helsinki, Hyvinkää, Iisalmi, Imatra, Joensuu, Jyväskylä, Järvenpää, Kerava, Keuruu, Kitee, Kotka, Kouvola, Kuopio, Lahti, Lappeenranta, Laukaa, Lieksa, Loviisa, Muurame, Mäntsälä, Naantali, Nokia, Oulu, Petäjävesi, Raahe, Raisio, Saarijärvi, Savonlinna, Taipalsaari, Tampere, Tohmajärvi, Turku, Uurainen, Vantaa, and Varkaus.

Our final thanks go to various organizations, which in their different ways contributed to the study and enabled it to take place. The following organizations assisted the DIALUKI project by making data collection instruments (e.g., published tests) and foreign-language textbooks available to the project: IEA (PIRLS), Kustannusosakeyhtiö Otava, OECD (PISA), Opetushallitus, Sanoma Pro Oy, Tammi, WSOY. We owe a special thanks to Pearson Language Tests for making several of their operational English reading and writing tasks available to the project and to the Jyväskylä Longitudinal Study of Dyslexia, which provided us with the Finnish-language versions of a range of psycholinguistic measures used in the study.

The authors and publisher wish to thank the following who have kindly given permission for the use of copyright material:

> Cambridge University Press for the book *Reading in a Second Language: Moving from Theory to Practice,* by William Grabe, Cambridge: Cambridge University Press, 2009, pp. 29, 40–41, and 44–45.
> Hong Kong Journal of Applied Linguistics for the article *Diagnostic Testing of Hong Kong Tertiary Students' English Language Proficiency: The Development and Validation of DELTA,* by Urmston, Raquel, and Tsang, *Hong Kong Journal of Applied Linguistics, 14*(2), 2013, pp. 63, 66, 67, and 77–78.

The DIALUKI study would not have been possible without the financial support of the Academy of Finland, the University of Jyväskylä, the UK Economic and Social Research Council (ESRC), the Leverhulme Trust, and Pearson Language Tests. The University of Jyväskylä also generously made space available for us in the Konnevesi research station where the authors retreated on three occasions to work on the manuscript of this book. More inspiring and peaceful surroundings for focusing on writing are hard to imagine.

1

DIAGNOSING READING IN A SECOND OR FOREIGN LANGUAGE

An Overview

Diagnosis can be defined as the "investigation or analysis of the cause or nature of a condition, situation, or problem" (Diagnosis, 2013). Although arguably most commonly associated with medicine, illness, and disease, diagnosis is used in many fields to identify cause and effect relationships, the cause of symptoms, or the solution to problems. In education, diagnosis is often seen as the task of classroom teachers, whose responsibility is to help their learners by constantly observing them, encouraging their efforts to learn, and identifying any obstacles to their progress. In language teaching and learning, diagnosis is sometimes called "the interface between learning and assessment" (Alderson, 2005). It should be mentioned at this point that diagnosis in the classroom is often indistinguishable from formative assessment, particularly if it is based on such informal methods as observing classroom activities and analyzing learners' homework. We will discuss the similarities and differences between diagnostic and formative assessment in more detail later in this chapter.

Yet, curiously, in the field of second or foreign language (SFL) education, there is very little discussion of diagnosis, of what it is, who does it, how it is done, and with what results. Until recently, there was virtually no research into how, what, and why SFL teachers diagnosed their learners' problems, the 'nature and causes' of their strengths and weaknesses. Certainly, in the literature on language assessment, there are many references to diagnostic testing, alongside proficiency, achievement, aptitude, and placement testing, but, again until recently, very few tests were available that were labeled 'diagnostic.' Some authors (e.g., Bachman, 1990) argued that the results of almost any language test could be used for diagnostic purposes, but authors rarely showed how this might be possible and what the results might be, nor were classroom language teachers given much advice on how to diagnose in class, or what tests to use to diagnose their learners' problems.

Given the supposed centrality of diagnosis to teaching and learning, why is this? Why is the diagnostic testing of SFL learners so underdeveloped, so under-researched, and so rarely problematized? One possible reason is the existence of a large and powerful examinations and testing industry, which, especially in second or foreign language education, has concentrated on developing proficiency tests that are used in a variety of gate-keeping functions (Bachman & Purpura, 2008). Language proficiency tests are used throughout the world to assess whether language learners have sufficient proficiency to be able to study in higher education institutions, where their native language is not the language of instruction. This is particularly the case in the proficiency of English, where millions of international students seek education in English-speaking countries and even in non-English-speaking countries where education is conducted in English rather than in the national language(s). Proficiency tests, especially in English, are also used to control entry into many professions, into business and commerce, and as part of the process of issuing visas for immigration, for citizenship, and more. Thus, proficiency tests are very powerful instruments with very high stakes and consequences, and they have generated a lucrative test-preparation industry around the world. As a result, it is argued, other forms of testing and assessment have become much less important, known as low-stakes tests. Even in secondary education, where foreign languages are on the curriculum, most tests and assessment procedures can be argued to be low stakes, at least in comparison with school-leaving examinations, which dominate the curriculum. And so, within this examination and testing industry, there is currently little or no use of diagnostic tests, which, in any case, rarely exist.

Surely, this is an unsatisfactory state of affairs. If diagnosis is the identification of the nature and cause of problems, diagnostic language testing should be an important part of the language curriculum, or at least of teaching processes. Yet, those entering the second or foreign language education profession are rarely taught in their pre-service courses how to diagnose their learners' strengths and weaknesses in formal assessments, and although the analysis of learners' needs may be a useful step in the direction of diagnosis, it is rare that teachers learn how to use, or interpret the result of, diagnostic tests. Even in-service professional development courses for language teachers rarely deal with diagnosis, be it classroom or test based, as we shall see in Chapter Nine.

Thus, the broad aim of this book is to problematize the lack of use of diagnostic tests and to make a case for research into how SFL diagnosis might be understood and developed. We envisage progress in SFL diagnosis to require progress in the design of diagnostic tools (tests) that can, for example, complement the other sources of feedback on teaching and learning that teachers gather through formative assessment procedures. More specifically, however, this volume sets itself the task of focusing on the diagnosis of reading in a second or foreign language. One can argue that the diagnosis of problems in SFL writing or speaking is not as difficult and, indeed, is both more widespread in classroom practice and second language acquisition research. This is partly because the learners' problems in these two so-called productive skills are more obvious: they can be seen in the students' writing and heard in their oral use of the language. The so-called receptive skills are much less amenable to inspection and research because they are typically internal to the learner/reader/listener. Thus, there is a more urgent need for understanding learners' comprehension problems. In addition, the ability to read in a second or foreign language is particularly important in the modern world, where the need for literacy is so widespread and central to education, to business and commerce, to the professions, and even to leisure and pleasure.

In this book, we talk frequently about different skills; we refer to reading skills and cognitive skills, to comprehension skills and technical reading skills, or to productive and receptive skills, as in the paragraph above. What is a skill? What does it consist of? These are not simple to define. For example, reading can be considered a receptive skill consisting of sub-skills, such as reading comprehension and basic decoding skills. Thus, there seems to be a hierarchical network of skills. However, reading can also be seen as an umbrella-like macro skill, which includes several micro skills, such as understanding the gist of a text or deducing the meaning of a word from the context. Reading comprehension or decoding in turn calls on different cognitive skills. Even though such cognitive skills are required by the reading micro skills, we would not call them reading comprehension sub-skills, since they are skills that are broadly used in all kinds of activities requiring cognitive functions, not just reading. Since comprehension of written language seems to involve abilities from several areas that are not clearly in a hierarchical relation to each other, unlike reading skills and sub-skills, we simply refer to such abilities as cognitive skills.

Our Approach to Diagnosis

At this point, it is useful to clarify how our definition of diagnosis and especially diagnosis of weaknesses in learners' language or, in particular, their reading skills, relates to other, more medically oriented views. Our approach in this book, as well as in the DIALUKI research project we will refer to on occasion, is rather broad. We are interested in both the strengths and weaknesses of the language learners, although it is fair to say that the weaknesses are probably more important to focus on if we wish to assist struggling learners to improve or catch up with others. However, those who struggle and have clear weaknesses in their performance do not form a uniform group, rather the reasons for such weaknesses can be quite varied. In particular, it is important to distinguish those learners whose weaknesses are related to learning disabilities from those whose weaknesses stem from other sources, such as inadequate SFL proficiency, cognitive overload, insufficient background knowledge, deficient teaching, or lack of motivation.

The type of learning disability that concerns reading specifically is usually called *dyslexia* or *developmental dyslexia*, although dyslexia is probably just the most common form of reading disability. As will be mentioned in Chapter Two, the World Health Organization (WHO) has published *The ICD-10 Classification of Mental and Behavioural Disorders* (WHO, 1992), which is also available online. The WHO classifies 'Specific reading disorder' (code F81.0) as a sub-type of 'Specific developmental disorders of scholastic skills' (code F81), which in its turn is a sub-category of 'Disorders of psychological development.' According to the WHO, reading disability can manifest itself in a variety of ways ranging from word recognition and oral reading to reading comprehension. Thus, it is not easy to judge from reading performance if a learner has a disability or if the problem is caused by something else. In dyslexia research, the identification of dyslexic readers is not a straightforward matter but involves an analysis of learners' performance on three or four standardized measures, such as the Rapid Automatized Naming test (see the neuropsychologist's interview in Chapter Two, and Alderson, Brunfaut, & Harding, 2014).

However, although teachers interested in the diagnostic assessment of reading need to be aware of learning disabilities, it should be very clear that the diagnosis of reading disabilities is not the purview of teachers of a second or foreign language but of reading specialists. Learners whose teachers suspect that they may have learning or reading disabilities should be referred to reading specialists or to educational psychologists, as indeed the teachers whose interviews we describe in Chapters Two and Nine reported that they do. This book is not about learning or reading disabilities but about identifying problems in reading in a second or foreign language (SFL), and in particular what SFL teachers need to know and be aware of in order to diagnose their learners' strengths, and particularly weaknesses, in their reading, in order to help them to improve. This applies as much to the use of formal and informal tests as to classroom assessment procedures.

However, diagnostic SFL testing, as opposed to diagnostic assessment, is very much in its infancy at present. Many specialists in diagnosis in other fields, as we will see in Chapter Two, work with individual clients, patients, or learners who have been identified in some way as having a problem. Individual learners in a classroom or a school might be identified as having particular difficulties in learning, which could be usefully diagnosed by a teacher with specialist skills on a one-to-one basis, but a model of diagnostic language assessment of individuals by teachers in SFL educational settings may not be common or practical in many circumstances. Certainly, the diagnostic tests that claim to be diagnostic, which we describe in later chapters, represent quite different models of language diagnosis from this approach.

It is said that some practitioners of dynamic assessment, which we describe in Chapter Three, are moving away from one-to-one assessment of a student's learning potential in order to explore an interventionist approach, which can be administered to whole classes or larger groups of learners. Certainly, the SFL teacher is more likely to have to deal with the diagnosis and treatment of learners' reading problems in classroom settings, as we discuss in Chapter Nine. However, we assume that there is a role for the use of test-based diagnostic instruments as well as more informal diagnostic procedures, both in the classroom and in formal testing settings such as those in which tests like DIALANG, DELNA (Diagnostic English Language Needs Assessment), and DELTA (Diagnostic English Language Tracking Assessment), which we introduce in Chapter Three, are used. Thus, it is the belief of the authors of this volume that a general theory of language diagnosis, which, as we discuss in Chapter Two, has yet to be developed, could include such large-scale diagnostic programs as those referred to in Chapter Three. We argue that although those tests are diagnostic in a somewhat limited sense, it is possible to enhance their diagnostic qualities through research into the basis of diagnosis of the sort that is currently being conducted in the DIALUKI project, to which we refer throughout this book. That project sees diagnosis as more than 'just' a classroom assessment activity, and the development of suitable diagnostic instruments is one of the aims of current research into diagnosis.

A question that arises when discussing diagnostic testing and assessment is the extent to which diagnostic assessment in the classroom is distinguishable from formative assessment or from Assessment for Learning (AfL) (Black & Wiliam, 1998). Chapter Three discusses the potential similarities and differences between formative and diagnostic assessment, but one way in which they might eventually differ is that teachers would have access to well-designed diagnostic tools to complement the other sources of feedback on teaching and learning that they gather through practicing AfL or other forms of formative assessment. The principles for designing assessment tools that can arise from the DIALUKI project are being developed in the Finnish educational context—for Finnish, English, and Russian, which we introduce below and describe in more detail in Chapters Four, Five, Six, and Seven—but there is every hope that assessment tools based on such principles could be adapted to other educational and linguistic contexts. Indeed, the principles on which such instruments are being based may well be universally applicable.

The DIALUKI Project

The participants of the DIALUKI project represent two different linguistic conditions. The Finnish-English (FIN-ENG) group consists of three subgroups of Finnish-speaking monolingual students learning English as a foreign language at school. They all have started to learn English at the age of 9 years in the third grade in primary school. The sub-groups represent beginning (Grade 4 students), intermediate (Grade 8 students), and advanced students (GYM, second year of gymnasium, or upper secondary school) of English.

The other group, the Russian-Finnish (RUS-FIN) group, consists of two subgroups of Russian-speaking bilingual students learning Finnish as a second language in Finnish schools and in a Finnish environment. The primary school sub-group includes 169 children and the lower secondary school sub-group 70 pupils with a Russian background. In Finland pupils with immigrant backgrounds are immersed in regular classes after a year of preparatory education in a separate class where the focus is on learning Finnish (or Swedish if the school is located in a Swedish-speaking region of the country). After the preparatory year, immigrant students can have a few weekly lessons in Finnish as a second language and, in some schools, even in their first language (e.g., Russian). However, the availability and extent of preparatory education, as well as teaching of Finnish as L2 and of the immigrants' L1 vary considerably from one school and municipality to the next. In addition, immigrant students can also be given extra support by a class assistant or special education teacher, again depending on the resources and practices of the school, if they struggle to follow the Finnish (or Swedish) language instruction in the regular classes.

The learners participating in DIALUKI represent the full range of abilities at the grade levels studied, as we did not set out to study struggling language learners only. However, we can deduce from the learners' and their parents' responses to background questions that a small percentage of the participants have clear reading and/or learning problems (e.g., reported issues with learning to read in L1, reading problems in the immediate family, participation in remedial teaching). Thus, it is possible to select such at-risk learners for a more detailed examination and for comparison with their peers. Alternatively, we can identify poor readers simply by looking at their SFL reading test performance or by combining the two sources of information in the selection.

Understanding whether a learner's reading problems stem from a disability or from something else seems to be an important starting point for a diagnosis, as the most effective treatment of weaknesses of reading disability may be very different from the treatment of, say, lack of motivation or inappropriate teaching or materials. Since the main underlying reason of learning disabilities is some dysfunction in the central nervous system, and since such problems are very persistent, their treatment is likely to be very challenging (see, however, advances made in the treatment of L1 dyslexia in Finnish and English as reported in Lyytinen, Erskine, Kujala, Ojanen, & Richardson, 2009; Kyle, Kujala, Richardson, Lyytinen, & Goswami, 2013).

Difference Between Research Into Reading in L1 and SFL

In the case of L1, the child already understands and speaks the spoken language. Reading is then a question of recognizing what they already know on the page, hence the importance of decoding, of phonemic awareness, of working memory and of fluency, as we shall see especially in Chapter Six.

In the case of SFL, however, the child usually already knows how to read, but in a different script or with different grapheme to phoneme rules. The child does not, however, know the second or foreign language—written or spoken.

So the first task has to be to get to know the words and the structure, and then to apply what he or she knows about the word and its sound to the unfamiliar script or the unfamiliar sound-symbol correspondence. Hence, the importance of knowledge of the language, as well as the ability to read in one's first language. Usually, in the case of an SFL, the learners are learning to read the SFL at the same time as they are learning to speak the language. Also, after having learnt to decode the SFL, they still do not necessarily comprehend what they have read because of their limited vocabulary, grammar, and other skills. For L1 readers, comprehending reading is arguably simpler.

SFL learners probably already know what comprehension is, because they can understand written text in their own language. Thus, the learner does not need to learn that texts have meaning but rather that texts in an odd script also have meaning.

The L1 learner/reader has automatized to a large extent the sound-symbol correspondence and has fluency in linking words to meanings and to building up meanings. But in the SFL, reading is a slow process, is not automatized until much later, and exposure to print is probably much less frequent than in the L1. Therefore, automatization and fluency come later. Similarly, the role of working memory is likely to be even more important in the SFL, as words and structures are less familiar, and meanings, as well as the rules governing morphology, are likely to be less strongly embedded in memory. Thus, the demands on working memory are likely to be higher in the SFL.

In a second language, as, for example in the DIALUKI project, where the Russian children are learning to read in Finnish in Finland, the situation is likely to be different again, since exposure to spoken Finnish will likely be much greater than is the case for Finnish children learning to read English, the sound-symbol correspondence in Finnish is much more transparent than in English, and exposure to written Finnish is also likely to be greater and more easily comprehended (a) because of context (b) because of the sound-symbol rules, and (c) because school work is in Finnish. It is, however, quite likely that the Russian children's L1 does not develop in the same way as it does in children of the same age in a Russian-speaking country because of the limited exposure to the Russian language in Finland. This makes the relationship between the L1 and the SL very different from that between the L1 and the FL.

Having made, however briefly, the case for more attention to diagnosis in general, and to the diagnosis of reading in a second or foreign language in particular, the remainder of this chapter will now turn to giving a general overview of the book, summarizing the essence of each chapter and relating the chapters to each other. Emphasis is placed on the central importance of applied linguistic constructs to diagnosis, and particularly to the role that second language acquisition research can play in identifying variables that might be relevant to assessing aspects of learners' ability to read in their second or foreign language.

Chapter Two: Understanding Diagnosis

Diagnostic testing of second or foreign language ability is an undeveloped field, and we currently have no theory of how SFL diagnosis should be carried out, what principles and procedures it should follow, and how practitioners should go about doing diagnosis. However, in many other domains, such as medicine, information systems analysis, or car mechanics, there are well-established procedures and diagnostic practices. This chapter explores how diagnosis is theorized and carried out in a diverse range of professions with a view to finding commonalities, which can be applied to the context of language assessment.

We report on a series of interviews with diagnosticians in order to get to the core of what it means to make a diagnosis. Naturally, every field has its differences; the summaries of the interviews highlight these differences and draw on them to develop a set of hypothesized features and principles, if not yet a theory, of diagnosis in language assessment. One aim of the chapter is to set an agenda and a direction for how such a theory might be realized.

The interviews were conducted with 10 informants: a car mechanic, a computer systems support manager, an oncologist, a general practitioner, a nurse, a neuropsychologist, a psychologist working on dyslexia projects, a teacher of learning disabled students who is responsible for diagnosing dyslexia in English as a second language, a primary school principal and literacy subject leader, and a primary school teacher who specializes in interventions for pupils with reading difficulties.

Summaries of the interviews are presented, and a range of issues common across the different interviews is discussed and compared with what appears to be the case in the area of diagnosis in SFL assessment.

Ten themes emerged and are described and discussed in this chapter: definitions of diagnosis, treatment and action, the role of technology, knowledge and experience, training, basic principles and complexity, support for diagnosis, self-report and self-assessment, normality, and methods and guidelines.

Most fields contrast the conditions they are examining, whether that is the way the car or computer is behaving or the functioning of a heart or a mind, with the way it normally functions. Diagnosis begins with a comparison with normal behavior. But what *is* normal behavior, and what is abnormal behavior in the SFL domain? What is normal in the case of an SFL learner would appear to vary with age, first language, SFL proficiency, and cognitive, motivational and attitudinal factors, and as a result, diagnosis in terms of comparison with norms appears non-existent in SFL.

All those interviewed mentioned methods, procedures, tasks, techniques, tests, and guidelines for the identification and categorization of problems. Every field except SFL has well-established methods and guidance for diagnosis. In contrast, the average SFL reading teacher seems to lack procedures for identifying, categorizing, or treating problems.

The chapter concludes with an emphasis on the need to build a knowledge base in SFL reading, similar to that in other areas, of problems and possible solutions, of technologies of various sorts, and for specific technical knowledge and practical experience of diagnosis. Training in diagnosis is essential, as is a thorough knowledge of the basic principles of SFL learning and SFL use.

Importantly, what appears to be needed is the development of a theory, a model, or a set of principles by which SFL diagnosis might be developed. Chapter Three begins to develop such a possible framework for SFL diagnosis.

Chapter Three: Research Into the Diagnosis of Second and Foreign Language Proficiency

Whereas Chapter Two explores how diagnosis is conducted in disciplines other than second or foreign language (SFL) proficiency, Chapter Three summarizes some of the theoretical and empirical literature relevant to diagnosis in an SFL and describes a number of tests of SFL proficiency that claim to be diagnostic.

The earliest accounts of SFL diagnostic tests we have come across are by Tim Johns of Birmingham University in the UK. We examine the rationale for and content of this Diagnostic Grammar Test, first developed in 1971.

We continue with an account of the speculative but often quoted work by Spolsky (1992), who claims that diagnostic tests relate closely to the language curriculum. Interestingly, he argues that the term 'diagnostic' is unduly negative, because it frequently relates to the identification and solving of problems, whereas Spolsky (1992, p. 32) argues that this connotation does not sit well with an approach to teaching that "seeks the good rather than the bad."

We then move on to Shohamy (1992), who looks at the place of diagnosis within teaching, learning, feedback, and assessment. She develops an assessment model that aims to provide diagnostic information to those who will carry out whatever change is deemed necessary, namely by teachers.

After a brief summary of the treatment of diagnostic testing in a number of handbooks on language testing more generally, we then describe speculation by Alderson (2005) about the sort of features that diagnostic tests might usefully contain, before turning to an account of dynamic assessment. This approach to assessment, which derives from a Vygotskian notion of socio-cultural development, has recently sought to bring learners and assessors together in an attempt not only to diagnose the learner's needs, but also to guide the learner's development.

This discussion is followed by an account of attempts to retrofit a diagnostic function to proficiency tests such as the TOEFL or the MELAB. Cognitive Diagnostic Assessment (CDA) seeks to apply sophisticated statistical analysis to the results of sections of proficiency tests. CDA is basically designed to provide more detailed information about learners' performance on proficiency tests than a simple total score. Expert judgments are collected about test item content, using somewhat traditional categories of sub-skills of reading. Sophisticated statistical models are then used to identify the extent to which individual test takers show evidence of the ability to engage in such processes when reading in the second or foreign language.

The problem with such approaches is that they are based on tests which are not specifically designed to be diagnostic, nor do they necessarily engage the sorts of linguistic sub-processes posited. A common finding is, therefore, that insufficient numbers of items can be said to measure such skills for reliable diagnoses to be made.

More fruitful would be attempts to design new diagnostic tests, examples of which are next described in some detail. These diagnostic test batteries include DIALANG, DELNA, and DELTA. They attempt to diagnose learners' strengths and weaknesses in a range of skill areas and to provide feedback and advice on how the learners might best improve their skills.

Finally, we report briefly on the ongoing research project, DIALUKI, already mentioned in Chapter One, which is investigating the second or foreign language reading and writing proficiency of school-age learners of English as a foreign language, or of Finnish as a second language. The project employs a mixed methods approach and uses a wide range of potentially diagnostically useful measures of cognitive and linguistic abilities, of background factors, and of motivation.

Chapter Four: What Is Reading?

Chapter Four is in many ways the central chapter of the book, since it addresses the construct of reading in a second or foreign language, and how it has been operationalized. The constructs to be operationalized are central to any test or assessment procedure, but this is especially true of a diagnostic test and particularly a diagnostic test of reading, since reading is essentially a private process that is internal to the reader and difficult to define, describe, externalize, and observe.

In Chapter Four we seek to define the reading construct by presenting a brief but focused account of the relevant literature on reading in both L1 and the SFL. A number of recent publications in SFL reading (Alderson, 2000; Koda, 2005; Grabe, 2009) have offered useful overviews of the main recent trends in L1 reading research and theories along with their implications for the teaching and testing of SFL reading.

In this chapter we also discuss the debates in the SFL reading literature as to whether SFL reading is a reading problem or a language problem (Alderson, 1984). Empirical research on the topic suggests that SFL reading is more of a language problem than a reading problem. However, the research also shows that there is a threshold of language proficiency beyond which L1 reading can transfer to the SFL, thus to some extent compensating for gaps in SFL knowledge, and below which SFL knowledge is essential (the short-circuit hypothesis—Clarke, 1980).

Following a description and discussion of the construct of second and foreign language reading, we then describe how the SFL reading construct has been operationalized in terms of the components of reading and task demands and effects. We concentrate on describing tests of reading in an SFL that have been used in the SFL test batteries DIALANG, DELNA, and DELTA, already introduced in Chapter Three, and provide somewhat more detail about DIALUKI, since this is a comprehensive research project rather than 'simply' a test development project.

The second half of Chapter Four is devoted to illustrating how reading is tested in these four test batteries, and how reading tests have been used as the dependent variables in studies that have sought to explore the main components in, and contributors to, overall SFL reading ability. In the following three chapters we illustrate how various linguistic, cognitive, background, and motivational measures have been used as independent variables to predict overall SFL reading ability.

Chapter Five: The Linguistic Basis of Reading in a Second or Foreign Language

Chapter Five discusses the linguistic basis of reading in SFL (i.e., the role particularly of vocabulary and grammar in reading). Understanding a written text requires some knowledge of the vocabulary and structure of the language in question, but how such knowledge is related to reading and whether one of the two is more important for reading are questions explored in the chapter.

The majority of research reviewed in Chapter Four has come to the conclusion that although vocabulary knowledge seems to be more important in reading than does grammatical knowledge, there are a few exceptions to this. That said, it appears to be the case that both types of knowledge are needed in reading, as grammar is also important in reading comprehension. The role of vocabulary versus grammar knowledge may, however, depend on several factors, such as the purpose of reading, the type of text and task, or learner characteristics.

We report on results from the DIALUKI study that are relevant to the discussion about linguistic predictors of SFL reading, as this study included several different vocabulary measures ranging from general vocabulary-size tests to measures of very specific aspects of word knowledge. The results from this study concur with the results from previous research in that general vocabulary tests were found to correlate strongly with reading comprehension measures. Also, findings from DIALUKI indicate that the speed of retrieval of words from memory, as measured by tasks such as reading a list of L1 or SFL words or naming simple objects or symbols is correlated with reading comprehension in SFL. An interesting finding was the strong correlation between reading in an SFL and performance on a segmentation task in L1 or SFL in which the learner has to mark boundaries between words in a short text, where all the words are written together without empty spaces. Furthermore, the findings suggest that the particular language one tries to diagnose and the learners' L1 can influence which types of linguistic measures are most strongly related with reading performance. Possibly, the results also differ between second and foreign language contexts.

The chapter presents concrete examples of vocabulary and grammar tests that claim to be diagnostic and aim at tapping into different aspects of those areas of language. Tests presented include the *Birmingham Assessment and Diagnostic Test* (BADT), which focuses on grammar; the DIALANG and DELTA vocabulary and grammar tests; the Martinez (2011) test of multiword expressions; and Shiotsu's (2010) test of syntactic knowledge. Although some of the vocabulary and grammatical tasks used in these tests are somewhat traditional and therefore limited, there are also interesting new openings that expand the notion of linguistic knowledge by adding new dimensions to linguistic knowledge that have not been traditionally considered in testing (e.g., tests of formulaic sequences). Finally, we discuss what automated analysis of the characteristics of texts might have to offer to diagnostic testing.

Chapter Six: The Cognitive Basis of Reading in a Second or Foreign Language

The cognitive nature of L1 reading has long been investigated, as well as the influence on L1 reading ability of weaknesses found in cognitive skills. However, our focus in Chapter Six looks at what different tests measuring cognitive skills might tell us about reading in a second or foreign language.

Although there are different views of what is happening cognitively during reading, the research distinguishes two different processing levels: lower and higher levels. The lower level reading processes, such as decoding and word recognition, make it possible to convert written letters and symbols into the words of a language. Efficient use of lower level reading processes involve readers' phonological awareness, fast word retrieval skills, and working memory capacity. Poor phonological awareness has been a strong candidate for the cause of dyslexia and thus a constant target of research. It is also one of the abilities that are tested for in diagnosis of dyslexia in L1.

However, to reach the main goal of reading—transforming written text into meaning—higher level reading processes are also needed which enable reading comprehension in which readers make inferences and combine their background knowledge with what is said in the text. However, the higher level processes are not efficient if the lower level processes do not function well and do not become more or less automatic.

The second part of Chapter Six introduces different methods used to examine the cognitive skills relevant for reading. Tests of phonological awareness, decoding, word recognition, rapid naming, lexical access, and working memory are described and discussed.

The last part of Chapter Six is dedicated to DIALUKI's exploratory study of how cognitive skills that are relevant for reading function in different linguistic settings and how these skills contribute to reading comprehension if the reading language is the first, second, or a foreign language. The cognitive skills that mostly differentiate weak and strong foreign language readers are also discussed. Chapter Six does not provide ready-made cognitive tests or set standards for different linguistic conditions. Instead, its purpose is to make readers aware of those factors that are usually invisible to reading instructors or language teachers, but that are essential for reading skills in general.

Chapter Seven: The Background Factors of Reading in a Second or Foreign Language

Background factors, such as learners' individual characteristics (e.g., age, gender, socioeconomic background) and attitudes as well as motivation toward learning an SFL have often been shown to be linked with performance on L1 and SFL reading comprehension tests. In Chapter Seven we summarize research on this topic, including recent findings from the DIALUKI project.

We first discuss different background characteristics that have been found to have a relationship with reading performance in previous studies, such as in international comparative studies of educational achievement (e.g., the Programme for International Student Assessment [PISA]). These factors include learners' place of residence (country or region, urban environment or countryside), their socio-economic status (parents' wealth and education), and the characteristics of the school that they attend. What the parents do can also be important. For example, the literacy activities the parents have engaged in with their children or their attitudes towards reading can affect how well the children read.

We then discuss the theoretical background of dimensions of motivation and describe how motivation is usually studied. Language learning motivation is seen as an important factor in SFL learning in that stronger motivation toward learning the SFL leads to better results in learning the SFL. Motivation can also change over time, which makes it interesting diagnostically, as it can potentially be influenced by teachers in particular.

Finally, we report the results of the DIALUKI study, where we focused on exploring the diagnostic value of a number of learner background and motivational factors. The parents were asked to report, for example, on their education, occupation, total household income, reading difficulties, reading and writing done at home, self-assessment of the SFL (in our case English or Finnish) skills, and engagement in pre-reading activities with the child. The children were asked to report, for example, on their mother tongue, languages used at home, languages they know, latest school grades, amount of homework, amount of reading in free time, attitudes toward reading, age when they learned to read, and use of English in free time. The background questionnaires included several questions that can be considered potential indicators of problems in L1 or SFL reading, such as participation in special education and occurrence of reading difficulties in the child's family.

In the DIALUKI study, we examined the following motivational dimensions by using questionnaires: Instrumentality, Intrinsic Interest, Motivational Intensity, Parental Encouragement, Self-regulation, Anxiety, and SFL Self-Concept.

The results of our study show that the background characteristics had at best only a relatively modest relationship with SFL reading. Especially for the youngest learners, few significant correlations were found. Associations between parents' socioeconomic status, learners' language use (e.g., free-time reading), number of different languages known, and their attitude to reading and SFL reading performance were found. Interestingly for diagnostic purposes, in all the groups investigated, a single reported difficulty in SFL reading was enough to distinguish between strong and weak readers.

The results concerning the motivational dimensions show that learners' SFL self-concept, anxiety, motivational intensity, self-regulation were related, to varying degrees, depending on the group studied, to learners' SFL reading scores.

From the diagnostic point of view, family background, age, gender, and other such characteristics may be useful predictors of good versus poor achievement in some cases, but they are not factors that the teacher or the school can change, and they are therefore of somewhat limited diagnostic value, even if the school and the teachers certainly have to consider these factors, too, when deciding what may be a feasible way forward for a particular learner. Factors that relate to the learners themselves are more likely to be diagnostically useful, as they can at least potentially be modified. Examples are how often the learners use the SFL in their free time and learners' motivation to study and use the SFL.

Chapter Eight: Feedback From Tests and Assessments

Diagnosis is usually followed by feedback to the learner, and so Chapter Eight presents an overview of feedback and related research. We start by reviewing different definitions of feedback and pay special attention to what makes feedback diagnostic and how feedback from diagnostic assessments might differ from feedback from other kinds of assessments. Feedback given by the teacher on learners' errors, or error correction, is the most common form of feedback in classrooms. However, feedback need not be limited to knowledge of the SFL that is being learned, but it may also focus on metacognition and beliefs that play an important role in acquiring new knowledge. Diagnostic feedback, in particular, may also contain hints or explicit proposals about the action the learners should take to remedy the problem identified in their performance. Feedback need not be limited to external sources, either, but may be generated by the learners themselves.

Research on feedback on SFL learning reflects what happens with reference to feedback in SFL classrooms: most studies focus on what learners produce and on its correctness rather than, for example, on the learners' cognitive processing or the strategies they use for speaking, writing, and comprehending. Feedback studies focusing on comprehension are particularly rare.

The chapter discusses in some detail the recent feedback model by Hattie and Timperley (2007), which takes a broad view of feedback and spans the entire learning process from planning learning and teaching through assessment of progress to deciding on what further action the learner should take.

Feedback is useful only if it relates to the goals of learning and moves the learner towards the goal. This can happen only if the goals are known and accepted by the learners and are concrete enough to be considered achievable. Clearly defined goals are thus an essential starting point for feedback that improves learning.

To understand how and why feedback works, it is important to consider the different levels that feedback can target, namely task (product), process, self-regulation, and self-levels. It is argued that feedback needs to go beyond the task level to the process and self-regulation levels in order for it to be effective and more easily generalizable across different tasks.

We then analyze a wide range of different kinds of feedback that tests and teachers give, and we also provide examples of feedback from reading items. It would appear that most forms of commonly used feedback concern the task level only. However, DIALANG provides learners not only with task-level feedback but also feedback focusing on the processing and self-regulation levels, which we therefore describe in some detail. Research on learners' perceptions of DIALANG feedback is also reviewed.

Finally, we discuss why giving feedback on reading is rarer and more challenging than feedback on speaking and writing; this has to do with the opaque, hidden nature of comprehension as compared with language production. This has implications for the development of appropriate feedback on reading.

Chapter Nine: Diagnosis From the Perspective of the Language Classroom

We saw in Chapter Seven the importance of learner motivation. At school, motivating pupils is the teachers' job, and thus in Chapter Nine we examine how teachers describe teaching reading in SFL, and what they say about learners' motivation when learning to read in an SFL.

We first review previous research on classroom assessment and diagnosis in L1 and SFL by teachers that has been carried out within the frameworks of formative assessment and dynamic assessment. Teachers are presumed to be best placed to know what their learners' strengths and weaknesses are—diagnosing learners' problems can even be said to be the teachers' responsibility. However, there is little empirical evidence as to exactly what or how teachers actually diagnose their students' proficiency in SFL reading.

We discuss in some detail an example from the L1 reading literature (the Reading Recovery Program by Clay, 1979, 1985) of what teachers of English as a first language do and how this can help teachers help learners in reading. The implications of this for teacher-based diagnosis of SFL reading are then discussed.

In order to find out more about how language teachers go about diagnosing their students' SFL reading skills, the DIALUKI project interviewed SFL teachers about how they teach reading, and what they can tell language testers about how they identify their learners' reading problems, as well as strengths.

Based on our study and the review of other studies reported in this chapter, we summarize the main challenges that language teachers face when attempting to diagnose their learners' problems in reading in an SFL. Perhaps the main challenge for diagnostic assessment in the classroom that emerges from the studies reviewed here is teachers' limited understanding of what reading involves. Thus, knowledge about the normal development of reading both in L1 and SFL, typical problems in this development and approaches to addressing these are the main factors that influence how successful a teacher's diagnosis of learners' reading is likely to be.

However, we discuss a range of other factors that can potentially affect the quality of teachers' diagnosis of their students' reading skills. These include experience in teaching in general, the opportunity to get to know the students, the size of classes, the systematicity of recording diagnostically useful information, the use of multiple techniques and sources of information, and consulting other teachers.

We complement the discussion by describing selected techniques that, in addition to those mentioned in the reviews of research, can help teachers to gather diagnostic information from their students, such as talking about reading, reading summaries, portfolios, and self-assessment.

Finally, we revisit the notion of language teachers' diagnostic competence and argue that a key component of that competence is an ability to interpret students' foreign language growth, which was identified as a key issue in teacher diagnosis at the beginning of the chapter. Therefore, teachers should develop an understanding of what is involved in reading in both L1 and SFL. That is, they should be helped to become experts in evaluating the process of literacy development. Becoming an expert in reading in an SFL is thus a cornerstone of a teacher's diagnostic competence.

Chapter Ten: State of the Art of the Diagnosis of SFL Reading and the Challenges Ahead

Finally, Chapter Ten first summarizes the key points of the book, particularly the main ideas that appear important for improving our understanding of how SFL reading might be diagnosed. We then discuss the whole diagnostic process from the identification of a problem to feedback followed by some action or remediation, because diagnosis is only useful if something is done with the information obtained from it. The remainder of the chapter addresses a range of issues and topics that arose from the review of research presented in the book. These issues also provide directions for future research.

Underexplored areas that have potential for diagnosing SFL reading include reading strategies. Strategies for reading have been studied quite extensively in reading instruction but what is lacking is an in-depth exploration of learners' reasons for a failure or an inadequate application of these strategies. Such studies could well lead to diagnosis and treatment of problems in SFL reading. Another area that has received scant attention in diagnostically oriented SFL reading research is reading speed, although it is an obvious, although admittedly a rather general, indicator of reading problems.

A further area for future research was in fact covered to some extent in the DIALUKI project, namely the role in SFL reading of psycholinguistic skills that relate to different technical aspects of reading. Measures of these skills proved to predict a certain amount of variance in reading comprehension, thus suggesting that they have diagnostic potential. However, the fact that the psycholinguistic measures administered in the SFL were better predictors than their L1 versions raises interesting and difficult questions about the language through which different diagnostic instruments should be administered.

We discuss some of the challenges that real-world SFL teachers face in their work when they attempt to diagnose learners' reading skills and point out the potential that teaching materials, if carefully designed, could have in supporting teachers' diagnostic decisions. We also touch on the practical issue of how much evidence is needed for reliable diagnosis; the answer is likely to relate to the importance of the diagnostic decisions to be made.

One of the great promises in diagnostic testing and assessment is the introduction of information and communication technologies. We single out adaptive feedback, feedback on the reading process, and automated analysis of learners' language and open-ended responses as particularly important and interesting lines of development in the computerization of SFL diagnosis.

We conclude the book by discussing a selection of general principles of diagnostic assessment and by introducing a topic of research, which is rather common in other areas of language testing but that has not yet been studied in diagnostic language testing, namely, test washback and impact. We suggest that a diagnostic test might usefully be validated, or at least its usefulness might be assessed, if the treatment that follows from the diagnosis and the feedback presented to the learner and teacher is effective.

2

UNDERSTANDING DIAGNOSIS

Diagnosis is common in many fields other than second or foreign language testing. Obviously, this is true for medicine, both in general practice and in medical specialisms like gynecology, oncology, and so on. It has become an established practice in car mechanics as well as in computer studies, programming, and systems support. Indeed, in first language reading studies, especially in the area of learning disabilities like dyslexia, diagnostic testing and assessment has been common for decades. So, one possible avenue of study is to explore how diagnosis is carried out in those other fields and to see whether the principles and practices of diagnosis in those fields can be applied in some way to second and foreign language (SFL) testing.

In order to begin such a study, we decided to conduct exploratory interviews with practitioners in a number of such domains. This chapter reports on the results of those interviews and speculates on what a theory of diagnosis might contain and what procedures or processes might be implicated. A detailed summary is given of interviews with 10 informants: a car mechanic, a computer systems support manager, an oncologist, a general practitioner, a nurse, a neuropsychologist, a psychologist working in dyslexia research, a teacher responsible for diagnosing dyslexia in English as a second language as well as with adult English first language speakers, a primary school principal and literacy subject leader, and a primary school teacher who specializes in interventions for pupils with reading difficulties.

The chapter concludes with a discussion of what factors are common to diagnosis across the various domains, and speculates on the relevance and implications for the diagnosis of second or foreign language proficiency in general.

Need for This Study

Diagnosis has long been recognized as an important function of tests and assessment procedures, including language tests, and diagnostic tests are almost always included in a taxonomy of test types (the others commonly listed include proficiency, achievement, progress, placement, and aptitude). A recent overview of definitions of diagnostic tests (Alderson 2005; Chapter One) cites sources such as the Association of Language Testers in Europe's (ALTE) multilingual glossary (ALTE, 1998); the *Dictionary of Language Testing* (Davies et al., 1999); Bachman (1990); Alderson, Clapham, and Wall (1995); Moussavi (2002); Bachman and Palmer (1996); and Hughes (1989, 2003) but concludes that "the language testing literature offers very little guidance on how diagnosis might appropriately be conducted, what content diagnostic tests might have, what theoretical basis they might rest on, and how their use might be validated" (Alderson, 2005, p. 10).

Interestingly, as far back as 1984, Bejar commented: "Although there is an increasing demand for diagnostic assessment little guidance exists as to how to conduct such assessments" (1984, p. 185). The situation appears not to have changed much in almost 30 years. However, as mentioned earlier, it is clearly the case that diagnosis per se exists in a number of professional and vocational fields, some with long and respected histories behind them, like medicine, others more recent, like car mechanics and computer systems. Language testing, even applied linguistics as a whole, could possibly benefit from studying how diagnoses are conducted in domains such as car mechanics, medicine, and first language reading.

This chapter attempts to provide insights toward the guidance Bejar felt was needed, by exploring accounts by practitioners of the process of diagnosis in other professional and vocational domains, in the hope of eventually contributing to a theory or framework for diagnosis.

Aim

The aim of the study, which was intended to be fairly small scale and qualitative in nature, was to provide insights into diagnosis from the perspective of the practitioners in various professional and vocational fields. It should be noted from the outset that it is emphatically not being claimed that diagnosis in car mechanics or IT support is similar to diagnosis in medicine or in education. Diagnosis in all fields can be seen as the identification of problems and as an attempt to understand their causes, or what underlies the problems or difficulties, in such a way that treatment or action might result. In that sense, understanding diagnosis across a range of fields has justification. The initial aim is thus to see what the process of diagnosis has in common across fields. A later stage might then explore how the various fields are different from each other, and what implications such differences might have for a theory of diagnosis within a field and across fields.

Informants

We decided to interview people whom the interviewer knew well who were working in a range of different fields and who had considerable experience and expertise in their field. Informants came from or had worked in countries as diverse as Australia, Finland, Germany, Hungary, Japan, Kenya, Sweden, and the United Kingdom. They were assured in advance that their participation was voluntary and any report would be anonymized. In all, 10 informants were interviewed: a car mechanic, a computer systems support manager, an oncologist, a general practitioner, a nurse, a neuropsychologist, a psychologist working in dyslexia research, a teacher of students with learning disabilities who was responsible for diagnosing dyslexia in English as a second language as well as with adult English first language speakers, the principal of a primary school who had long been interested in the teaching of reading in children's first language (in this case, English), and a primary school teacher.

Method

Data were collected by a semi-structured interview, beginning with a broad explanation of our interest in diagnosis in general and in learning from other fields, and then asking the informant how diagnosis in their field is defined and practiced. Probing and follow-up questions were not prepared in advance, but related to issues raised during the interview, or to clarifying understanding of what had been said. Toward the end of each interview, informants were asked what training, if any, they had in diagnosis, the role of subject knowledge and experience in diagnosis if the informant had not already addressed those topics, whether they thought that the treatment and feedback that followed on from the diagnosis validated the diagnosis itself, and if not, how the diagnosis could be validated. Each interview lasted about 1 hour. The interviews normally took place in the interviewer's office or in the informants' house, but in the case of the car mechanic, it took place at the garage where he worked and included his demonstrating the various machines and computer programs he used.

Analysis

All interviews were audio-recorded with a high quality Edirol R-09HR digital recorder, and the recordings were transcribed by a professional company. The transcripts were double-checked while listening to the recordings, and a few minor corrections were made. The transcripts formed the basis of the analysis, which was intended to be a grounded theory approach. This involved initially making rough notes about the content, categorizing different sections, highlighting relevant quotes on the transcripts and adding notes to them, then summarizing the main issues arising and identifying suitable quotations from the transcripts. The resulting summaries were then sent to each informant with a request to correct misunderstandings or misinterpretations, and to add any relevant information they might feel was missing. The resulting corrected summaries formed the basis for the briefer accounts of each interview, which follow. Each summary gives details of the informant's experience and expertise, followed by a description of the diagnostic process as related by the informant, and a brief description of example diagnostic tools or procedures. After the 10 interviews and descriptions, we then summarize the issues arising and draw some implications for the diagnosis of reading in a second or foreign language (see also Alderson et al., 2014).

The Car Mechanic (Alan)

Alan has been a mechanic for 47 years but thinks the job today is for younger people who have taken courses in electronics, which he has not. Diagnosis in car repairing requires specific knowledge and practical experience. Much is now diagnosed via computer, but he acknowledges that experience is still important, as is knowledge of basic principles "is there a spark, is there fuel?"

Alan sees himself as the first line of diagnosis, together with his electronic aids, but he can refer to colleagues' electronics expertise as well as their knowledge of particular makes of car, when necessary. Although computers can remove the need for retaining detailed information in one's head or looking it up in car manuals, they do not replace the basic expertise, experience, know-how, and understanding of basic principles of how things work. Alan mentions that problem-solving experience, sometimes based on trial and error, is essential—but even so, one's diagnosis may not always be correct, or the diagnosis may be correct but the remedy may be wrong.

Approaches to Diagnosis

All cars now have a Controller Area Network (CAN) electrical system, which has made the electrical system in modern vehicles much more complicated than before. Nowadays, Alan's first question to the customer is: "Has the engine management system light gone on?" If it has, then he goes straight to the computer to see what it has to say. If that light has not been illuminated, then the problem is mechanical, not electronic.

Alan demonstrated a computer program that has replaced car manuals with a checklist of problem–cause–remedy. The database contains records of all makes of cars and their components, developed in collaboration with the car and component manufacturers to record faults that are known to occur in particular cars.

The IT Systems Support Manager (Brian)

Brian has been managing IT systems for university departments and faculties for 24 years. He has always been interested in working with computers, from as young as 13, and has developed a knowledge base from experience. He never had a mentor or formal training in computer diagnosis. However, changing technology in computer hardware and software programming has been both rapid and complex and has changed the way that people diagnose problems. The need to hold all necessary information in one's head has been largely superseded by the development of knowledge bases and use of the Internet to access information. But humans' knowledge, experience, and ability to solve problems, based on an understanding of basic principles of computer programming and how computers work, are all also necessary in order to diagnose and fix problems.

Brian reports that the first level of support for users is the call desk operators, who are expected to solve 80% of the problems brought to them by consulting knowledge databases. The second level of support is the trained technicians, who may fix the problem remotely or work on the user's computer. The third level of support can be either a generalist like Brian, who understands principles and systems, or specialists in particular aspects of IT design whom he can consult.

Approaches to Diagnosis

When solving a problem with a computer, Brian first asks himself whether he has any specific knowledge relating to the problem. Is the problem what the client thinks it is? If he sees an obvious solution, then he tries it immediately. The problem may be a common one he has experienced, possibly with other clients reporting the same thing at around the same time.

The second stage, if he cannot work out an obvious solution, is to go back to first principles. Computers may have multiple (underlying) problems, so he tries to fix other things as he goes along. There may be missing security updates or updates to the operating system, and he systematically fixes the problems as he finds them. The third stage is to research via the Internet or local knowledge bases possible solutions to similar reported problems, or to consult with specialists.

The Oncologist (Cyril)

Cyril has three specializations, namely, oncology, pharmacology, and internal medicine, and has been practicing medicine as an oncologist for 27 years. He reports that there are various ways in which he diagnoses a patient he has not seen before. He often uses what he called "the Blick approach" (*Blick* is German for *glance*, and this method is sometimes known as the one-glance diagnosis), which involves making a diagnosis on first sight according to the patients' behavior. He does not check the laboratory notes in advance because they may be misleading and may bias his diagnosis. After noting the patients' behavior, like holding their hands to their chest, he asks patients what they feel and what the reported problem is. In this situation, the oncologist is looking for patterns of symptoms of known problems.

If the patterns do not match any known problems, there is a danger that doctors may try to fit the reported symptoms into known diseases without being open-minded to the possibility that the patient may have two or three diseases at the same time. If the patterns do fit the doctor's experience, then he or she double checks with the laboratory reports, magnetic resonance imaging (MRI) scans—the 'objective data'—and confirms or disconfirms the hypotheses as to the underlying problem by asking probing questions. Unfortunately, general symptoms (e.g., headache) do not indicate specific problems.

Approaches to Diagnosis

Cyril lists four different approaches to diagnosis. The first approach is referred to as *probabalistic*, because frequently occurring diseases are more likely to be the cause of the problem. University students should learn how to diagnose rare diseases because the frequent ones will certainly be encountered during their medical practice, whereas the rare ones are unlikely to be part of their experience.

The second approach is *casuistic*, that is, looking for causes based on physiological examinations (e.g., tachycardia: an ECG examination can confirm such diagnoses objectively).

The third approach is the *deterministic* approach using algorithms, which is increasingly popular. This approach is good for university students who need to learn how to diagnose based on case studies. The algorithm is an aid but not an approach to be followed blindly.

The most interesting approach is *heuristic*, that is, based on experience, but it is not logical; rather it is intuitive, a gut feeling, based on past memories by very experienced clinicians, plus knowledge that is holistic and integrated.

The General Practitioner (GP) (David)

David has more than 30 years in general medical practice, is the senior partner, and is also an adviser to the regional and national health committees. He notes that diagnosis is essentially evidence based and derives from the doctor's knowledge, but it need not lead to action because there may be nothing one can do about the problem. David identifies different stages of medical diagnosis. The first is labeling the problem and the second is taking account of important contextual factors. The former includes all the features that the doctor needs to know in order to take the correct action. The latter is deciding what in the patient's circumstances might influence the decision to be taken. The action taken will depend upon the GP's degree of certainty of the diagnosis.

David says that diagnosis has to take account of patients' self-report but also their fears about their condition. In medical school one learns standard questions to ask patients about their condition, and there are different ways of conducting consultations with patients. Communication skills are also taught.

David acknowledges that general medical practice can be an isolating experience, and it is important to know when to consult with somebody else about a diagnosis. Laboratory tests, x-rays, ultrasound, and blood tests are all important aids to reaching a diagnosis. Computers have massively helped the maintenance of patient records, which also aids diagnosis. A diagnosis is a prediction of outcome, and a diagnosis is not a diagnosis if one is uncertain about what will happen next.

Approaches to Diagnosis

The World Health Organization publishes a *Guide to Mental and Neurological Health in Primary Care* (WHO, 2004) as an aid to GPs. Checklists cover areas such as sleep problems, depression, and anxiety. An example of the latter follows:

"A. Feeling tense or anxious?
 B. Worrying a lot about things?
If Yes to any of the above, continue below.

1. Symptoms of arousal and anxiety?
2. Experienced intense or sudden fear unexpectedly or for no apparent reason?
   - Fear of dying
   - Fear of losing control
   - Pounding heart
   - Sweating

Summing up
Positive to 1 and 2: indication of panic disorder
Positive to 2 and 3: indication of agoraphobia
Positive to 3 and 4: indication of social phobia"

The Nurse (Ethel)

Ethel has been a nurse for over 35 years. She worked on a coronary care unit for some time and is now also an advanced life support instructor and provider for the Resuscitation Council UK. As a senior nurse, she is involved in mentoring medical students when they are doing their hospital internship. Ethel reports that in nursing, as in other domains, knowledge and experience are fundamental to diagnosis, but diagnosis can occur at quite different levels—from recognizing a patient's basic physical needs, such as the use of a bedpan, to diagnosing a heart attack.

Nowadays, nurses are trained in diagnosis and often have specializations that allow them to replace some of the work of the GP (e.g., running asthma clinics or well-men programs). Ethel says that much diagnosis is pattern recognition, which comes with experience. Mentoring trainee doctors on the wards concentrates on teaching them to recognize patterns of behaviors and physical or verbal signs. Also important is that the mentor teaches trainees how to communicate with patients in order to understand both their needs and their concerns.

Ethel points out that making a diagnosis involves making decisions that may affect patients' lives. Therefore, being certain about one's diagnosis can be difficult, especially if faced with a different diagnosis made by a more senior colleague.

Approaches to Diagnosis

Recent developments in nursing include structured algorithms of treatment post-diagnosis but also ways of observing patients and reporting changes in their condition. One example given was the Physiological Observations Track and Trigger System (POTTS) chart, where nurses track their physiological observations. When the observations reach a certain criterion level, this triggers actions that need to be taken. She says that not everybody has the experience and skills to recognize when a patient's condition is deteriorating, and so the POTTS chart is an aid to diagnosis.

The Neuropsychologist (Frank)

Frank is 53 years old, an experienced university researcher, and a former member of a psychological test-development institute. In neuropsychology, diagnosis is defined in much the same way as in medicine. Unlike other mental disorders, however, dyslexia does not have to be certified by a medical doctor, and a diagnosis is arrived at by combining the results of a learner's performance on three or four standardized tests. Within neuropsychological practice the cut-off point for a severe disorder is about two standard deviations below the mean, but that varies from disorder to disorder and from country to country.

Frank says that reading is a skill composed of a number of processes, and a problem in reading may be due to a variety of different background processes that are not functioning normally. There are various procedures, such as Rapid Automatized Naming (RAN) or Backward Digit Span Tests, that are used to diagnose processes underlying reading disorders, but psychologists are still unsure what the underlying processes are that affect performance on such tasks.

He argues that diagnosis and treatment are quite separate concepts, and diagnosis is validated by the tests that are used to diagnose the condition, although this would seem to be an operational definition rather than a validation procedure. Poor performance in RAN and Backward Digit Span could be identified as precursors to a reading disorder rather than as predictors per se. Diagnosis is not the prediction of future events or conditions: prediction takes place by identifying the precursors of a condition, which may not be part of the condition but which simply co-occur with it. Diagnosis involves establishing that the problem or disorder exists, and a good diagnostic method will lead to the disorder being identified.

Approaches to Diagnosis

Disorders are categorized according to the *International Classification of Diseases* (ICD-10) (see WHO, 1992) and carry an identifying letter and number. This contains clinical descriptions and diagnostic guidelines and was produced by "a vast number of individual experts and institutions all over the world, who actively participated in the production of the classification and the guidelines" (WHO, 1992, p. vii). It is far too detailed and extensive to cover here, but it is worth mentioning F81.0: Specific reading disorder (WHO, 1992, p. 245) and F81.1: Specific spelling disorder (WHO, 1992, p. 247), for which there are paragraph-length descriptions and typically a page or more of diagnostic guidelines. Bullet-point summaries for the former are as follows:

- *Includes*:
  o "backward reading"
  o developmental dyslexia
  o specific reading retardation
  o spelling difficulties associated with a reading disorder
- *Excludes*:
  o acquired alexia and dyslexia (R48.0)
  o acquired reading difficulties secondary to emotional disturbance (F93)
  o spelling disorder not associated with reading difficulties (F81.1) (WHO, 1992, p. 247).

The Psychologist/Dyslexia Expert (Gail)

Gail is a 48-year-old university professor who researches dyslexia and related matters, including intervention studies, with more than 20 years of research experience. She points out that in academic L1 reading research, the term *diagnosis* is not used. Diagnosis depends on one having a very clear idea of what the disorder is and what has contributed to it. Diagnosis is the product of an assessment, usually of cognitive abilities, and IQ is also measured in order to assess whether the person also has underlying problems that are not related to written language. It can be difficult to distinguish between being a poor reader and being dyslexic.

She says that there are many different ways in which what is called 'dyslexia' may manifest itself, and there is a reluctance among academic psychologists to use the term *dyslexia*. Reading disorders are thought to be due to phonological problems, but some researchers think visual problems may be implicated, and others consider memory problems to be important. A family history of dyslexia may also mean one is likely to be dyslexic, and several genes are thought to be related to aspects of dyslexia.

Diagnoses can be validated by experimental-control type research, but a diagnosis is not necessarily validated by a treatment because diagnosis and treatment are quite separate concepts. The emphasis in diagnosis is on weaknesses, not strengths, although weaknesses in some areas can perhaps be compensated by strengths in other areas.

Approaches to Diagnosis

The cognitive skills assessed include memory skills, receptive vocabulary, word decoding skills, phonological awareness, segmentation, speech perception skills, word spelling, pseudo-word reading, Rapid Automatized Naming, phonological awareness, and rapidly presented words. Depending on the research question one might also assess attention, motor skills, and so on. IQ is tested in order to rule it out as a problem, as might be auditory or visual skills.

The Dyslexia, Learning Disabilities and ESL Teacher (Helen)

Helen teaches both native English speakers who might be dyslexic and non-native speakers of English. She has a PhD in inclusive education and more than 20 years' teaching experience, both abroad and in the UK. She makes an important distinction between holistic screening, which is often ad hoc and intuitive, and diagnosis that is more systematic, quantitative, test based, and statistical in its analysis. She notes that teachers can refer those of their learners who they believe might have reading problems to educational psychologists for objective testing and analysis. The screener looks for specific behaviors and difficulties with tasks they have often designed themselves. The problems that both L1 and SFL learners have are varied. Furthermore, many learners may even have difficulty expressing what their problems are.

Helen notes that in many languages there are no standardized diagnostic instruments and procedures, so the diagnostician has to try to adapt those that exist in English. However, it is important to avoid specifically linguistic problems within the adapted instruments (she points out that most diagnostic instruments in English assume proficiency in English). The screener looks for patterns across the various activities that have been devised to explore reading, visual, auditory, and memory problems. Experience of similar problems with a wide range of learners from different backgrounds and languages helps one decide whether the learner is typical or atypical of those the screener is familiar with. She says that teachers are not taught how to design tests or how to diagnose, but they need to be familiar with theories of language acquisition, reading development, and with normal reading behavior and development. However, experience with learners in classrooms with reading problems is invaluable.

Approaches to Diagnosis

Screening interviews may use a self-report from the learner based on a checklist of issues, problems, and background details as a basis for a probing discussion with the learner. Typical questions in such checklists include the following:

- Do you confuse visually similar words such as *cat* and *cot*?
- Do you lose your place or miss lines when reading?
- Do you confuse the names of objects (e.g., *table* for *chair*)?
- Do you get confused when given several instructions at once?
- How easy do you find it to sound out words such as e-le-phant?
- How easy do you find it to recite the alphabet?
- How hard do you find it to read aloud?

The Head of a Primary School and Literacy Subject Leader (Ingrid)

Ingrid has been a primary school teacher for 25 years, including 12 years as a deputy headmistress in two schools and headmistress in her current school for 1 year. During her teacher training she learned about the diagnosis of English L1 reading, the stages of reading development, the expected route for the normal child and problems that might occur and how they might manifest themselves. Although she learned about early reading and phonics, the course did not go beyond 'barking at print' to cover comprehension, higher order skills, or strategies, nor did it deal with treatment or interventions. Ingrid only learned about such matters when training to be a literacy subject leader, including covering assessment and diagnosis.

She mentions that informal diagnosis is what teachers do every day, but she considers 'diagnosis' to be more of a formal event or procedure carried out by experts trained in appropriate procedures. She believes that treatment of reading difficulties can be given without formal diagnoses, and the aim of such treatments is not necessarily to cure or overcome difficulties but to help individuals manage them.

She says that there are many recognized diagnostic and screening procedures, and literacy subject leaders are trained in their use as well as in aspects of reading theory, the nature of comprehension, higher order skills, and reading strategies.

In-service courses are also available for school staff who feel the need for continuing professional development in these areas. Teaching assistants are specifically trained in carrying out interventions with small groups of children on a daily basis, using highly structured programs. External support is available through the Reading and Language Service and from county-level educational psychologists, who can screen for dyslexia.

Approaches to Diagnosis

There are numerous tools for working with children with reading difficulties, such as the Toe by Toe scheme (www.toe-by-toe.co.uk) and the UK Government's Literacy Strategy (established in 1997 but discontinued in 2011). There are also many recognized diagnostic and screening procedures, for example:

- The Schonell Reading Test (Schonell & Goodacre, 1971), which is still in use.
- The *Salford Sentence Reading Test, Third Edition* (Bookbinder, Vincent, & Crumpler, 2002).
- Running records (see Chapter Nine on Clay's, 1979, research.
- The English Year 1 Phonics Screening Check (www.gov.uk/government/uploads/system/uploads/attachment_data/file/230810/Phonics_assessment_framework.PDF)

However, Ingrid is very critical of the UK Government's new phonics test since it is not suitable for many children, especially those who are reading for meaning. It does not assess comprehension. Other tests and assessment procedures are used to track progress according to national curriculum levels, but the UK Government is now abolishing these, so it is unclear how progress will be tracked in future.

The Primary School Teacher (Judith)

Judith earned a diploma in social anthropology, followed by a Certificate in Teaching English to Speakers of Other Languages (CELTA), and a 1-year teaching qualification for primary school pupils. She has 10 years' teaching experience: having worked as a general primary classroom teacher for 4 years, she then became a specialist literacy teacher, conducting interventions with groups of four to five ESOL children.

Judith defines diagnosis as looking for something and putting a name to it. The most difficult thing about diagnosis is

> having enough data to work with . . . a lot of diagnoses are based on one assessment, whereas you need constantly to be monitoring. And particularly if you are a classroom teacher and you've got 30 children, to keep your head around 30 children is hard.

Diagnosis and treatment operate in parallel, but she considers that one can diagnose without knowing what the treatment should be. Small-group, regular interventions follow referrals based on diagnoses or screenings, and such treatment often has to do with test-taking skills, with children becoming aware that the answer to questions lies in the text being read.

Formal training is available for those who wish to become Reading Recovery teachers, and school-based in-service training is available as well as support from more experienced teachers within the intervention team. However, there was no training in literacy or diagnosis on the CELTA course that Judith took.

Approaches to Diagnosis

Numerous diagnostic tests, screening tests, and the use of running records are available to teachers of English reading and are used with non-native speakers as well as with native speakers of English. Early interventions deal with pre-literacy awareness and decoding issues, later ones with comprehension, answering different types of questions, vocabulary development, and strategies. Tests used include the *Test of Reading Comprehension* (TORCH, 2003, p. 2). Its purpose is "to identify comprehension levels, to measure progress and to use content-referenced interpretation to identify those skills requiring further instruction. The test consists of a set of twelve reading passages graded in order of difficulty, varying in length from 200 to 900 words, including fiction and non-fiction texts. Students read a passage and then use a cloze answer sheet to retell the passage, filling in the gaps in their own words to demonstrate understanding."

Summary of Approaches to Diagnosis

Definitions

Different views emerged from these interviews of what diagnosis is:

- "diagnosis is evidence-driven,"
- "diagnosis is labeling a condition,"
- "diagnosis is pattern recognition,"
- "diagnosis is the product of an assessment,"
- "diagnosis is finding the problem,"
- "diagnosis is finding the cause of a problem,"
- "diagnosis is problem solving,"
- "trial and error has a role in fixing the problem,"
- "a diagnosis is not a diagnosis if one is uncertain what will happen next," and
- "diagnosis is not treatment."

Although in some areas examined, strengths were also occasionally mentioned as possibly compensating for the known weaknesses, usually diagnosis was seen as identifying problems and weaknesses, not strengths. In second or foreign language reading (SFL), diagnosis is most often defined simply as 'identifying strengths and weaknesses' without further problematization or discussion.

Treatment and Action

Diagnosis was seen to lead to decision making, usually regarding what action to take, but it may also include a decision not to take action. Diagnosis and treatment are separate but related concepts. The diagnosis may be correct and the fix or treatment solves the problem. Diagnosis may be correct, but the treatment does not solve the problem. The diagnosis may be incorrect, but the treatment solves the problem anyway. The diagnosis may have been incorrect, and the treatment does not solve the problem, so new diagnoses are needed. The treatment may be related to the causes diagnosed, or it may not be, as there may be no known treatments, and trial and error are needed.

In SFL reading diagnosis, there tends to be more emphasis on the treatment than on the diagnosis. Diagnosis is seen as being useful for feedback and remedial treatment, and the relationship between diagnosis and treatment is more usually assumed than questioned.

The Role of Technology

In many of the fields discussed, technology has become an essential aid to diagnosis. As the electronics of cars become more complex, as computers become more sophisticated, as knowledge bases continue to be developed with respect to specific known problems, and as the specialists' understanding of problems becomes more sophisticated, new technologies such as complex blood tests are used, and complex machines like MRI scanners and brain imaging techniques are developed and are increasingly useful in diagnosis.

In SFL diagnostic testing of reading, little use has been made to date of the computer, with the exception of the DIALANG suite of programs (Alderson, 2005; Alderson & Huhta, 2005), which delivers tests over the Internet as well as results and feedback regarding possible treatment. It could, however, be argued that computer-based testing has resulted in overblown claims being made for the diagnostic basis and value of the results of proficiency tests like the TOEFL iBT or MELAB, as well as computer-based placement tests like DELNA and OOPT (Oxford Online Placement Test), with no theoretical basis for the 'diagnoses' reported. However, recent advances in the use of technology for identifying errors in learners' writing—such as Pearson Knowledge Technologies' *WriteToLearn*, or Educational Testing Service's e-rater and *Criterion*, or Vantage's *My Access*—may herald the advent of computer-based diagnosis of SFL writing problems, if not yet SFL reading problems.

Knowledge and Experience

It has been seen in all the domains examined that diagnosis requires both specific knowledge in the particular area and practical experience of diagnosing and solving problems. In every case examined in this study, it was said that computers do not replace the need for the knowledge, expertise, experience, and problem-solving abilities of humans.

In the case of SFL diagnosis, it is often assumed that diagnosis is the responsibility of the classroom teacher. To date there is very little empirical research showing exactly what it is that teachers diagnose, and, despite Edelenbos and Kubanek-German's (2004) claim that teachers need "diagnostic competence," this is rarely defined. Research has so far only looked at *how* teachers diagnose and *when*, rather than *what* it is that they diagnose (see, for example, Leung & Mohan, 2004; Rea-Dickins, 2008).

Training

Expertise in diagnosis in various professions may come from on-the-job training, as in car mechanics' apprenticeships, or it may be the result of mentoring with observation of the mentee by the mentor, or of the mentor by the mentee. It may be the result of specific academic training, as in the case of medicine and (neuro)psychology, or it may be more the result of trial and error together with experience over many years.

In the case of SFL teachers, training in diagnosing second and foreign learners' reading problems is not even in its infancy (see Chapter Nine). In fact, it is virtually non-existent, and where it might exist, it is almost certainly based on anecdote and intuition rather than a theory of how or what to diagnose, what the causes might be of supposed weaknesses, and what possible underlying processes might give rise to observed conditions. Indeed, even in second language acquisition research, where there is said to be a growing emphasis on and interest in processes of learning, very little attention has been paid to second and foreign language reading, rather than to the more easily researched areas of speaking and writing.

Basic Principles and Complexity

A point repeatedly emphasized in the interviews was the importance of a knowledge of basic principles within the particular domain, either the role of an electric spark and fuel in car mechanics; how computer systems work in principle; one's knowledge of anatomy and how the heart, lungs, liver, and kidney work; or, less certainly, how the brain and the mind work. Such basic principles seemed to be essential to the education and knowledge of those doing diagnoses.

However, there is an increasing degree of complexity as one moves from domain to domain. Basic car design has not changed much in 100 years, although the advent of electronics and in-board computers has made them more complex than they were. IT systems and software programs are hugely complex, much more so than the car.

But both cars and IT systems were designed by human beings and thus there is somewhere a deep repository of knowledge as to the design and functioning of mechanical and electronic systems. However, no human being or group of humans designed the human body, so the designer cannot be consulted. Humans are individuals, not machines, and they are even more complex than machines, making diagnosis more difficult and the requirements of research, knowledge, and experience even more crucial. The mind is even more complex than the body, and we know even less about how or why it works.

There is a great deal of research into first language reading, and the diagnosis of first language reading is reasonably well understood, although why first language readers have problems in the first place is less well understood. The fact that reading is typically silent and the processes of word, morphological, syntactic and semantic recognition, and comprehension are internal makes true diagnosis difficult, and the advent of modern technology has had relatively little impact to date on diagnosis.

In SFL reading, however, there is very little research into diagnosis, and the nature of SFL reading problems is not well understood. Nor are diagnostic procedures well documented or researched. Applied linguistics is a new field, as is language testing in the modern sense, and the knowledge base of both fields is therefore relatively small. More research and theorizing are needed in second language acquisition studies, in language teaching and instruction, in understanding the nature of the cognitive processes, and in the skills that underlie SFL reading and its acquisition. Moreover, the fact that individuals may not be able to read in their first language, that their first language may be very different from the target language and may be written in completely different scripts, all make SFL reading considerably more complex even than first language reading. Moreover, most normal human beings can speak their first language and understand its spoken version: their task is to relate the spoken version to the written version; but second language readers vary enormously in their proficiency in the second language, and indeed may not be able to understand or use the spoken version at all.

Support for Diagnosis

Given the complexity, even of cars, it is important that those in the first line of support have higher levels of assistance available to them in the event of any difficulty in diagnoses. The car mechanic had colleagues available who were expert in electronics. IT help desks are the user's first line of support, and trained technicians are the second line of support, themselves aided by a third level of experienced generalist managers, or specialists in particular areas of IT. GPs have the support of technical services such as phlebotomists, pulmonologists, and oncologists, and in the case of nursing, there are specialized nurses, senior nurses, and doctors available to provide advice and diagnoses if necessary. Classroom teachers suspecting L1 reading problems have potential support from special education teachers and educational psychologists who can provide 'objective' tests. Similarly, online learning tools in science and mathematics education have diagnostic features (conceptual definitions, procedural checklists, reminders for checking assumptions, formulae, calculations, etc.).

What are the levels of support available to the SFL reading teacher? Given the lack of research and knowledge in the area of SFL reading, not much practical or even theoretical support is presently available. Teachers can certainly read research articles, but these are not typically designed to help classroom teachers diagnose. Textbooks on second language reading are increasingly informative, but diagnosis is usually glossed over, if addressed at all, and more emphasis is provided on instruction and remediation than on diagnosis in the first place.

Doubtless some experienced SFL teachers have experience and expertise in diagnosis, but at present the field knows little about such expertise. Far more research is needed in classrooms, both observational research and interviews with teachers on what they diagnose and why, and detailed studies are needed of the effects of interventions in SFL reading classes to see what light the results can throw on the causes and precursors of reading difficulties and disorders (but see Chapter Nine for an exploration of this issue).

Self-Report and Self-Assessment

A common theme across the various domains is the occurrence of self-report. Patients refer themselves to the general practitioner and report their perceived symptoms. They have presumably made some form of self-assessment before going to see the doctor. The diagnostician pays attention to the self-reports but also questions the patient in order to assess the plausibility of the self-report, in order to reach his or her own conclusion about the condition, the symptoms reported or found, and the diagnosis to which such symptoms might be pointing. Importantly, the patient has not been trained in self-assessment, and therefore the self-report can be challenged or ignored in light of further tests and an examination of the patient. (Of course, in the case of cars or computers, it is the driver of the car or the user of the computer that is reporting and describing the symptoms of the perceived problems.)

In SFL teaching and testing, self-assessment is often couched in terms of can do statements, as contained, for example, in the Common European Framework of Reference (Council of Europe, 2001) and in many language portfolios. In language teaching, self-assessment is associated with the advocacy of autonomous learning, and it is often argued that learners need to be trained in carrying out self-assessments. In diagnosis, however, it is less clear that faith can be placed in the validity of any self-report, since SFL learners may simply not be aware of their problems or of their lack of achievement. In diagnosis, it is perhaps more likely that learners might be aware of what they *cannot* do (yet), or do not yet know, and therefore, perhaps self-assessments should be couched in terms of can–not–do statements.

Normality

A common theme underlying the discussion of diagnosis is the need for a precise definition of what is normal. This is relatively straightforward in the case of the car mechanic or the computer specialist, but more complex in health care in general, and rather difficult to define in the case of education. Diagnosis can be seen as the synthesis of everything that has been investigated in the domain concerned, and compared to what is thought to be normal in that domain. In judging both what is normal and what is abnormal, it is important to bear in mind that the average might not represent any of the individual data. This is clearly important in the interpretation of any kind of test results.

In first language reading, for example, norm-based judgments have involved comparing a reader's reading age with his or her chronological age. Although such a procedure has become somewhat controversial in recent years, in second and foreign language reading there is virtually no basis at present for establishing norms for an SFL reading age. Moreover, what is normal in the context of SFL reading will likely differ according to individual ability and background variables such as age, first language, cognitive factors, educational level, and maybe even personality and motivation.

Methods and Guidelines

Finally, all informants mentioned methods, tasks, techniques, tools, categorizations of disorders, and guidelines for their identification. Engine management systems and databases are used to check for problems. Knowledge bases, the Internet, and remote diagnostic tools are increasingly used in the diagnosis and fixing of problems in IT systems. The oncologist outlined four different approaches to diagnosis but also uses ancillary objective tests and physical examinations, as well as other colleagues' opinions, to help him diagnose. The GP described two different stages in diagnosis that are needed and briefly explained the different models of how a consultation may be carried out, with or without checklists or standard questions. The nurse has structured algorithms that must be followed, especially in the case of heart attacks and for reporting problems to senior colleagues, as well as a set of observations of blood pressure, temperature, pulse, and the like, to follow. Psychologists have a range of standardized tests they must use and norms to help them interpret the results. Dyslexia experts also have a set of test tasks that they can administer and procedures for combining the results of two or more similar tests in order to arrive at a confident diagnosis.

What diagnostic tools do SFL reading teachers, experts, or testers have to aid them in their task of diagnosis? There are no checklists, no agreed-upon definitions of SFL reading problems or disorders, no standardized diagnostic tests or procedures, no defined approaches to consultations with learners, or observations of behavior in classrooms or in consultations. Everything seems to be intuitive, 'holistic,' ad hoc (see also Chapter Nine). There is little or no expert advice available, and the tests available claiming to be diagnostic are in fact proficiency or placement tests. Although it is asserted by practitioners and testing experts alike that diagnostic information can be gained from any test, that seems to be stretching the definition of diagnosis too far; it is too opportunistic, not founded on any theory of the ability being diagnosed, and certainly not based on a body of knowledge of successful diagnoses.

What would perhaps be very useful would be a list of the common SFL reading problems a teacher might come across. Therefore, one way forward in assembling advice and exploring steps toward creating a diagnostic tool set for classroom teachers might be to interview teachers about the main issues that they face in identifying, labeling, diagnosing, and treating their learners' problems, in a similar way to what has been reported in this chapter from other domains (see Chapter Nine). A useful additional procedure would be to observe teachers teaching and diagnosing SFL reading and, together with the teachers themselves, reflecting on what they do and why.

Summary

To summarize thus far, there are many different ways of defining diagnosis, but in most diagnostic situations there is an emphasis on the identification of problems and weaknesses, which are contrasted with, and rely upon, a knowledge of what is 'normal.' Diagnosis leads to decisions on whether or not to treat the problem, or to seek further diagnoses from higher levels of support or from objective data. Technology of various sorts has a special and important role in modern diagnostic techniques, but specific technical knowledge and practical experience of diagnosis on the part of the human diagnostician are essential. Training in diagnosis is also essential, be that academic training, on-the-job apprenticeships, or mentoring. A thorough knowledge of the basic principles of the machine or organism and how it functions is clearly important, especially as the complexity of the machine or organism increases.

Self-assessment and self-report can be an important contribution to the diagnosis, but there is a need for guidelines for, and the establishment of, empirically justified methodologies of diagnosis to assist the diagnostician and help that person reach a decision about the problem. One thing that might be said to be characteristic of diagnosis is that it can be done in different phases: to detect a problem, to follow the development of the problem or condition, to make post-treatment diagnoses, and to evaluate the success of the treatment. However, what and how to treat the problem diagnosed depends on the nature of the problem and the diagnosis, and treatment itself is not an essential component, per se, of diagnosis.

Toward a Theory of Diagnosis

Diagnosis (1987) is defined in *Collins COBUILD English Language Dictionary* as follows: "Diagnosis is the discovery and identification of what is wrong with someone who is ill or with something that is not working properly" (p. 388). The above discussions have hopefully provided opportunities for more nuanced thinking and exploration of the nature of diagnosis than that. Indeed, it can be seen from the summaries above that there seems to be an important distinction between machines that are malfunctioning, bodies and minds that might be said to be ill, and poor readers in a second or foreign language.

Bejar (1984) made a distinction between two different approaches to diagnosis, the medical and the educational. He argued that in medicine patients are assigned to a disease category on the basis of a pattern of indicators, the co-occurrence of several symptoms that point to a diagnosis, whereas in education diagnosis either focuses on learners' weaknesses (the deficit approach) or on the kinds of errors the learner makes (the error analysis approach).

In education, a problem is identified when there is a discrepancy between expected and actual achievement, or when achievement in one content area is 'out of phase' with achievement in other content areas. In SFL contexts, this is often referred to as a jagged or uneven profile of achievement. In the latter case, the student is his or her own reference point, unlike in norm-referenced testing. "Self-referencing is what distinguishes diagnostic assessment from other assessment procedures such as standardised achievement testing" (Bejar, 1984, p. 176).

Some Implications for the Diagnosis of SFL Reading

Experienced diagnosticians first ask themselves whether they have any specific knowledge that relates to the problem encountered. This might be something that experienced SFL reading teachers do, should do, or could do. Just as the computer specialist tries to fix other problems as he goes about diagnosing a problem, experienced SFL teachers work on a range of different aspects of language and other factors that might affect learning (see Chapters Nine and Ten), arguably in the hope that strengthening these various areas might help the learner to tackle a specific problem or lack of specific knowledge. Indeed, language teachers probably behave rather similarly to doctors who diagnose problems at first sight, but the problem might be that, unlike doctors, many SFL teachers lack the knowledge and tools to go beyond their first impressions.

Similarly, just as doctors develop their knowledge and experience through case studies, one effective way of developing language teachers' diagnostic skills might be through the use of specific case studies in initial and ongoing teacher training. Moreover, the situation where a GP can do nothing about the problem diagnosed might be analogous to the language educator who lacks the resources or the knowledge of how to approach remediation. Once diagnostic SFL reading tools or tests become available to identify particular problems, teachers themselves need to know what should be done, or at least the diagnostic tool should provide such information.

The notion that diagnosis can occur at different levels is relevant to the diagnosis of SFL reading problems, which can exist at the level of letter-sound correspondence or at the higher level of reading skills or strategies. In addition to the notion of different levels of problems, it is likely that many SFL reading problems relate in some way to different first languages, in which case one implication might be that useful diagnostic tools should also be specific to a particular L1, rather than attempting to address the problems of learners of one target language (especially a widespread language like English) regardless of the L1 of the learners.

Tests are not the only diagnostic tools, and diagnosticians have a number of different, non-test-based assessment procedures in their armory. Indeed, a lot of what actually happens in schools on a day-by-day basis probably involves spotting learners who are slow to learn to read or have problems with language. The class teacher will try out a number of things in the hope (based on experience, in many cases, of what has worked in the past) that the procedures work, without any clear idea of why the problem arose in the first place and what are its causes.

Of course, the average SFL classroom teacher is faced with many learners, and diagnosing, or even remembering, which learner has which problem is an enormous task. Hence, computer-based diagnosis, and the keeping of electronic records tracking diagnosis, treatment and progress, should be tools that every SFL teacher has available and knows how to use. Good record keeping is surely essential, which argues for a portfolio-like system (preferably electronic) but with various pieces of advice and guidance on what and how to observe and record problems, misunderstandings, and errors, and how to identify sources and types of relevant and useful feedback and remediation, which is the subject of Chapter Eight.

Conclusion

In this chapter we have explored how diagnosis is carried out in a range of professional fields through exploratory interviews with practitioners, and we have considered whether the principles and practices of diagnosis in those fields can be applied in some way to the diagnosis of second and foreign language reading. We discussed which factors are common to diagnosis across the various domains and speculated on the relevance and implications for the diagnosis of second or foreign language reading.

We have thereby laid the ground for the development of a possible framework for the creation of diagnostic tests of SFL reading, which is the subject of the next chapter.

3

RESEARCH INTO THE DIAGNOSIS OF SECOND AND FOREIGN LANGUAGE PROFICIENCY

In Chapter Two, we explored how diagnosis was defined and conducted in disciplines other than second or foreign language (SFL) proficiency. In this chapter, we will summarize relevant literature and describe a number of tests of SFL proficiency that claim to be diagnostic.

Early Treatments of Diagnosis in Language Testing

The first reference to diagnostic English language testing we have come across is in an undated manuscript by Tim Johns (n.d.), of Birmingham University, UK, in which he describes Vera Adamson using the Chaplen test before 1971 for placement into university language courses for non-native speakers of English, and that the test "was based on a mixture of syntactic and lexical items" (Johns, n.d., p. 1). He reports Elizabeth Ingram suggesting that, although the test was intended to be diagnostic, "the diagnostic intention had somehow got lost along the way" (Johns, n.d., p. 1). Unfortunately, he does not describe the nature of the test or why it might not be considered diagnostic.

However, in the same document, Johns describes the design of the first version of the *Birmingham Assessment and Diagnostic Test* (BADT), written in 1971. The test, used to identify learners' strengths and weaknesses in English grammar, was revised several times, once in 1976, then in 1984, 1991, and 1999. Johns describes the original version of the test as containing 130 items "to achieve test stability," consisting of four-option multiple-choice items, whose diagnostic areas (initially 12) were based on several criteria:

- Importance in written academic discourse.
- Problematic for learners of English from a wide range of L1 backgrounds and levels of competence.

- Covering areas which are not normally taught explicitly in English courses or which are badly taught ("on the assumption that if a student is able to obtain a good score on such areas, that must be a result of language acquisition (e.g., from extensive exposure to/use of English," Johns, n.d., p. 1).

Scores were reported to two sets of users: (a) "to departments, giving scores separately for undergraduates and postgraduates; (b) to students giving their overall score, an indication of those diagnostic areas on which they fall below a criterion score, and the (Remedial Grammar) classes in which those areas will be dealt with" (Johns, n.d., p. 4).

In another unpublished document, Johns (1976) presents a rationale for diagnostic testing that, he claims, is intended to relate specifically to features of students' entry behavior, which "arises from **previous learning** of L2: (a) What is **not** known?, (b) How does what **is** known differ from target behaviours? (problem of 'interlanguage')" (p. 1, emphasis in the original).

Johns (1976) asserts that

> it is fundamental to diagnostic testing that students learn a second language differentially within the general constraints of the human Language Acquisition Device, and those differences come from exposure to a previous teaching programme or to differences in the language learning process between individual students. Given that the student's interlanguage is idiosyncratic, diagnostic testing is intended to provide a profile of scores on different measures for individual students or groups of students, as an indication of where particular remedial help may be needed in order to attain target behaviours.
>
> (p. 1)

Furthermore, Johns distinguishes between macro-diagnosis (a profile on the basis of overall language skills) and micro-diagnosis on the basis of the "various discriminations which the student needs to command within the system of the target language" (p. 2). An example of the micro-diagnostic syntactic profile provided by an early version of the BADT is shown in Table 5.2 in Chapter Five.

Another early contribution to a general discussion of diagnostic testing was a presentation by Bernard Spolsky in an unpublished paper given at a workshop in diagnostic testing, organized by the *Interuniversitäre Sprachtestgruppe* in 1981. It is unfortunate that none of the papers presented are available, but fortunately a revised version of Spolsky's thoughts was published in 1992.

In that chapter, Spolsky (1992) claims that diagnostic tests can be classified as educational/curricular types of tests, but argues that "the traditional interest in curriculum did not lead to a concern for diagnosis, which was assumed to be a matter for the classroom teacher" (p. 30). Interestingly, he also suggests that this may be due to the negative connotation of the term 'diagnostic,' which is associated with looking for the cause of a problem, like why someone is ill or a car or computer will not work. "Its very negativity is ill-suited to an approach to teaching that expects not problems but potential, that seeks the good rather than the bad" (p. 30). However, Spolsky does not extend this thinking to diagnosis of reading problems in one's first language, which was and still is an active area of research and test development, as well as for teacher training.

He further argues that diagnostic tests are different from other types of language tests in four ways:

- The diagnostic tester and the diagnostic test user are the same person: the teacher.
- The test taker is defined as a foreign language learner.
- The test purpose is modifying in some way the teaching process.
- The linguistic content is defined by the curriculum.

It is interesting to reflect how well these distinctions hold in the 21st century. Spolsky (1992) then turns to discussing issues of test form and test content, asserts that diagnostic tests are linked to a curriculum and concludes that diagnostic tests will "cycle back and forth between the testing of discrete items, . . . their integration into larger contexts . . . and the performance of integrative functions. . . . The obvious implication is that teachers must be closely involved at all stages" (p. 36).

Finally, Spolsky (1992) argues for the use of self-assessment in diagnosis, provided that two conditions hold, namely that there be no need to give inaccurate answers, and that the question being asked in self-assessment be within the experience of the answerer. The more precise the question, the more it is within the experience of the subject, and the more likely the answer is to be accurate. He closes with a repetition of the argument that

> diagnostic and formative assessment is typically curriculum-driven. The function of diagnostic testing, then, is to shadow, as it were, the implementation of the curriculum and provide feedback to teachers and learners on progress. Its use remains an art, for it requires imaginative balancing of ratios (How much feedback do specific teachers or learners need? How much time can be spent on the process?) and creative implementation (How can it remain fresh and interesting?).
>
> (p. 36)

Shohamy (1992) expands upon the claim that diagnostic testing is central to the curriculum, which ensures that tests become sources of meaningful information about the improvement of foreign language learning. She argues that while external (proficiency) tests influence teaching, and are used to impose new curricula, she is skeptical about the extent to which "the introduction of tests *per se* can bring about meaningful improvement in learning and teaching" (p. 514). Instead, she claims, what is needed is the involvement of those who will carry out the change—the teachers. She develops an assessment model grounded in a number of principles and recommendations:

- focus on both achievement and proficiency
- provide diagnostic information
- connect teaching with learning
- involve the agents of change
- provide comparative information
- develop communicative tests.

A pilot experimentation with Shohamy's (1992) model was based on a collaboration between the pilot schools' teachers and the university assessment team. Shohamy says that the diagnostic information provided was full, detailed, and innovative and involved a variety of language dimensions within the four skills. She notes that the learners' language performance was reported on five dimensions: general performance in each of the language skills; specific performance in sub-skills within each skill; comparative performance relative to other schools; and both item and qualitative assessment of all individual test items, focusing on strengths and weaknesses of the school. Each school interpreted its own results and drew its own conclusions and implications for action and change. According to Shohamy, the assessment was intended to be repeated so that changes could be monitored over time.

Shohamy's (1992) appendices give details of the reading comprehension test specifications, with a range of different text types, whose reading objectives are as follows:

- identify main idea
- identify key words
- arrive at conclusions
- make inferences.

There is also a 'General Table' of objectives, which include the following:

- comprehend vocabulary in context
- identify grammatical functions
- identify logical relations
- follow sequence of events
- discern between relevant and irrelevant
- locate specific information
- identify main idea/message
- make inferences
- hypothesize.

Few results of Shohamy's (1992) experiment are available, but she reports that a validation study was taking place at the time and initial findings indicated that there were differences in impact across schools and over time. She also noted that some schools did not utilize the information provided, but others rethought the curriculum and made changes, and "it was found that a strong need exists to train school faculty in skills for utilising empirical information for making decisions at the school" (p. 519).

To summarize, Spolsky's paper and Shohamy's study emphasize the necessary link between the school curriculum and the content of diagnostic tests and assessment. In the next section, we will review the literature on diagnostic testing, especially in language testing handbooks.

Language Testing Textbooks' Treatment of Diagnosis

In a volume on language test construction and evaluation, Alderson, Clapham, and Wall (1995) define diagnostic tests as follows:

> Diagnostic tests seek to identify those areas in which a student needs further help. These tests can be fairly general, and show, for example, whether a student needs particular help with one of the four main language skills; or they can be more specific, seeking perhaps to identify weaknesses in a student's use of grammar. These more specific diagnostic tests are not easy to design since it is difficult to diagnose precisely strengths and weaknesses in the complexities of language ability. For this reason there are very few purely diagnostic tests. However, achievement and proficiency tests are themselves frequently used, albeit unsystematically, for diagnostic purposes.
>
> (p. 12)

Hughes (1989, 2003) is more specific than any of the previous authors in describing in some detail what diagnostic SFL tests should look like, and suggests that computer-based testing might offer a solution to the numerous problems posed by designing a diagnostic test of a student's strengths and weaknesses. Designing diagnostic tests is very difficult, since when testing grammatical structures, for instance,

> we would need a number of examples of the choice the student made between two structures in every different context which we thought was significantly different and important enough to warrant obtaining information on. A single example of each would not be enough. . . . As a result a comprehensive diagnostic test of English grammar would be vast (think of what would be involved in testing the modal verbs, for instance).
>
> (p. 13)

Interestingly, Hughes (2003) also says that

> the usefulness (and indeed the feasibility) of a general diagnostic test of vocabulary is not readily apparent . . . we would not normally require, or expect, a particular set of lexical items to be a prerequisite for a particular language class. All we would be looking for is some general indication of the adequacy of the students' vocabulary. The learning of specific lexical items in class will rarely depend on previous knowledge of other, specified items.
>
> (p. 179)

However, Alderson (2005) points out that

> until we have developed tests of grammatical knowledge across the range of contexts which Hughes asserts are essential, we will not know whether it is indeed essential to include so much variation, or whether many of the items or contexts are redundant.
>
> (p. 10)

And, of course, the same must apply to all the other linguistic and skill areas, as well as text types and language functions that, a priori, we might be interested in testing. In short, there is clearly a great need, both for clarification of what a diagnostic test should look like and what it should contain, and for empirical research into the performance of such tests and validation of them. There is even a degree of uncertainty about how one might go about validating a diagnostic test rather than, say, a proficiency test or an achievement test.

Hypothetical Features of Diagnostic Tests

In order to bring a more focused discussion of what the characteristics of a diagnostic test should be, Alderson (2005) lists a set of hypothetical features of diagnostic tests, which might guide further thinking about the design of and research into diagnostic tests. It should be pointed out, however, that some of these 'features' contradict other features, and, more importantly, that they constitute a potential agenda for research rather than a set of definitive statements about what is necessary and possible. These hypothetical features include the following:

1. Diagnostic tests are designed to identify strengths and weaknesses in a learner's knowledge and use of language.
2. Diagnostic tests are more likely to focus on weaknesses than on strengths.
3. Diagnostic tests should lead to remediation in further instruction.
4. Diagnostic tests should enable a detailed analysis and report on responses to items or tasks.
5. Diagnostic tests thus give detailed feedback which can be acted upon.

6. Diagnostic tests provide immediate results, or results as little delayed as possible after test-taking.
7. Diagnostic tests are typically low-stakes or no-stakes.
8. Because diagnostic tests are not high-stakes they can be expected to involve little anxiety or other affective barriers to optimum performance.
9. Diagnostic tests are based on content which has been covered in instruction, or which will be covered shortly.
10. Diagnostic tests are based on some theory of language development, preferably a detailed theory rather than a global theory.
11. Thus, diagnostic tests need to be informed by second language acquisition research, or more broadly by applied linguistic theory as well as research.
12. Diagnostic tests are likely to be less 'authentic' than proficiency or other types of tests.
13. Diagnostic tests are more likely to be discrete-point than integrative, or more focussed on specific elements than on global abilities.
14. Diagnostic tests are more likely to focus on language than on language skills.
15. Diagnostic tests are more likely to focus on 'low-level' language skills (like phoneme discrimination in listening tests) than on higher-order skills, which are more integrated.
16. Diagnostic tests of vocabulary knowledge and use are less likely to be useful than diagnostic tests of grammatical knowledge and the ability to use that knowledge in context.
17. Tests of detailed grammatical knowledge and use are difficult to construct because of the need to cover a range of contexts and to meet the demands of reliability.
18. Diagnostic tests of language skills like speaking, listening, reading and writing are (said to be) easier to construct than tests of language knowledge and use. Therefore the results of such tests may be interpretable for remediation or instruction.
19. Diagnostic testing is likely to be enriched by being computer-based. (pp. 11–12)

It should be stressed that this list is tentative, and can only be confirmed by empirical research, once an adequate definition of what diagnosis is and what it entails has been agreed upon.

A recent innovation in thinking about the relationship between assessment and learning which provides another perspective on diagnosis is dynamic assessment, which we introduce in the next section.

Dynamic Assessment

There are various definitions of dynamic assessment in the literature, but in general it is understood to be an interactive approach to conducting assessments in psychology, speech/language, and education that focuses on the ability of the learner to respond to intervention. Key elements in the definitions are active intervention by testers and assessment of test takers' response to intervention (Haywood & Lidz, 2007).

Dynamic assessment (DA) is based on Vygotsky's (1978) socio-cultural theory of cognitive development which he had already introduced in the 1930s. According to Ableeva (2010), the Vygotskian approach to understanding the relationship between instruction and cognitive development differs significantly from the Piagetian view. For Piaget the developmental readiness of individuals determines the type of instruction that is appropriate for them. In contrast, the Vygotskian view tries to understand how instruction influences development and what kind of instruction might promote development.

The key concept in Vygotsky's theory is the zone of proximal development (ZPD), which Vygotsky (1978) refers to as "the distance between the actual developmental level as determined by independent problem-solving and the level of potential development as determined by problem-solving under adult guidance or in collaboration with more capable peers" (p. 86).

According to Vygotsky, learners' actual level of development can be identified on the basis of their independent, unassisted performance, whereas the ZPD reflects what learners can do with the help from the teacher. The ZPD also involves cognitive functions that are not yet fully developed. Instruction and assessment should focus on both the actual and potential (proximal) zone of the learner's development. To assess the learners' ZPD and, thus, their potential for learning, typically requires interaction between the learner and assessor, the use of leading questions, and gradually presented prompts or hints. The proponents of DA argue that assessing performance in this way enables the evaluation not only of the products of learning but also the process. Related to this, the proponents also claim, the approach makes it possible to assess learners' ability to transfer what is gained through mediation to other related but different tasks.

In the literature on DA, the approach is often contrasted with traditional (static) assessment or testing, where the test (or the tester) presents items, one at a time or all at once, to test takers who have to answer them without any help or feedback—assistance during the test would usually be regarded as cheating.

DA is often subdivided into interventionist and interactionist types. Interventionist DA is the more formal, planned, and standardized approach of the two and, as the name suggests, it involves intervention of the tester during the assessment procedure. For example, if the tester notices that the test taker has a problem, the tester intervenes and asks leading questions or gives hints. Such intervention is typically planned—and the tester's prompts may even be scripted in advance—to cover the most likely problems, but it also has to be flexible to some extent as it is obviously not possible to anticipate everything that might happen during face-to-face interaction. Also, certain tests—typically computerized tests—represent interventionist DA. Naturally, computerized DA has to be fully scripted in advance. The key features of computerized and human-mediated interventionist DA are, however, similar: They both implement features such as guiding questions and graduated or adaptive feedback (e.g., the CODA test described below; see also Poehner & Lantolf, 2013). Two somewhat older computerized tests that included DA-based measures of language aptitude (Güthke, 1982; Güthke & Beckmann, 2000; Jacobs, 2001) employed a somewhat simpler approach to mediation as they included only tutorials that were presented to the test takers whenever they encountered problems in completing the tasks, instead of carefully graded prompts.

Interactionist DA entails mediation emerging from the interaction between the tester/teacher and the learner. Unlike in interventionist DA, leading questions, hints, or prompts are not planned in advance, rather, they emerge from the interaction. Computerized tests based on interactionist dynamic assessment do not appear to exist, presumably because of the mostly unplanned nature of the way mediation can take place in interaction between the teacher and learner. Both types of DA can be carried out individually or with groups (for more information, see Sternberg & Grigorenko, 2002; Poehner & Lantolf, 2005; van Compernolle & Kinginger, 2013; Davin, 2013; Poehner & Lantolf, 2013).

Dynamic assessment is mostly applied in classroom contexts where learners and teachers can interact face-to-face and where the teacher can provide the kind of mediation (support) to the learner performing tasks that is at the heart of this approach. In interaction, the teacher can first find out what the learner can do alone, independently, and then what the learner can do with assistance. The approach predicts that what the learner can do with assistance at the time of assessment is what he or she will be able to do alone, without assistance, in the future.

In the area of second and foreign language assessment, dynamic assessment is a relatively new approach. Examples of studies on dynamic assessment in SFL instruction are Lantolf and Poehner (2004), Poehner and Lantolf (2005), Ableeva (2010), van Compernolle and Kinginger (2013), and Davin (2013). Most of the studies have concerned productive language skills, especially speaking, which is quite natural given that the most common form of dynamic assessment of any type takes place in face-to-face interaction between the teacher and the learner. Research, however, suggests that dynamic assessment can reveal problems in learners' language skills that may escape other types of assessment. For example, Gibbons (2003) showed how traditional assessment could lead to an underestimation of students' ability to use scientific terminology in content-language integrated teaching. Learners' progress was only revealed by the use of dynamic assessment procedures (see also Poehner & Lantolf, 2013). On the whole, there is still rather little dynamic assessment research in second and foreign language learning. It is thus likely that the same conclusion holds for DA in SFL as was drawn by Grigorenko and Sternberg (1998) for DA in general, that is, that it is still too early to be sure if the approach is better than the traditional, static testing. More systematic and larger scale research is needed.

An example of the operationalization of dynamic assessment principles in testing reading and listening comprehension is the *Computerized Dynamic Assessment of Language Proficiency* (CODA), designed by the Center for Advanced Language Proficiency Education and Research (CALPER) at Pennsylvania State University in the United States. It is currently available for French, Russian, and Chinese (see http://calper.la.psu.edu/dyna_assess.php?page=exams). According to information on the CODA website, "It is an online formative assessment tool designed to provide more fine-grained profiles of listening and reading comprehension abilities than possible with traditional tests by offering graduated assistance to student test-takers." These online comprehension tests provide the teacher who uses the system with information about the number of test items that his/her learners answered correctly vs. incorrectly on the first try, and they also give an estimate of the amount of support each learner required to complete the test. The item format used is five-option multiple choice.

Each CODA item comes with up to three pre-scripted prompts that are presented to the test taker if their attempts at answering the item are incorrect. No help is given on their first attempt. If the first attempt is a failure, the learner receives an implicit hint, and the hints grow more explicit in the second and third levels of assistance. Learners can also choose to see an explanation of the answer after completing the item, even when they answer the item correctly on their first try.

The sample reading task available through a video guide at the CODA website is a multiple-choice question on a text about a researcher experimenting on how rats learn to run a maze. Unlike the real test items, the sample consists of a question and text in English with only four options, and therefore only two levels of hints are exemplified. The sample question asks the test taker to identify the type of rats that learned to run the maze more quickly. The first level hint is phrased like this: "That's not the correct answer. Read the highlighted part again."

The hint is displayed next to the item and the learner's incorrect choice. The text to be comprehended is also shown and the key portion relevant to the correct choice is marked in green to draw the learner's attention to it. The area of the highlighted text is relatively large, that is, several sentences.

If the learner makes a second unsuccessful attempt at answering the item, the second level hint could be like this: "This is still not the correct answer. Re-read the passage again, noting the author's comparison with the phrases 'pressure of hunger' and 'non-crisis conditions.'" Again, the learner's incorrect reply is shown to him or her. Additionally, the two phrases mentioned in the hint are marked in the text in orange. According to the video guide, the final level of assistance, if this were a true five-option item, would be to pinpoint the key place in the text even more precisely by marking the key word(s) in red. The exact wording of the hint is not given in the guide, but presumably it would refer to rats being either hungry or not, as the text reported hungry rats learning to run the maze more quickly than rats with their bellies full of food.

To give some concrete examples of graduated feedback, we reproduce a table (see Table 3.1) from a recent intervention study that aimed at improving English language learners' ability to construct questions by providing them with graduated/adaptive feedback through an online learning and assessment system (Leontjev, submitted). The domain of language knowledge differs from reading, the focus of the current book, but we hope the example illustrates the levels of feedback that are often used

TABLE 3.1 Examples of graduated (adaptive) feedback in dynamic assessment of the ability to construct questions in English (reproduced from Leontjev, submitted)

Level	Description	Example
0.	An indication that the response is correct	*Your sentence:* When does he come to work?
		Correct!
1.	An implicit hint that there might be something wrong with the answer	*Your sentence:* When did it appeared in your shop?
		Think more carefully. Try to complete the next question—it will be similar to this one.
2.	The location of the error is narrowed down	*Your sentence:* How long **does it sleeps**…?
		Look at the highlighted part of your sentence. The following question will be similar to this one.
3.	The location of the error is further narrowed down, the nature of the error is identified, and metalinguistic clues or elicitations are provided	*Your sentence:* How often **do** you're clean the shop?
		You used the correct helping word. But do we need the verb **are** here?
		The following question will be similar to this one.
4.	Examples of the correct structure are given	*Your sentence:* How many times must **eat the puppy** every day?
		Not quite right. Look at the following examples:
		How are they different from your sentence?
		How **could** you do that?
		What **might** you answer him?
		Where **could** he go?
		The following question will be similar to this one.
5.	The correct response is provided with the explicit indication of what was wrong	*Your sentence:* When **you're took** the picture of the puppy?
		Sorry, you need **did** before the word **you**; the verb **are** is not needed; and you had to use **take** instead of **took**.
		The correct answer is:

in dynamic assessment (see also Aljaafreh & Lantolf, 1994). The feedback in Leontjev's study consisted of two parts: a reproduction of the question that the learner had selected from the options given to him or her, and the actual feedback message.

The CODA tests produce two scores for the learner. Each item is worth four points and if the learner manages to reply to the item correctly on the first attempt he or she receives four points. Thus, the score based on the number of correctly answered items is equivalent to a total score from a traditional language test. The second is a mediated score where each failure to reply to an item reduces the score by one point.

In Chapter Eight, where we discuss various types of feedback, we present other examples of item level feedback to test takers, some of which bear some similarity to the hints typical of tests designed in the dynamic assessment framework. The key difference between the item-level feedback in DA and most other types of tests is that in DA tests hints are graded in systematic (although probably to some extent varied) ways and provide learners with increasingly explicit guidance.

We note that dynamic assessment is somewhat similar to aptitude testing, as they both try to evaluate a person's potential for learning something. They are, however, based on different theoretical considerations and assumptions. Traditionally, for example, foreign language aptitude has been considered as a rather static, unchangeable characteristic of a person (cf. Robinson, 2005) whereas dynamic assessment does not appear to take a clear view on the changeability of learners' learning potential. Clearly, the two approaches differ in that language aptitude tests are static measures of learners' current abilities that are thought to predict the facility or speed with which learners are likely to learn new languages. On the contrary, dynamic language tests aim at improving learners' language proficiency during the testing or assessment procedure. They also produce a quantitative measure of learning potential by taking into account, in the final (mediated) score, the amount of help the learner needs to complete the tasks (see the CODA example above).

There is, however, some interplay between aptitude and dynamic testing in the area of test development. A new type of second language aptitude test developed by Grigorenko, Sternberg, and Ehrman (2000) "utilizes the dynamic paradigm of testing by tapping the processes of knowledge acquisition at the time of the test, and . . . provides diagnostic information that might be suitable for devising optimal teaching and learning strategies" (p. 393). The focus of the new test, CANAL-FT (Cognitive Ability for Novelty in Acquisition of Language as applied to foreign language testing), is on the learners' ability to deal with novelty and ambiguity. The test makes use of both immediate and delayed recall tasks administered after the following types of tasks: (a) learning meanings of neologisms from context, (b) understanding the meaning of passages, (c) continuous paired-associate learning (learning to associate English words with words from an invented language), (d) sentential inference (figuring out syntactic and morphological rules from examples), and (e) learning language rules (learning words and grammatical rules of an invented language) (Grigorenko et al., 2000, p. 394).

In the next section, we look at another recent development relevant to diagnostic testing, namely the retrofitting of proficiency tests to a diagnostic function.

Retrofitting Proficiency Tests Through the Use of Statistics

Recently, there have been developments in research into SFL diagnosis in a somewhat different direction from speculations about how diagnosis might be defined, characterized, or related to curricula. Efforts have been made to retrofit proficiency tests to diagnostic purposes (sometimes also known as reverse-engineering tests intended for quite other purposes). Proficiency test developers like the Educational Testing Service (developers of the TOEFL family of tests) and the University of Michigan (the developers of MELAB—the Michigan English Language Battery) as well as associated researchers have sought to provide test users with rather more refined information about test takers' results than a single score or even separate scores for the three or four skills tested in their assessment batteries

As Lee and Sawaki (2009a) state

> a great number of large-scale assessments designed for high-stakes decision making often report a single score for each test section or for an entire test. For a test to inform intervention or learner self-learning, however, more fine-grained information about learner performance, such as a skill (or attribute) mastery profile based on learner performance within a test section, is required. For the purpose of contextualization, suppose, for instance, that a reading test reports a single score of reading proficiency for each test taker. Although this score provides some information about the overall level of reading proficiency for a particular test taker, it does not provide any further insights into the specific areas of reading that require further improvement on the part of the examinee. In contrast, imagine another reading test that reports a profile of mastery states of the reading skills required for the test. Such a skill mastery profile provides fine-grained information about the test taker's strengths and weaknesses in reading (e.g., she is relatively strong on vocabulary and understanding specific information but relatively weak on distinguishing main ideas from details). In the contexts of language learning and instruction, the availability of such diagnostic feedback at this finer grain size would allow the instructor to identify the learner's specific reading deficiencies and plan instruction that is tailored to the needs of the particular learner.
>
> (pp. 239–240)

In fact, as we shall see below and in the next chapter, this is precisely what tests like DIALANG and DELTA aim to do, but they are *designed* to make such diagnosis possible. Proficiency tests like TOEFL iBT or MELAB are not designed from the onset to be diagnostic. The aim, however, of Lee and Sawaki and others is to make such proficiency tests diagnostically useful by retrofitting them through the use of recent statistical models, known collectively as Cognitive Diagnostic Models (CDM), Cognitive Diagnostic Assessment or Cognitive Diagnostic Analysis (confusingly, both are abbreviated CDA).

In fact, applications of Cognitive Diagnosis Models to proficiency tests are not new. One early Cognitive Diagnosis Model, the rule-space model (Tatsuoka, 1983, 1990) was used to create and evaluate a Q-matrix. The Q-matrix is simply a two-way table of items in the rows and item attributes in the columns with 1 or 0 indicating presence or absence of the particular attribute or sub-skill, or whatever content aspect is considered relevant from the perspective of the test developer or the test construct. Test data (0/1 results on individual items) are then analyzed and matched to the Q-matrix (Buck & Tatsuoka, 1998; Buck, Tatsuoka, & Kostin, 1997; Buck, Tatsuoka, Kostin, & Phelps, 1997). More recent approaches have also first built a Q-matrix, and then applied one or more psychometric CDMs to the data. Lee and Sawaki (2009b) explore three such models (the general diagnostic model—GDM, the fusion model—FM, and latent class analysis—LCA) based on data from the TOEFL Internet-based test (iBT) of reading and listening, with similar, and promising, results.

Jang (2009a) applies the Fusion Model to data from the TOEFL test preparation practice tests *LanguEdge*, argues for the validity of the feedback that results from that analysis, and concludes that "the results offer useful information about the potential challenges and conditions for future application of cognitive diagnostic assessment" (p. 31). However, there is a clear caution in her account of the limitations of this approach because it was based on tests that were not designed to be diagnostic in the first place. Thus, the information provided by the psychometric analyses may be fundamentally flawed.

> The results suggest that the CDA approach can provide more fine-grained diagnostic information about the level of competency in reading skills than traditional aggregated-test scoring can. While various empirical evidence [*sic*] supported the dependability of the skill profiling process, the results also raised some concerns about the application of the CDA approach to a test developed for non-diagnostic purposes, most significantly, a lack of diagnostic capacity of some of the test items with extremely easy or difficult levels.
>
> (Jang, 2009a)

Alderson (2010) provides a critical commentary on several of the articles in the 2009 Special Issue of *Language Assessment Quarterly* on Cognitive Diagnostic Assessment, which he claims is 'a landmark publication.' Lee and Sawaki's (2009b) is the first paper in that Special Issue, which Alderson considers to be a very useful overview of CDA and its various models and methods. He is, however, critical of a lack of reference to methods of content analysis, which needs to be addressed in future research (Alderson, 2010).

The second article, Sawaki, Kim, and Gentile (2009), reports on a study involving six judges analyzing the content of two prototype forms of the Reading and Listening tests in the *LanguEdge* test-preparation software and two TOEFL iBT test forms. We are not told what the test specifications contained that was of relevance to diagnosis specifically, although we do learn that the specifications define three constructs for Reading (Basic Comprehension, Inferencing, and Reading to Learn). Unfortunately, we are not given any sources for the coding categories used by the Q-matrix creators, and it is unclear whether any theories of reading in a second language were consulted, and if so, which aspects were found to be most useful. Disappointingly, the attributes that were the object of multiple meetings and discussions among the judges are very traditional, and are not particularly fine-grained. The Reading attributes are as follows:

1. Understanding Word Meaning
2. Identifying Information: Search and Match
3. Understanding Information within Sentences
4. Understanding and Connecting Information within a Paragraph
5. Understanding and Connecting Information across Paragraphs
6. Understanding the Relative Importance of Information and Relationships among Ideas.

Moreover, Skills 4 and 5 were later combined into one category—'Connecting Information'—after rounds of coding and discussion; and Skills 2 and 3 were merged into the category 'Understanding Specific Information,' resulting in only four 'Skills,' which can hardly be said to be 'diagnostic.'

Indeed, the authors recognize that for proper diagnosis it is necessary "to look more deeply into various types of linguistic sub-processes that are thought to underlie L2 comprehension" (Sawaki et al., 2009, p. 207). (Examples of some such processes are given in Chapter Six of this book.) They point out that "current theories of reading . . . suggest the importance of the efficiency of lower-level processes for rapid and accurate reading . . . comprehension of text." Thus, it is unclear why such theories were not utilized when deciding which attributes to code. Nevertheless, the authors recommend that, when designing 'a true diagnostic assessment,' a range of psycholinguistic knowledge and skills should be taken into account, acknowledging the complexity of comprehension processes.

One reason for the above-mentioned reduction in the number of skills is that there were relatively few items in the proficiency tests examined. "In the present large-scale assessment context, identifying stable coding categories that can consistently be supported by sufficient numbers of items for score reporting across test forms was of prime importance" (Sawaki et al., 2009, p. 206). This points yet again to the problem of trying to retrofit a proficiency test into diagnostic uses. As Hughes (2003) points out, to be suitably diagnostic, tests need to contain multiple items of any one targeted attribute.

The third article, Jang (2009b), makes a more substantial contribution to understanding what is involved in diagnosing reading in a second language as she deals at greater length with research and theories of reading in a second language than the other articles in the Special Issue reviewed here.

Jang (2009b) points out that "test developers' skill specifications are useful but not sufficient for providing a comprehensive picture of reading processing skills" (p. 213). After an extensive review of the literature on textual variables, test specifications, text-related and test-taking-related reading skills and strategies, and a detailed analysis of eleven learners' retrospective verbal protocols, Jang identified nine skills, each with at least three further sub-skills. These skills (see Jang, 2009b, p. 223) were then used by five raters to categorize all 37 items in the Reading test. It would be useful to replicate Jang's study using her list of skills, because there were problems with insufficient numbers of items testing some skills for statistically reliable results. This indicates yet again the problem with trying to reverse-engineer through psychometric means a proficiency test into a diagnostic function. Despite this limitation, the nine skills are usefully illustrated by reference to the results of the verbal protocol analysis. For example, the following insights into the inferencing skill seem useful for diagnostic purposes:

> Items measuring the inferencing skill proved to be more cognitively demanding and required test-takers to use multiple skills simultaneously. Items associated with the inferencing skill included difficult vocabulary and complex sentence structures. Further, the inferencing skill involved some degree of synthesizing textual information at the global level by connecting textual information to background knowledge including both formal schemata (associated with knowledge about text genres and rhetorical organizational structures) and content schemata (associated with the knowledge of textual content).
>
> (Jang, 2009b, p. 225)

Lee and Sawaki (2009b) claim that a typical procedure of Cognitive Diagnostic Analysis is as follows:

1. identifying a set of skills involved in a test (*they do not detail how, with justification, this should be done—authors' comment*)
2. demonstrating which skills are required for correctly answering each item in the test (*it is unclear how this can be done—authors' comment*)
3. estimating the profiles of skill mastery for individual examinees based on actual test performance data using the CDM

4.   providing score reporting and/or diagnostic feedback to examinees and other stakeholders (*this is not described in any detail—authors' comment*).

(p. 175)

One further study attempting to retrofit a proficiency test to diagnostic uses is Li (2011), using the University of Michigan's MELAB test. However, once again, there were too few items testing particular sub-skills to be analyzed statistically, and Li admits that it is important for there to be a balance between the number of sub-skills being measured and the number of items in the test (i.e., more items should be included if more fine-grained diagnostic information is of interest). Li concludes (2011) that

the present study shows that it is possible to extract richer diagnostic information than the MELAB reading test was designed to elicit. However, retrofitting CDMs with existing tests is by no means an optimal approach for diagnostic assessment. In order for a test to generate detailed diagnostic feedback, it is essential that it be built for a skills-based diagnostic purpose (DiBello, Roussos, and Stout, 2007). Thus, a successful cognitive diagnostic assessment of reading comprehension largely depends on test development, which again depends on more insightful understanding of the cognitive processes underlying reading comprehension.

(p. 40)

We could not agree more. This problem and limitation is inevitable if one is reverse engineering an existing proficiency test which has been designed with a certain number and mix of items for a quite different function. We repeat: better to design a test to be diagnostic than to attempt retrofitting a proficiency test by statistical means. CDA may be useful, but not, clearly, for reverse engineering. What we would prefer to see is the application of CDA to truly diagnostic tests that meet at least some of the hypothetical features listed by Alderson (2005) in an earlier section.

Examples of Tests Designed to Be Diagnostic

In what follows, we describe and illustrate several testing projects which sought to develop diagnostic reading tests, in order to understand better the design process of diagnostic testing. The tests we present are DIALANG, DELNA, DELTA, and DIALUKI.

DIALANG

DIALANG (www.lancaster.ac.uk/researchenterprise/dialang/about.htm) is an online multilingual suite of diagnostic tests, based on the Common European Framework of Reference (CEFR), and co-funded by the European Commission's

Directorate General for Education and Culture from 1997 to 2004, and supported by 22 European universities and institutions. The project was managed by a consortium of the Universities of Jyväskylä, Finland; The Free University of Berlin; Lancaster University; and CITO, a Dutch testing agency. The suite consists of tests of reading, listening, writing, vocabulary, and structures in 14 European languages, namely, Danish, Dutch, English, Finnish, French, German, Greek, Icelandic, Irish, Italian, Norwegian, Portuguese, Spanish, and Swedish.

Users of DIALANG first select the interface language (from the 14 listed above) in which they wish to read the test instructions, the self-assessment statements (taken from the CEFR), and the extensive feedback. Having selected the interface language, they then decide in which one of the five skills or language elements they wish to take a test. For example, they might take a test of German reading with the interface language in Greek, or a test of Spanish listening with the instructions in Icelandic.

Users are then given the option to take a Vocabulary Size Placement Test (VSPT) in the target language—this is a yes-no test, where real words in that language are mixed with a number of pseudo words that follow the phonological constraints of the target language (see Chapter Five for more details and examples). This is intended to provide an objective estimate of the user's vocabulary and is complemented, again optionally, by a set of self-assessment statements adapted from the CEFR scales, with which the user has to agree or disagree. For example, the following are examples of can-do statements for reading:

- I can follow short, simple written instructions, especially if they contain pictures.
- I can go quickly through long and complex texts, locating relevant details.

The combination of the VSPT and the self-assessments is then used to assign the user to an easy, medium, or difficult set of items that have been calibrated to the CEFR through specially devised standard-setting procedures (for an introduction to standard setting, see Cizek & Bunch, 2007). The reason for this is to give the user a test most suited to his or her level, because there is no point giving an advanced learner easy items or a beginning learner very difficult items. If, however, the user decides not to take the VSPT or do the self-assessment, then he or she is immediately routed to the test they have chosen, at a medium level of difficulty.

Users then take the test—usually consisting of around 30 items on a wide range of texts—and receive extensive feedback on their performance. Immediate feedback on performance on each item is available, or it can be switched off. The user can choose which feedback to read and which to ignore. This feedback is in the administration language for ease of processing. Brief feedback is available on their performance on the VSPT, and their self-assessment is compared with their test result (the test result is not a score, but one of the six levels of the CEFR, together with an explanation of what that level means). Users are also provided with a set of explanations that they can explore as to possible reasons why their test results and their self-assessments do not match, and they can also explore a range of advice on what they might do to improve their level. DIALANG currently does not provide an individualized set of advice about what sort of action to take or activities to engage in, but the system does provide feedback on whether users got each item right or wrong, what skills were tested by each item, and users can compare their response to each item with the correct response. Thus, the test is diagnostic at the macro level of the CEFR level (A1 to C2) of their ability in each skill and at the micro level of each item. Self-assessment is considered a very important part of the system and is intended to encourage learner autonomy and the opportunity for learners to reflect on their learning as well as what is involved in learning a language.

Users can then, if they wish, take a test of a different skill or in a different interface language. The system is available free of charge, online at any time or place, and can be downloaded (www.lancs.ac.uk/researchenterprise/dialang/about) to the user's computer, from where it interacts with the DIALANG secure server.

The opening screen, where they first choose the interface language, looks like this (see Figure 3.1):

FIGURE 3.1 DIALANG opening screen

Users then proceed to choose the target language and skill or language element they wish to be tested on (see Figure 3.2).

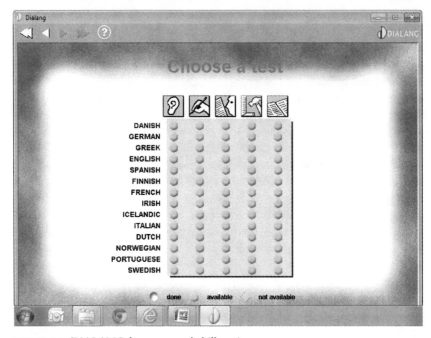

FIGURE 3.2 DIALANG language and skill options

Figure 3.3 shows the feedback menu where users can inspect their results on the Vocabulary Size Placement Test and their self-assessment as well as on the skill test chosen and their answers to each skill test item, together with the correct answer. They can also explore advice on improving their language skills.

Figure 3.4 is an example of the test result screen, where the user is presented with their CEFR level and a brief description of what sort of texts they can understand.

Figure 3.5 is an example of the explanations that are given about why self-assessment and the test result may not match. Users can click on the menu on the left-hand side for a range of different suggestions, including

- How often you use the language
- How you use the language
- Situations differ
- Other learners and you
- Other tests and DIALANG
- You and your targets
- Tests and real life
- Other reasons.

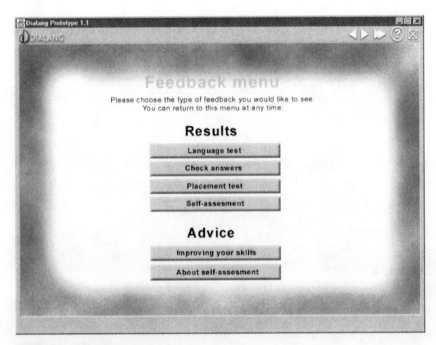

FIGURE 3.3 DIALANG feedback menu

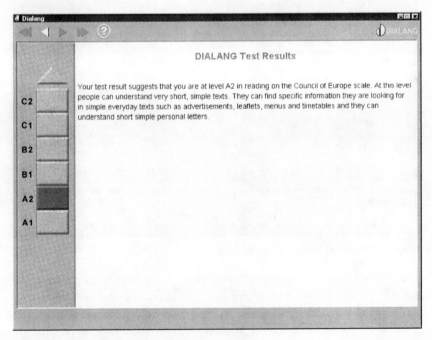

FIGURE 3.4 DIALANG test result (an example)

Explanations of self-assessment

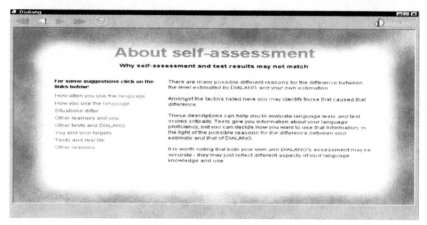

FIGURE 3.5 DIALANG explanations of self-assessment

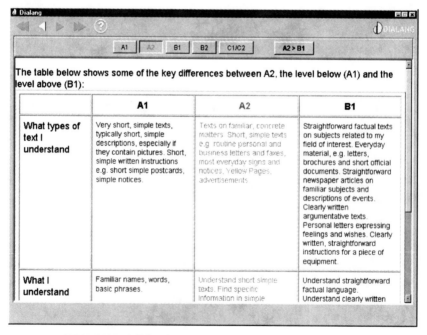

FIGURE 3.6 DIALANG skill level descriptions

Figure 3.6 presents examples of the skill level descriptions, showing users how the level the user has reached (in this case A2) differs from the level below (A1) and how the level above differs from the level reached (in this case B1), in terms of what type of text the learner at each level can understand, what they can understand, and under what conditions and with what limitations.

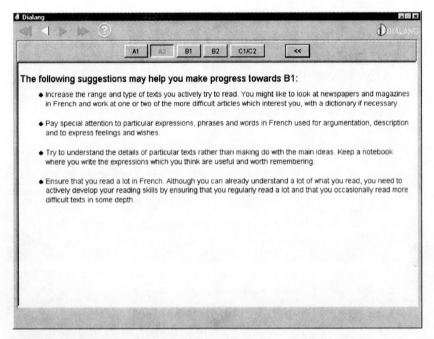

FIGURE 3.7 DIALANG suggestions for improvement

Figure 3.7 provides suggestions which may help the user progress from their current CEFR level towards the next level above (in this case, from A2 to B1). In both Figures 3.6 and 3.7, the user can click on the buttons labeled with the CEFR levels and explore how to progress from any chosen level to the next highest level.

What is interesting about DIALANG in terms of diagnosis is not only that users can received feedback in any of the 14 test administration languages but also that this feedback is at different levels (more about this in Chapter Eight). There is generalized feedback about one's reading (or other skill) level on the six-level CEFR scale, as well as feedback on the six-level Vocabulary Size Placement Test scale. But there is more fine-grained feedback on the sub-skills of reading (or other skills) and also feedback on one's performance on each test item, with a comparison between the individual's answer and the correct answer. The generalized feedback is rather similar to the traditional feedback given on placement tests, and indeed the evidence is that DIALANG is actually largely used for placement purposes at the beginning of a course, whereas, as we shall see in Chapter Eight, users tend not to pay much attention to the more fine-grained feedback. As will be evident in subsequent sections of this chapter, this tension between diagnostic intent and use for placement also exists in other tests that claim to be diagnostic.

Diagnostic English Language Needs Assessment (DELNA)

DELNA (www.delna.auckland.ac.nz/uoa/) is an adaptation of the University of Melbourne's DELA test (Elder & Randow, 2008) developed by the University of Auckland in 2000. DELNA is a test of academic English skills. It consists of two components—a 30-minute Screening Test, which is a computer-based assessment and consists of vocabulary tasks and a timed reading task, and a 2-hour DELNA Diagnosis.

Three possible outcomes of the Screening Test are:

1.   If the outcome shows that the student's English language proficiency is 'very good,' then they are expected to develop their academic literacy independently during their studies.
2.   If the results show that the student's English Language Proficiency is 'satisfactory,' then they "will be directed to the language enrichment options on campus, where they will be able to brush up language skills."
3.   If the results of the screening assessment suggest that the student may need language support as they begin their studies, they will be asked to take the DELNA Diagnosis.

No score appears to be reported and the screening test is clearly rough and ready screening only. Profiles describing students' skill level in terms of 'bands' (see below) are sent to them approximately eight days after they sit the 2-hour Diagnosis. The band descriptors are summarized below.

Summary Band Descriptions (for reading only)

Bands 8 & 9: Proficient or highly proficient user.
Recommendation: No support required. Unlikely to experience any difficulties with academic English. A typical student at this level reads efficiently and with ease, extracting and synthesizing both abstract and factual information from linguistically complex texts, even when these are not on familiar topics.

Band 7: Independent user.
Recommendation: English is satisfactory and no support is required. The student may, nevertheless, benefit from further practice in one or other skill area. A typical student at this level can read and interpret most important information in academic texts, with only occasional lapses in understanding.

Band 6: Adequate user.
Recommendation: English is mainly satisfactory but would be advised to seek concurrent support in one or more skill areas. A typical student at this level can generally understand academic texts but may take some time to draw out the necessary information or to interpret parts of the text, particularly those which are linguistically complex or deal with abstract ideas.

Band 5: Limited user.
Recommendation: May be at risk with academic study due to limited English skills. Needs intensive English language support. A typical student at this level reads academic texts with difficulty. May be able to get the gist but important concepts/information may be misunderstood or overlooked.

Band 4: Very limited user.
Recommendation: Is likely to be at severe risk of academic failure due to inadequate English. Needs intensive English language support. A typical student at this level reads very slowly and has difficulty extracting meaning from academic prose or following a line of argument due to inadequate knowledge of English vocabulary and grammar.

These outcomes resemble proficiency test bands rather than the detailed information that diagnostic tests are hypothesized to provide. This test might be more appropriately classified as a placement test, as it is unclear how DELNA can be classified as a diagnostic test in terms of the definitions and hypothetical features presented in earlier sections. Further details, with examples of test items, are available at www.delna.auckland.ac.nz/webdav/site/delna/shared/documents/delna-handbook.pdf.

Diagnostic English Language Tracking Assessment (DELTA)

The DELTA (http://gslpa.polyu.edu.hk/eng/delta_web/) consists of tests of listening, reading, grammar, and vocabulary (and writing and speaking tests are currently under development). It was originally developed at the Hong Kong Institute of Education as the Tertiary English Language Test (TELT) as a paper-and-pencil placement test, but from 2009 was re-developed as a web-based diagnostic assessment by the English Language Centre of the Polytechnic University of Hong Kong (HKPU), and is now run by a consortium of the HKPU, Lingnan University and the City University of Hong Kong. Table 3.2 gives details of the various components of DELTA.

The assessment lasts 90 minutes, as per Table 3.2 taken from Urmston, Raquel, and Tsang (2013, p. 63). The tests are marked immediately by computer. Rasch-based analyses are then generated on the test items, and individual student Component Skills Profiles are produced (see Figure 3.8). The numbers on the vertical axis show the DELTA measures as points on the DELTA proficiency scale, which ranges from 0–200 using Rasch-based logits converted onto the DELTA proficiency scale. The figures correspond to the test-taker's performance on the skills tests shown on the horizontal axis. Thus this student scored 107 for Listening below the overall mean of 113 for the test as a whole, and 118 for Reading, which was above the overall mean.

After taking the test, students receive a detailed diagnostic report on their performance, where the language sub-skills tested by each item on the test are recorded in the student's DELTA Report, together with statements of the student's

TABLE 3.2 Components of DELTA

Component	Parts	Composition	Difficulty	Time Allowed
Listening	Part 1	1 Recording + 4–6 MCQ items	Easier to More difficult	20–25 minutes
	Part 2	1 Recording + 6–8 MCQ items		
	Part 3	1 Recording + 6–8 MCQ items		
	Part 4	1 Recording + 6–8 MCQ items		
Vocabulary		20–25MCQ items	A range	65–70 minutes
Reading	Part 1	1 Text + 4–6 MCQ items	Easier to More difficult	
	Part 2	1 Text + 6–8 MCQ items		
	Part 3	1 Text + 6–8 MCQ items		
	Part 4	1 Text + 6–8 MCQ items		
Grammar	Part 1	1 Text + 10–15 MCQ items	A range	
	Part 2	1 Text + 10–15 MCQ items		

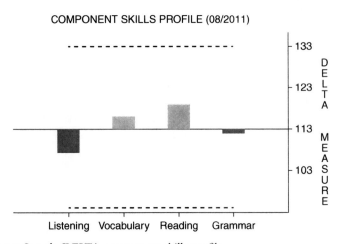

FIGURE 3.8 Sample DELTA component skills profile

strengths and weaknesses (see Figure 7 in Sample DELTA Component Report on Reading, http://gslpa.polyu.edu.hk/eng/delta_web/doc/Sample_Report.pdf).

The sub-skills tested in the reading section of DELTA are as follows:

1. Identifying specific information
2. Interpreting a word or phrase as used by the writer
3. Understanding main ideas and supporting ideas
4. Understanding information and making an inference
5. Inferring the writer's reasoning

6. Interpreting an attitude or intention of the writer
7. Understanding grammatical relationships of words or phrases across text
8. Identifying text type.

An important, indeed unique, feature of DELTA is that because DELTA measures are points on an IRT proficiency scale, each time a student takes DELTA, the performance is measured on the same scale. Therefore, progress can be tracked over time on the same scale.

Urmston et al. (2013) describe the main function and the future challenges facing the DELTA system as follows:

> The main function of the DELTA is to inform students about their English language proficiency and to help them to monitor their progress as they seek to improve this proficiency while they are at university. To this end it is vital that the DELTA is supported through providing DELTA-dedicated learning resources, such as teacher/advisor support and self-access learning provision, both physical and online. These resources are gradually being put in place at the three institutions through initiatives such as the Inter-university Collaborative Online Self-Access (ICOSA) project, which is developing an online repository of self-access English language learning resources for Hong Kong university students.
>
> Perhaps the greatest challenge of the DELTA is to be able to predict growth in English language learning in students so that they will know just what they need to do to get to where they wish to be in terms of proficiency at graduation. As more students take the DELTA repeatedly, the data gathered will facilitate the modeling of the typical growth patterns of students who start at a particular proficiency level, engage in particular language learning activities through both a formal curriculum and extra-curricular activities and study in particular universities in particular pro-grams. It is anticipated that in this way, the DELTA can make a significant contribution to facilitating students' learning of and through English while they are at university.
>
> (pp. 77–78)

DIALUKI

DIALUKI (www.jyu.fi/dialuki) is a research project located in the Centre for Applied Language Studies at the University of Jyväskylä, and funded by the Academy of Finland, the University of Jyväskylä, and the UK Economic and Social Research Council. The project is currently investigating the diagnosis of reading and writing in a second or foreign language and includes researchers in language testing, applied linguistics, psychology, and dyslexia. The project began in 2010 and the current phase ended in December 2013.

The informants are in two language groups: Finnish-speaking learners of English as a Foreign Language and Russian-speaking learners of Finnish as a Second Language. The project began by studying the English learners when they were in Grade 4 (age 10), Grade 8 (age 14) and the second year of upper secondary school (age 17). There are two groups of Russian speakers, the primary school group and the lower secondary school group.

There are three major components to the project. Study One is a cross-sectional study of the learners at these different ages, and some 850 learners have taken part in that study. In it we are exploring the value of a range of L1 and SFL measures in predicting SFL reading and writing in order to select the best predictors for further studies. We give further details in Chapter Four.

Study Two is a longitudinal study which started in 2010 and continued until the end of 2013. We are studying the development of SFL literacy skills, and the relationship of this development to the diagnostic measures we used in Study One. In addition, several language lessons in the participating schools were observed and the interaction between the teachers and students was recorded.

Study Three is a series of intervention studies, aimed at examining the effects of training on SFL reading and writing.

DIALUKI employs a multi-method or mixed method approach to studying reading and writing in an SFL. In practice this means that both quantitative and qualitative methods are used in the gathering and analysis of data. The quantitative aspects of the project relate to the administration and analysis of a range of language and other tests, as well as background and motivation questionnaires to the learners participating in all three Studies of the project. The qualitative methods include interviewing a considerable number of language teachers during Study One and Two and observing language classrooms in Study One. The results of the teacher interviews are discussed in Chapter Nine, which focuses on diagnosis in the classrooms.

Study One used a range of L1 and SFL measures of reading (and writing), as well as cognitive and linguistic tests, again in both L1 and SFL, in order to see which measures, in which language, best predict abilities in reading (and writing). In addition there are measures of self-assessment, and motivation and background questionnaires for the learners as well as background questionnaires for their parents.

Chapters Four, Five, Six, and Seven describe in detail the background to the various constructs upon which the DIALUKI research is based and the linguistic, cognitive, background, and motivation instruments used in the cross-sectional Study One.

Summary

In this chapter we have briefly discussed some of the literature on diagnostic SFL language testing and cited some hypothetical features that diagnostic SFL tests might have, which could form part of a framework for the development of diagnostic tests. We then described a somewhat related type of assessment known as dynamic assessment and exemplified how it might be embodied in a computer-based test by looking at the CODA test. Next, we examined a number of fairly recent attempts to provide diagnostic information by statistical analysis of the results of proficiency tests. However, we concluded that such retrofitting of a diagnostic function was very limited in its usefulness, because the tests had not been designed with a diagnostic function in mind. Finally, we described and illustrated four interesting tests and projects—DIALANG, DELNA, DELTA, and DIALUKI—that claim to be diagnostic. It is for the reader to judge to what extent these tests can be said to embody the hypothetical features of SFL tests presented in this chapter.

In the next chapter, we will describe and discuss the construct of reading that might underlie a diagnostic test of second or foreign language reading.

4

WHAT IS READING?

In a literate society, it is not always realized how complex the act of reading is. Although children have to learn to read, most do so easily and with relatively little effort. And if the act of reading is second nature to most adolescents and adults, then what could be easier than testing the ability to read? Just take a text, ask a few questions about the text, and you have a valid test of reading! However, it is not so simple. What text should be selected? Will any text serve the purpose, about any topic? Handwritten or word-processed text? How long should the text be? How familiar should the words be? What grammatical structures should the text contain, what sort of organization should it have? What genre should be used? A narrative or story, an expository text about an experiment? A poem? A newspaper article? And what sort of questions should be asked? Who should ask them? Should they be about details of the text, or about hidden meanings? Should questions be asked that require the reader to detect irony? Humor? Should the reader be required to summarize the text, to make an interpretation of the text, to criticize or make a judgment about the text?

In fact, of course, assessing one's ability to read is a complicated process and reading is far more complex than is perhaps generally appreciated. And assessing one's ability to read in a second or foreign language (SFL) is even more complicated because it involves not only the ability to read but also the knowledge of and the ability to use the second or foreign language. In order to assess or test a person's ability to read and understand texts in an SFL, it is important to know what comprehension is, and what one has to know and do in order to be able to read. Without knowledge of what reading involves—what is technically known as the construct of SFL reading—one cannot develop a valid test of reading. In other words, in order to test the ability to read, one needs to have a theory of reading. And in order to be able to diagnose a person's strengths and weaknesses in SFL reading, one needs to know what sort of strengths and weaknesses may be involved in reading. Therefore, in this chapter, we will attempt an overview of what is known about SFL reading.

Research Into Reading

There is a great deal of research into reading, especially into reading in one's first language, and particularly into reading English as one's first language. Far from being a simple activity, research has shown how complex first language reading actually is. There are many theories of what is involved in reading and in learning to read, and there are many controversies as to which is the best or better theory. Clearly, reading involves getting meaning from print, but how does one 'get meaning'? It is generally acknowledged that reading involves recognizing words, and word recognition involves relating print to sound. In alphabetic languages, this means being able to link phonemes to graphemes—the relationship between sounds and letters is, however, not always one to one. In so-called transparent orthographies, such as Finnish or Spanish, there is indeed a more or less one-to-one relationship between sounds and letters. However, other languages, such as English, French, Arabic, or Hebrew, have what is known as a deep orthography, and the relationship between sounds and letters is much more opaque and complex. Other orthographies, such as Japanese *hiragana* and *katakana*, denote syllables rather than phonemes, and logographic orthographies such as Chinese have no direct relationship between symbols and sounds, rather logograms represent words or morphemes.

But there is more to reading than 'merely' recognizing the sounds of a language through print. The grammar of a language is important for conveying meaning: A text is not simply a collection of words, because text has structure and structure is governed by the language's grammar and the rules of organization at sentence and paragraph levels. The meaning of text is not simply the meanings of words in combination. Readers have to apply their knowledge of the world to text in order to develop an understanding of text; however, readers also have to be able to infer meanings that are not explicitly stated, but which readers can agree are available, hidden, in the text. Understanding text involves drawing inferences, making subjective interpretations, as well as recognizing explicit statements.

Thus, reading researchers often refer to different levels of meaning and of understanding. Distinctions are made between literal understanding, inferred meanings, global comprehension, and more. It is also increasingly common to refer to a text model of meaning and a situation model (Kintsch, 1998). A text model is what the writer of the text intends his or her readers to understand, whereas a situation model describes the meanings that readers create for themselves from the text. Thus, texts do not simply contain meaning, which is to be 'mined' from the text by a reader, but they give rise to meanings in the head of the reader, and that meaning, which the reader creates, will vary with the readers' purpose for reading, the degree of attention they pay to the text, their knowledge of the world and the culture in which the text is embedded, their skill as readers, and their ability to think critically and creatively about the text being 'read.'

First and SFL Reading

However, reading in one's first language (L1) is not the same as reading in one's SFL, yet most research into reading has been done on L1 reading. In fact, L1 reading is a huge area of study and the research literature is vast, much too large to be fully understood by one person or even one team of researchers. Nevertheless, a number of recent publications in SFL reading (Alderson, 2000; Koda, 2005; Grabe, 2009) have offered useful overviews of the main recent trends in L1 reading research and theories and their implications for the teaching and testing of SFL reading. In addition, research into the testing of SFL reading is not insubstantial and is growing steadily, even though very little work has been done specifically into the diagnosis of SFL reading ability.

The existence of a vast literature on L1 reading, but a much smaller and younger literature on SFL reading, unfortunately often means that L1 reading research and L1 reading theories are taken to apply to SFL reading. Certainly from the 1950s to the 1970s, SFL reading theory was derivative of L1 reading theory, and it was only in the 1980s and beyond that SFL reading became a discipline in its own right. Although much L1 reading research and theory may indeed apply to SFL reading also, this should not be taken for granted. It is obvious, for example, that SFL reading involves knowledge of the SFL itself, be that in oral or written form. And SFL reading is likely to be less skillful, for most readers, than their L1 reading. In contrast, L1 reading research usually takes it for granted that the reader 'knows' the language, and interest focuses on how the ability to read develops. The child learning to read already has a firm mastery of the spoken language and its grammar, together with a rapidly developing vocabulary, and thus the child has a well-developed ability to understand and use the spoken language. What the child needs to learn is the relationship between what he or she already knows, and its written form. No such assumption can be made for SFL reading, and in SFL reading much discussion and some research has examined whether SFL reading is a reading problem or a language problem (Alderson, 1984).

It is often asserted that L1 reading ability transfers to SFL reading and that the reason why some readers have problems with SFL reading is because they are poor readers in their L1. The solution to the problem of poor SFL reading, it is argued, is to improve one's L1 reading so that transfer can take place.

However, most SFL research into this question has shown that SFL reading is more of a language problem than a reading problem, and that there is a 'threshold' of SFL proficiency that a reader has to reach and surpass, beyond which L1 reading can transfer to the SFL and to some extent can compensate for gaps in SFL knowledge, but below which SFL knowledge is essential (this is the so-called short-circuit hypothesis; Clarke, 1980). There is evidence (Sparks, Paton, Ganschow, Humbach, & Javorsky, 2008) that many L1 reading problems transfer to SFL reading, but not all do transfer. It is also likely, though far from adequately researched to date, that SFL reading problems vary across different L1 backgrounds, and hence findings from research into the reading problems of learners from one language background should not be assumed to generalize to readers from other language backgrounds. Moreover, the 'threshold' varies according to the type of SFL text, the text topic, the reader's purpose, their knowledge of the world, and so on, such that the threshold is clearly not fixed but is flexible and variable for any one individual.

SFL reading, then, is not simply a matter of being able to read, nor is it simply a matter of knowing the SFL. Clearly, one can be fluent in speaking the language but not be able to read in it. More commonly, perhaps, one's SFL profile may be peaked, that is to say that one's reading ability may be better than one's writing ability, or one's listening ability may be more limited than one's ability to speak the language. However—and this is true for L1 reading as well as for SFL reading—the reading process itself is usually hidden: it is internal to the reader, it is private and not easily examined. Of course, one can ask a reader to read aloud, but the reading aloud process is arguably not the same as silent reading— indeed, it is sometimes known as 'barking at print.' One can, after all, read aloud without understanding what one is reading. Nevertheless, one procedure, known as 'oral miscue analysis' (Goodman, 1969) was very popular in L1 reading studies in the 1970s. Miscues are incorrect guesses at words when reading aloud, and miscue analysis involves looking closely at the types of reading strategies a reader uses. Use of miscue analysis carried over into SFL reading, although it is clear that mistakes one makes when reading in one's SFL may not be indicative of one's silent reading ability, especially for a language such as English, with its opaque orthography.

In addition, it is useful to make a distinction between second language reading and foreign language reading, although the distinction is frequently ignored. A second language is typically one that is learned or acquired and spoken in a country where it is used by native speakers as their L1. A foreign language is one that is not used as an L1 by the majority of the population of a country. Thus, English may be learned as a second language in the United States or Britain, but as a foreign language in Spain or Hungary or China. Of course, with increasing globalization the distinction may be blurred in some urban areas or within certain professions or workplaces (aviation, for example, or the tourism industry or import–export businesses). On the whole, however, one is likely to have far more exposure to English in a second language context such as Australia or Canada than one is in a foreign language context, such as secondary education in most European countries. Thus, reading in a second language may be more of a survival necessity than is reading in a foreign language. Therefore, it may be the case that problems in reading in a FL are different from (although not necessarily more or less important than) SL reading. That is, for example, one reason why the DIALUKI Project, to which frequent reference is made in this book, is studying problems of reading in English as a foreign language in Finland *and also* problems of reading in Finnish as a second language for Russian-speaking immigrants to Finland.

Process and Product

In the study of reading, as in other areas of applied linguistics, it is useful, and fairly commonplace, to make a distinction between process and product. The product of reading is typically what one has understood: The comprehension that one exhibits, for example, in one's answers to comprehension questions or summaries of a text one has read. The process of reading, however, as we have already indicated, is normally silent, invisible, internal to the reader, and rarely externalized. It is also highly likely that the process of reading is more variable than the product: how one has reached a given understanding, especially in an SFL, is likely to vary across individuals and occasions, even though the product of the process, the comprehension, may be the same across individuals and occasions. In other words, two individuals can receive the same score on a reading task, but the questions they got correct may differ.

Of course, this is not to assert that the process is always more variable than the product any more than the product never varies across individuals. It is well known that two people can derive or create very different meanings and understandings from the same text—that is what is implied by the notion of a situation model. And the text model does not necessarily imply that the product is unitary. Indeed, the author may well not be aware of all the possible understandings that can legitimately arise from a reading of his or her text.

The distinction between process and product is, however, very useful for the study of reading and reading problems. Researchers, and diagnosticians in particular, want to know what a reader has understood, or misunderstood, and why. The problem is that *what* one has understood may well be influenced by *how* the researcher has elicited the (mis)understanding. The classic case is the use of multiple-choice questions in a test of SFL reading, where the incorrect options are intended to cause problems for the unwary reader. Had the product, the understanding, been elicited by some other means, for example, by questions requiring a two- or three-word answer, then the comprehension may have been different. Summaries, for another example, are often advocated as a 'more pure' measure of understanding, yet summaries obviously involve one's ability to write in the SFL, and to express one's understanding in a coherent manner that can be understood by an examiner or rater. Yet, it is clear that such a product risks being as much a test of one's ability to write as it is a test of one's reading ability.

Indeed, some will argue that any *test* of understanding will not necessarily reveal the understanding that a person reading for information or for pleasure will arrive at. The problem is how else to elicit comprehension in a more natural, less invasive manner. It is often asserted that a deep understanding of a text cannot be elicited; it is only experienced by a reader's complete absorption in the text, without any outside interference (see Fransson, 1984). Therefore, extensive reading, where the reader selects texts they wish to read and which they typically read outside the classroom is often advocated as a means of enhancing one's ability to read as well as being motivating. Full engagement in reading a text is said to be a hallmark of a good reader (Guthrie & Wigfield, 1997), but how can it be examined without changing the nature of the reading process and probably the reading product?

How to study reading processes and reading products? Eye trackers, which measure the point of gaze and the movement of the eye, are increasingly used to reveal aspects of the reading process, yet they are surely invasive. Test questions intended to tap different reading sub-skills (see below and Chapter One) may well be answerable without actually testing the intended skill, and readers can get an answer correct for the 'wrong' reasons or can get the answer wrong and yet still have the skill being tested. These, then, are some of the dilemmas a reading researcher faces, be it of an L1 or an SFL, and they clearly pose a problem for the validity of a diagnosis of reading difficulties, especially in an SFL. It is said that a reader needs to be familiar with as much as 98% of the words in a text in order to 'understand' that text (Schmitt, Jiang, & Grabe, 2011). So an SFL reader may depend far more on his or her vocabulary size than an L1 reader, and thus be more likely to give the impression of poor comprehension simply because of one or two key words in a text.

Components of Reading

One approach to diagnosing the problems that an SFL reader might have is to consider what skills and components of reading are involved in understanding written text. We have touched upon the topic of skills above, and indeed the notion that reading involves a variety of different sub-skills has a long history in reading research. Urquhart and Weir (1998), for example, cite several examples of reading skills taxonomies by Davis (1968: four skills); Munby (1978: 18 skills); Lunzer, Waite, and Dolan (1979: eight skills); and Grabe (1991: six skills). It is clear from examining even a selection of such taxonomies that there is little consensus on the number or content of such skills, and there would appear to be considerable overlap among them, even given the variation in terminology.

Nevertheless, the notion that reading sub-skills are components of the reading process is a persuasive one, and test developers in particular have tried to isolate and test such skills separately. In one of the first attempts at devising an online diagnostic testing system in a number of European languages, DIALANG sought to isolate and test three major (and generally recognized) skills: identifying main idea, reading for detail, and inferencing (Alderson, 2005).

Another recent diagnostic test battery, the Diagnostic English Language Tracking Assessment (DELTA), includes the following sub-skills of reading (Urmston, Raquel, & Tsang, 2013):

- Identifying specific information
- Interpreting a word or phrase as used by the writer
- Understanding main ideas and supporting ideas
- Understanding information and making an inference
- Inferring the writer's reasoning
- Interpreting an attitude or intention of the writer
- Understanding grammatical relationships of words or phrases across text
- Identifying text type.

Research to date has not shown convincing evidence (a) that expert judges can agree on what sub-skills are being tested (at least in proficiency test batteries, although it may yet prove to be the case that such skills can be isolated and identified in diagnostic test batteries); (b) that such skills are organized in a hierarchical relationship, such that some skills are more easily and quickly acquired than others and that there is an implicational scale of such skills; and (c) that there is a clear relationship between being a good reader and one's ability to master all or most of the posited skills. In short, more research is needed into the extent to which the presence or absence of such skills may explain strengths and weaknesses in SFL reading.

A somewhat different but parallel approach to identifying components of SFL reading is to look at the relationship between performance on SFL reading tests and performance on tests of linguistic abilities. Most commonly, such abilities are divided into grammar (or structure) and vocabulary (lexical abilities). While it is usually acknowledged that having a wide vocabulary is associated with good reading performance, recently some doubt has been cast on the primacy of the lexical component by research that claims that grammatical abilities account for more of the variance in reading test performance than do lexical abilities (Shiotsu, 2010). However, other research has recently questioned whether there really is a distinction to be made between grammar and lexis, and it has been claimed that lexicogrammar, and especially the use of formulaic phrases and a knowledge of collocations, is an important component of SFL reading ability (Alderson & Kremmel, 2013). It is thus asserted that a simple dichotomy between vocabulary and grammar cannot be maintained.

Be that as it may, it is clear that knowledge of grammar, and having a wide vocabulary, are related in some way to SFL reading proficiency. The challenge to the developers of diagnostic tests is to explore the nature of this relationship in order to tease out exactly what linguistic factors contribute to strengths and weaknesses in SFL reading. Indeed, recent research has revealed that there is a difference between high-proficiency and low-proficiency readers in their use of lexicogrammatical knowledge. This knowledge plays a much greater role in determining reading ability at the lower levels of proficiency, whereas at higher levels of proficiency lexicogrammatical knowledge is automatized and therefore has less of an impact on reading ability (Purpura, 1998; Urquhart & Weir, 1998). In Chapter Five, we will explore in more detail which linguistic features might provide useful diagnostic information.

Levels of Processing

It is relatively uncontroversial to say that reading consists of at least two sorts of processes, commonly called low-level and higher-level processes (Grabe, 2009), and both levels of processing should be relevant to diagnostic testing. Low-level cognitive processes contribute to word recognition and will be described in more detail in Chapter Six. These processes include orthographic, phonological, morphological, syntactic, and semantic processes important at the level of word recognition and are described in Grabe (2009, Chapter 2). Higher-level processes involve a set of skills and resources (such as background, topical, and cultural knowledge) as well as strategies, inferences, and the ability to monitor ongoing comprehension. In higher-level processes, it is common to make a distinction between the ability to extract the meaning that the writer has attempted to convey (the text model of comprehension) and the interpretation that readers make, which is affected both by readers' knowledge and their purposes in reading (the situation model).

Lower-level processes include word recognition, syntactic parsing, and encoding meaning as propositions. Working memory, which is essential for these processes, will also be dealt with in Chapter Six. As Grabe (2009) points out, calling these skills lower-level does not mean that they are simple: rather, they are skills that can become automatized, which is a requirement for fluent reading. Each skill is, however, complex, and these skills can operate simultaneously and in interaction, at least some of the time.

Word recognition and, in alphabetic languages, learning letter–sound correspondences are essential to predict later reading abilities. Fluent reading requires rapid and automatic recognition and a large vocabulary, and therefore problems with word recognition can be expected to be diagnostic of reading problems. Lexical access is not the same as word recognition, especially for beginning SFL readers, who may be able to pronounce an unknown word but have no idea what it means. Skill in morphological processing (Kieffer & Lesaux, 2012), that is, processing affixes, is associated not only with word recognition but also with superior comprehension as well as efficient syntactic parsing. Contrary to common beliefs in SFL reading textbooks, guessing words from context is characteristic of weaker readers: Fluent readers do not usually need the support from context. Only when there are problems with processing, or with a word that is not well known, might contextual information provide another layer of support. Indeed, Grabe (2009) points out that the information provided by context is usually not very explicit.

Syntactic parsing clearly contributes to reading comprehension, and we need the information provided by articles, prepositions, tenses in addition to nouns, verbs, adverbs, and adjectives in order to process sentences rapidly and accurately. Grabe (2009) gives several examples of this:

> "Man fired rifle factory screamed boss" is harder to process than "The man fired from the rifle factory screamed at his boss." "Tom chewed on the dog's leg" is not the same as "The dog chewed on Tom's leg." Garden path sentences (sentences that are easily misunderstood—they lead you down the garden path) show how we have to use our knowledge of grammar to disambiguate or to parse such sentences. Contrast "The man lent the money to a needy friend" with "The man lent the money to gamble lost it all." Problems with processing sentences like these, especially with more complex and ambiguous structures, slow down processing and are good candidates for diagnostic tasks.
>
> (p. 29)

Learners, and SFL learners in particular, need a great deal of practice in using these lower-level skills in order to read faster and with better comprehension. Extensive and frequent reading is essential with texts that increase gradually in length and have few unknown words and whose content is motivating to read. Thus, an important element of diagnosis is to establish how fast, and with what degree of comprehension, learners can read.

Higher-level comprehension processes involve one's ability to make mental connections across events and propositions in text to create a coherent idea of what the text is about. Such higher-level processes are not necessarily automatized, although they can be. Frequently, they require the reader to pay conscious attention to features of text. Important elements of such processing include strategies; goals and purposes; inferencing; the use of background knowledge, both consciously and unconsciously; and the monitoring of one's comprehension as one progresses through a text.

Building a text model of comprehension involves making connections and linkages across text into a network of meaning, recognizing overlapping elements, and removing from one's ongoing model less important or more detailed information. It also involves inferencing and restructuring one's internal summary of the text as more information comes into the mental network. Identifying at what points a reader has made incorrect linkages of information, has failed to suppress less relevant information from memory, or has made an incorrect inference are all potentially useful features of diagnosis at these higher levels. Similarly, identifying the reader's growing situation model of text interpretation and exploring where, when, and why that model contains inaccuracies or 'misunderstandings' can throw important light on comprehension difficulties. Grabe (2009) lists those factors that influence the construction of a situation model:

- Reader purpose
- Task expectation
- Genre activation
- Similar story instances
- General background knowledge resources
- Evaluation of the importance of information, its enjoyment value, its interest value (and its truth value)
- Attitudes (and inferences) toward writer, story, genre, episode
- Inferences needed for interpretation (of genre, episode, hierarchical organization, purpose).

Classic research into the importance of the activation of relevant background knowledge by Bransford, Stein, and Shelton (1984), as well as of the impact of cultural differences by Steffensen, Joag-Dev, and Anderson (1979), are relevant to understanding how readers actively create their own interpretation (and misinterpretation) of text, and are especially relevant in SFL reading.

Grabe (2009) gives a graphic illustration of how a situation model might be built up, and it is worth quoting this at length, for it not only illustrates possible mental operations, but also provides an example of how introspection can provide insights into text processing and how processing might go astray.

Grabe presents a four-sentence (six clauses) text and demonstrates how a situation model might be built up. The reader might like to introspect on how he or she processes these first four sentences at the beginning of a story: "*The man could not find the map to the treasure. He saw an edge of paper under the professor's chair and looked the professor in the eye. 'Give me the map,' said the man. The professor raised a gun, and the man leaped out of the window*" (pp. 40–41).

Grabe (2009) continues:

As we begin reading the episode, and even perhaps before beginning to read, we activate a wide range of background knowledge. We activate previous instances of similar stories from long-term memory. We decide on our purposes for reading and our more immediate goals (using the executive processing mechanism in working memory). We begin to activate attitudes and emotions related to our expectations about the story to be read. We activate knowledge about the genre, and what we can expect with respect to discourse structuring, in this case an action adventure story. We also leave many of the informational expectations vaguely specified because we know that events, characters, objects and places will all be filled in to some extent in a fictional world. Thus, at the moment that we start to recognize the first words and begin the first parsing of the clause, we already have information activated to some extent and ready for further activation. In effect, we are prepared to build the situation in which the information unfolds.

On reading Sentence 1, we know that an episode is beginning and the problem has been announced. We might think that this is an uninspired opening, or we might be anticipating the opportunity to 'escape' into a story. We might think that the story is not well written but we will give it a try. We might imagine what 'the man' might look like (Indiana Jones) and how old the map might be (300 years old), although we might just let the text itself fill in these details. We certainly will set up slots in our interpretation for 'the man' and a 'map' based on our prior knowledge of this type of information. Sentence 2 introduces an unusual place for a piece of paper, a chair, and possibly a professor. Sentence 3 introduces two protagonists face-to-face and a standard conflict of characters has now been activated. By the time we have read through Clause 6, we have begun to fill in details about the situation, protagonists' personalities, the encounter taking place in a room, the causes for the protagonists' actions, and so on. We may also have (a) made further supporting inferences as necessary, (b) evaluated the episode for its excitement potential, (c) decided whether to continue reading or not, (d) considered how these protagonists match up with characters from other stories by this or other authors, (e) considered how much we like this story, and (f) decided if our goals for reading are being met. As readers, we build our own interpretive framework around the actual episode information being processed.

(Grabe, 2009, pp. 44–45).

The sort of text being read—a narrative or an informational text—will influence one's purpose for reading, one's expectations and how one evaluates the text as it progresses. It will also influence whether one builds a text model or a situation model. Informational texts, especially those on topics where the reader has little background knowledge, will tend to the building of a text model, whereas narrative texts will tend to the building of a situation model, especially where the reader has extensive background knowledge of the topic or the author and is expecting to evaluate the text. This notion that texts can lead to a text-based mental model, or an interpretive situation model, helps explain the different ways we can read a text, the different sorts of meanings that texts can have for readers, and may help explain the various difficulties that weaker readers experience.

Task Demands and Effects

The products and processes of reading are likely to be affected by the demands of the tasks that are set to assess SFL reading. Reading tasks operate on a wide variety of texts, and obviously the choice of text—genre, topic, style, language, organization—affects task difficulty. Readers with low background knowledge tend to produce text models when writing summaries, making simple recalls or answering multiple-choice recognition questions. Readers' comprehension of text tends to increase when the task involves the sort of model building that would otherwise not occur. Information-sorting tasks, for example, often require the making of many inferences, which leads to a situation model of understanding.

When texts and tasks do not fit with existing background knowledge, or when the context does not provide sufficient information, or when the linguistic difficulty of text requires greater attention, then readers need to be able to cope with such difficulties. They need to recognize the structure of the discourse to help them cope; they need to apply effective comprehension strategies and they need to monitor their comprehension and adjust their goals in order to cope. Such metacognitive awareness (of their comprehension problems, of the need for more effective coping strategies, or of adjusting their goals and expectations) are the hallmark of skilled readers, and weaker readers are less likely to monitor their comprehension or to adjust their approach to the task and text.

Similarly, metalinguistic awareness can support comprehension when faced with difficulties, by becoming aware of word-learning skills or devising new definitions for known words; disambiguating text meanings through an awareness of syntactic structures, and recognizing discourse patterns in the text.

Interestingly, weaker readers who have difficulty developing a text model of comprehension may, possibly because of weaker vocabulary, tend to rely on a situation model of comprehension, by grasping at the straws offered by a few known words and building an incomplete or inaccurate situation model. Weaker readers are also less likely to monitor their (in)comprehension effectively and accurately.

Grabe (2009) points out that readers are not simply bottom-up or top-down readers. Readers have to be both bottom-up and top-down readers at the same time. They need to be able to recognize words automatically and fluently, and parse text accurately and expeditiously. They need to continuously use their background knowledge, to set their goals, use effective comprehension strategies and monitor their developing comprehension. Problems with word recognition or with text interpretation can be experienced by any reader, even fluent ones, depending on the text, the task, the purpose for reading, and the need for higher-level inferencing or critical judgment. All readers experience difficulty at some point: the problem for diagnosis is to know when difficulties are due to wider problems with text processing, with underlying skills or with linguistic, cognitive or strategic competences, or with something completely different such as lack of motivation (see also Chapters One and Seven).

All readers need extensive exposure and practice, and the development of positive attitudes to reading, the motivation to read and the willingness to persevere despite occasional difficulties, or to adjust one's approach, can only be achieved by long and wide experience with texts, but weaker readers can hopefully be helped through accurate diagnosis of the underlying reasons for the difficulties they experience and appropriate feedback, treatment, or other interventions.

From Construct to Assessment

Having briefly explored what is involved in SFL reading, we now turn to describe and exemplify how the reading construct and its various components can be, and have been, operationalized (i.e., turned into test items or assessment procedures). We will briefly present the reading component from DIALANG, DELNA, and DELTA and provide somewhat more detail about DIALUKI, since this is a more comprehensive research project rather than 'simply' a test development project.

In all cases, however, the test development process is similar in that it follows the processes of identifying learners' needs; developing test specifications and item-writer guidelines; identifying suitable texts; drafting test items and tasks through a process of writing, editing, moderating, and revising tasks until they are considered to be ready for trialing (also known as piloting or field trials), as recommended in most language testing handbooks (see, for example, Alderson et al., 1995; Hughes, 2003).

Suitable samples of test takers are then identified, administration procedures are developed, the pilot tests are trialed, marked and analyzed statistically, either with Classical Test Theory procedures, and/or with Item Response Theory methods. Suitable test tasks are then selected or revised in light of the results, and delivered for real to target candidates. Once the tests have been administered in the main trial, they are marked and analyzed again, typically including inferential statistics and expert judgments, in order to examine to what extent the intended constructs have been successfully operationalized. In addition, detailed feedback is given to the test takers, together with advice on what action, if any, they might be advised to take in order to correct or compensate for weaknesses identified.

Below, we briefly review how four rather different projects have approached the testing of SFL reading.

DIALANG

The online and freely available DIALANG reading tests (see Chapter Three for more information about the DIALANG system) are based on the Council of Europe's Common European Framework of Reference (CEFR—see Council of Europe, 2001), which, however, does not contain any description of a reading construct or an underlying theory. Indeed the CEFR, according to Alderson (2005)

> virtually dismisses any psycholinguistic approach to understanding foreign language proficiency, and does not consider, much less describe, the sorts of mental operations that a reader might undertake when reading . . . DIALANG therefore had to have recourse to other sources for insight into what sort of operations or processes that might be involved in reading that could provide useful diagnostic information.
>
> (p. 121)

As a result, DIALANG developed the DAS—DIALANG Assessment Specifications—for reading, as well as for the other skills, and was instrumental in developing the Dutch Grid for Assessing Reading and Listening (Alderson et al., 2004, 2006) to complement the scant information on Reading in the CEFR (see www.lancs.ac.uk/fss/projects/grid/ for an explanation of the Grid and how it can be used when basing one's reading and listening tests on the CEFR). The reader is advised to consult Alderson (2005, Chapter 9) for more details of the text types in DIALANG, the factors considered that affect item difficulty and the skills tested (also briefly mentioned above).

Below are screenshots of reading items and of the sort of feedback that is available. Clearly, not all readers will be familiar with all of the 14 languages that are tested in DIALANG or in which the test instructions and are presented. The reader is therefore encouraged to download any reading test from the DIALANG website (www.lancs.ac.uk/researchenterprise/dialang/about) and examine the test and the feedback at leisure in whatever test or administration languages they feel most comfortable.

Different test methods are used in the reading tests: Figure 4.1 shows an example of a short-answer item (note that the item has a floating 'keyboard' containing the letters needed in the test language—Italian in this case—that are not found in the standard QWERTY keyboard; the test takers can input those letters in their responses by clicking on the particular letter).

Figure 4.2 is an example of a constructed response item where the box for the required word is embedded in the text rather than in response to the item.

Figure 4.3 shows an example of a multiple-choice item with immediate feedback (i.e., given before the test taker moves on to the next item):

The following screen-shot (Figure 4.4) is an example of feedback on a learner's performance on the items in the reading test (where the right-hand column is wrong and the middle column is correct). The items are grouped according to the skill being tested, which is one of DIALANG's features.

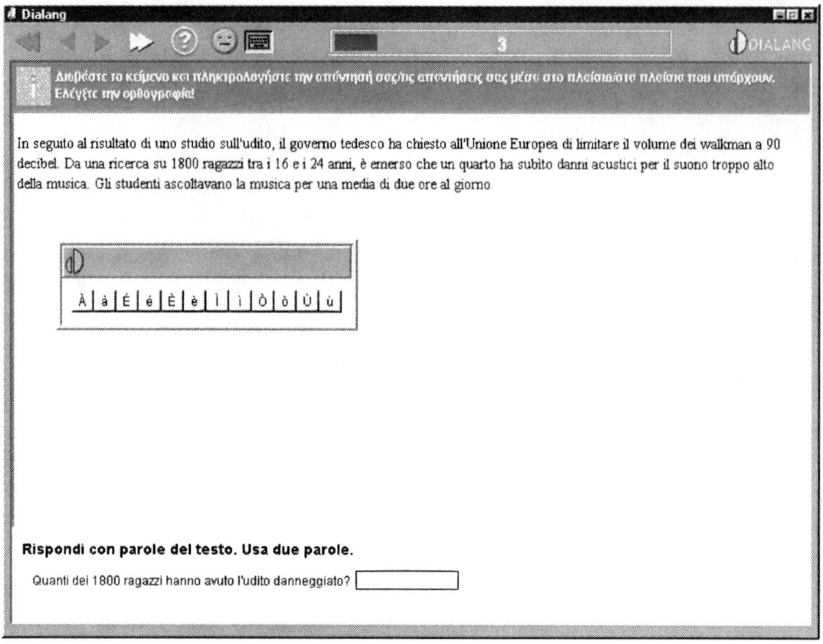

FIGURE 4.1 DIALANG short-answer item in Italian

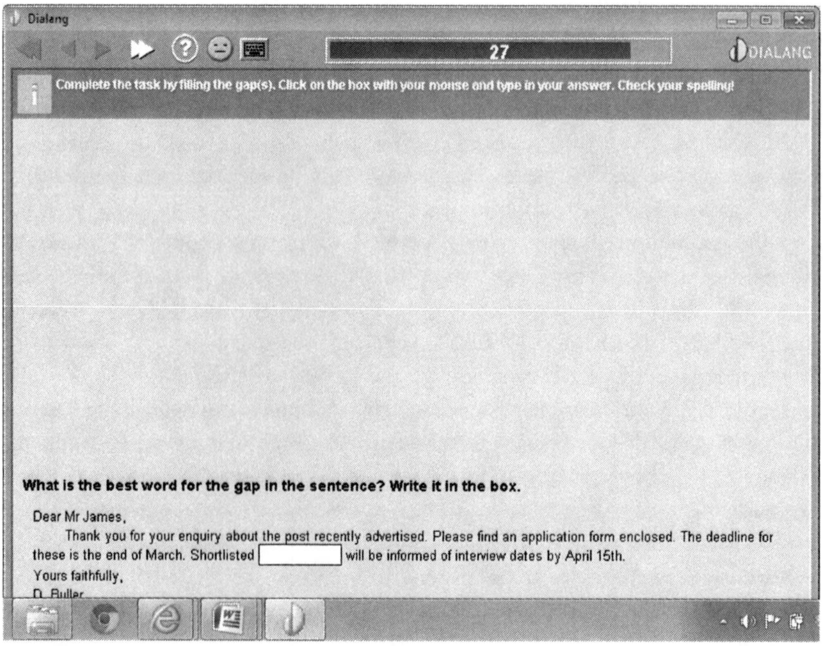

FIGURE 4.2 DIALANG short-answer item in English

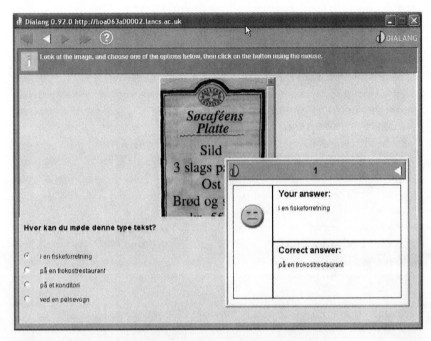

FIGURE 4.3 DIALANG multiple-choice item with feedback

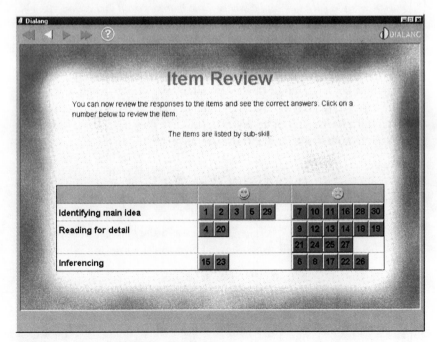

FIGURE 4.4 DIALANG example of feedback

Diagnostic English Language Needs Assessment (DELNA)

As explained in Chapter Three, DELNA consists of two components—a 30-minute screening test, which is a computer-based assessment and consists of vocabulary and timed reading tasks—and a 2-hour DELNA Diagnosis. The aim of the screening test is to see whether the learners need some form of language development, in which case the longer DELNA Diagnosis is administered to identify in detail the learners' needs.

In the Screening Test's Timed Reading Task, learners are allowed practice time and 10 minutes for the actual test (which is 73 lines long). Students are presented with a text that has been 'doctored' to include one additional word in each line. The task is to read the text as quickly as possible, and to click on the word in each line 'that does not belong.' (This is the so-called cloze-elide technique, developed by Manning,1987, based on a speed-reading test developed by Davies in the 1960s as part of the English Proficiency Test Battery, Form A.)

Sample instructions and a passage of text from the timed reading task are given below.

In the following passage there is a word in each line that does not belong. Click on that word in each line and it will become highlighted. If you change your mind you simply click on another word and that is then the highlighted word. Practice on the text below then check your answers with the passage beneath. The word that you should have highlighted will be in yellow.

Some public libraries have developed ways to personal capture the attention print and interest of younger library patrons. One library in the United Kingdom has space on its website for can teenagers to write book and music reviews you of library materials and they are encouraged to participate from in the development of library collections.

Answer

Some public libraries have developed ways to **personal** capture the attention **print** and interest of younger library patrons. One library in the United Kingdom has space on its website for **can** teenagers to write book and music reviews **you** of library materials and they are encouraged to participate **from** in the development of library collections.

Clearly, this 'reading' test is an integrated task, which we have argued in Chapter Three is unlikely to be suitable for diagnostic purposes, as it is not clear what exactly is being tested by the individual items. No description of the construct is given in the Handbook.

If the screening test results suggest that a student needs some form of further language development, they discuss their results with the DELNA Language Adviser, in order to identify the most suitable course of action. They may be recommended to take the DELNA Diagnosis, which is a 2-hour test consisting of three components: Listening, Reading, and Writing, in paper and pencil form, and results are available within 8 days.

The first subtest is the Reading test, which is described as follows:

TASK 1: READING TASK

Time allowed: 45–55 minutes

There will be one or two reading passages in the Reading task booklet. The total length of the texts is approximately 1,200 words. They will be on a topic of general interest that does not require specialist subject knowledge. You are asked to answer a variety of questions which assess what you have understood. A range of question types is used, including cloze, summarizing, matching ideas, information transfer, multiple choice, true/false and short answer. Examples of most of these question types are included later under the heading "Diagnostic Task Examples."

In this reading task, you are being assessed on the following skills:

- Speed
- Ability to find specific information
- Ability to locate causes and effects, sequences, contrasts
- Ability to distinguish between main points and evidence or supporting ideas
- Ability to select words which fit the meaning and the grammatical construction of the text (cloze)
- Ability to summarize main topics
- Ability to draw a conclusion based on information in a passage
- Ability to distinguish between fact and opinion
- Ability to organize information in a passage in another way (e.g., insert in chart, graph, map, diagram).

If students have any difficulty understanding what these skills mean, they are advised first to try the sample questions and then, if necessary, consult a teacher of English.

The following three examples (of the different possible item types) are offered;

Example 1 (multiple choice): A section of the text reads as follows:

> Until the early 1970s, no one cared about energy conservation. Very few knew what it meant. This apathy was caused by apparently ever-increasing quantities of fuel available at decreasing prices. However, the western world was suddenly jolted into reality by the 'OPEC oil crisis,' which clarified many of the reasons for bothering with energy conservation.
>
> **Question:** The 'OPEC oil crisis'
>
> A. made westerners aware of the need for energy conservation.
> B. increased westerners' apathy about energy conservation.
> C. made more fuel available at lower prices.
> D. caused the western world to reject high fuel prices.
>
> **Answer:** A

Example 2 (short answer): A section of the text reads as follows:

> Political leaders and the media often express concern about the possibility of cuts in oil supplies due to political unrest in the Middle East. When this is coupled with Australia's dwindling local oil reserves, then clearly the longer we can make our present reserves last the less vulnerable we will be to external conflicts in the future.
>
> **Question:** What two factors may make Australia vulnerable to outside events?
>
> **Answer:** 1. political unrest in the Middle East
>   2. dwindling local oil reserves

Example 3 (summary gap-fill): A section of the text reads as follows:

> We should also try to reduce our dependence on local energy sources such as gas and electricity. For example, a person who lives in a well-insulated house with solar water heating will be less inconvenienced by power restriction than other people while someone who lives close to work, shops and other facilities will never be affected by disruptions to transport services. Someone who walks or rides a bicycle never needs to worry about petrol supplies.

Question: Below is a summary of the passage. Select appropriate words from the box to complete the summary and write the corresponding letter in the numbered space to the right. Note that there are more words given than you will need. Each word may be used once only.

If you . . .$^{(1)}$. . . your house and . . .$^{(2)}$. . . solar water heating, problems with the power supply will . . .$^{(3)}$. . . you less than others . . .$^{(4)}$. . . non-motorized forms of transport also avoids problems . . .$^{(5)}$. . . with transport and fuel disruptions.

A.	depend	H.	protect
B.	associated	I.	sell
C.	avoid	J.	caused
D.	convenience	K.	insulate
E.	using	L.	affected
F.	inconvenience	M.	together
G.	install	N.	driving

Answers

1. K   2. G   3. F   4. E   5. B

Diagnostic English Language Tracking Assessment (DELTA)

As explained in Chapter Three, the DELTA Test of Reading contains four parts. Each part requires the test taker to read a text (of between 400 and 800 words) and answer a set of multiple-choice questions about the text. The four parts are of different and increasing difficulty levels, such that the first part is the easiest and the last the most difficult. The texts are of different types (e.g., news or magazine articles, extracts from academic papers, essays, etc.) and different topics.

A sample text and two sample items are also presented, together with a brief description of what each item is testing:

Sample text:

The task of standardizing English on Chinese menus is a much more daunting task, however. This is a very important and sensitive task. How appetizing do many current translations sound, such as 'stewed bean curd'; 'badly cooked starch cubes'; 'fish in first position' and 'chicken toenails in soy sauce'? They are all out there for public consumption. The committee is currently collaborating with the Beijing Institute of Tourism and they have gathered over 10,000 menus to study. A dedicated committee has now been set up consisting of volunteers, including local English professors, food and beverage managers as well as 'foreign experts,' mainly English instructors from the USA. The aim is to come up with 1,000 dishes most commonly found in 200 of Beijing's restaurants with ratings of three stars or above. This endeavor is vital says Professor Feng Dong Ming because, "food names are a very sophisticated part of our culture and we must deliver proper meanings to the foreigners in bundles that cannot be too long or too short." This is quite hard to do especially when the common dumpling called Won Ton actually has the literal meaning of 'swallowing clouds.' And what about the many variations of the names of such staple dishes as 'yu xiang ru si.' Would that be 'fish flavored shredded pork', 'slivered pork in garlic sauce' or just 'Sichuan sliced pork'? Adherence to this new set of translations isn't mandatory, but the committee is hoping that if the names are adopted in the more upmarket establishments, they will spread to smaller, unrated and even unlicensed restaurants in Beijing (around 40,000) and then beyond to the whole of China. And just in case the language and cross cultural understanding get left at the kitchen door, plans are afoot to train waiters to take orders in standardized English.

Sample items:

3. **The writer believes that standardizing English on Chinese menus**
   _____.
   (Understanding main ideas and supporting ideas)
   A. cannot be done
   B. is harder than expected*
   C. does not result in accuracy
   D. is hard to do for all Chinese dishes
4. **The committee hopes that eventually the new translations will**
   _____.
   (Identifying specific information)
   A. not be applied to 3-star restaurants
   B. be used only in expensive restaurants
   C. spread to 40,000 unlicensed restaurants
   D. gradually become more widely used all over China*

The correct answer is indicated by an asterisk *

No further information is available, but it can be seen that the text is an expository text on a topic likely to be familiar in general in the Hong Kong context, taken probably from an English language newspaper or magazine, or a textbook for students of tourism and hotel management, or the like.

	Subskills tested	Text type	Theme
✗	Identifying specific information	News article	Animal ethics
✗	Understanding main ideas and supporting ideas	Academic article	History and culture
✗	Understanding information and making an inference	News article	Environmental issue
✗	Interpreting an attitude or intention of the writer	Fiction	History and culture
✗	Understanding main ideas and supporting ideas	Academic article	History and culture
✗	Interpreting a word or phrase as used by the writer	Academic article	History and culture
✓	Identifying specific information	News article	Environmental issue
✗	Identifying specific information	News article	Animal ethics
✗	Understanding main ideas and supporting ideas	News article	Animal ethics
✗	Understanding main ideas and supporting ideas	Academic article	History and culture
✗	Interpreting a word or phrase as used by the writer	News article	Animal ethics
✗	Identifying specific information	Fiction	History and culture
✓	Understanding main ideas and supporting ideas	News article	Animal ethics
✓	Understanding information and making an inference	Academic article	History and culture
✓	Identifying specific information	News article	Environmental issue
✓	Understanding information and making an inference	Academic article	History and culture
✗	Identifying specific information	Academic article	History and culture
✓	Identifying specific information	News article	Environmental issue
✓	Interpreting a word or phrase as used by the writer	Academic article	History and culture
✗	Identifying specific information	Fiction	History and culture
✓	Interpret a word or phrase as used by the writer	News article	Environmental issue
✗	Inferring the writer's reasoning	Fiction	History and culture
✓	Understanding main ideas and supporting ideas	Fiction	History and culture
✓	identifying specific information	News article	Environmental issue
✓	Understanding information and making an inference	Fiction	History and culture
✓	Interpreting a word or phrase as used by the writer	News article	Environmental issue
✓	Identifying specific information	News article	Environmental issue

(axis labels: More / Difficulty / Less; DELTA 113)

FIGURE 4.5 The reading sub-skills tested in DELTA

Figure 4.5 presents the reading sub-skills tested in DELTA and indicates which sub-skills learners performed poorly on (indicated with an *x*).

Finally, in this exemplification of reading tests intended to be diagnostic, we now turn to a rather different project, which is researching various aspects of second or foreign language reading, using reading tests in the first language of informants as well as other reading tests in the second or foreign language. In the case of DIALUKI, we are not claiming that the reading tests used are themselves diagnostic. Rather, we are interested in exploring what linguistic, cognitive, motivational, and background variables predict performance on the reading tests we describe in the next section.

DIALUKI

As mentioned in Chapter Three, DIALUKI is a research project with two different groups of informants—the L1 Finnish/English FL group and the L1 Russian/ L2 Finnish group, at different levels in the school system. Table 4.1 sets out the details of these learners.

TABLE 4.1 Participants in DIALUKI Study One

Group	Subgroup	Age
FIN-ENG	Primary Grade 4	9–10 years
	Lower secondary grade	13–14 years
	Upper secondary	17–18 years
RUS-FIN	Primary school (Grades 3–6)	8–13 years
	Lower secondary school (Grades 7–9)	13–17 years

TABLE 4.2 First language reading measures

L1	Target group	Measures
Finnish	Primary school group	Selected parts of ALLU test (of Finnish)
	Lower secondary group	PISA test of Finnish
	Upper secondary group	PISA test of Finnish
Russian	Primary school group	Two texts (21 items) in Russian from PIRLS 2006
	Lower secondary group	2–3 texts (7–11 items) in Russian from PISA (OECD 2010).

DIALUKI uses reading tests in both the learners' L1 and their SFL. Where these exist, standardized tests are used whose properties are well known, and which, in some cases, have parallel versions in the two language pairs. Obviously, however, because learners at different ages are the object of study, different reading tests have to be used, which are as suitable as possible for the particular age group.

First Language Reading Measures

Table 4.2 sets out the details of the various L1 Finnish or Russian reading tests used in DIALUKI Studies One and Two.

In what follows, we describe in some detail the tests mentioned in Table 4.2, organized by group of participants. Again, the reader is reminded that these tests are not intended to be diagnostic. They are 'simply' tests of reading used as the dependent variables in the research to explore which measures best predict performance on these tests.

The L1 Finnish Primary Group

The primary fourth grade (age 10) L1 Finnish reading test was a narrative text from the Ala-asteen Lukutesti (henceforth ALLU) test battery (Lindeman, 2005) for Finnish primary pupils. In the ALLU battery there are different tests for each grade in primary school. The narrative text chosen is one of the reading comprehension tasks for fourth graders. The text is 188 words long, followed by 12 four-option multiple-choice questions, which are intended to test comprehension of the text in general as well as comprehension of certain infrequent words and phrases.

The ALLU tests are intended for 7- to 13-year-old children who are native speakers of Finnish. The standardization of the results is based on the test performances of 12,897 children in 651 classes around Finland. The tests are used as follows:

- to assess the child's level of reading skills
- to track the child's development in reading skills
- to identify children with difficulties in reading.

There are separate tests for each grade, intended to test two types of technical reading skills: word recognition and reading comprehension.

In the word recognition task (for Grades 4–6) learners have to mark word boundaries (2–4 words are written together without intervening spaces). The time limit is 3 minutes, 30 seconds. In the reading comprehension task learners have to read one informational text and answer 12 multiple-choice questions; there is no time limit but reading the texts and answering the questions takes approximately 15 to 20 minutes. There are five types of questions:

- detail/fact
- cause and effect/order
- interpretation/conclusion
- word/idiom
- main idea/purpose.

More information about the ALLU test can be found here: www.otuk.utu.fi/tiedostot/ot/english/index_eng.html

The Secondary L1 Finnish Groups

The lower secondary and upper secondary group both took 3 L1 reading tasks in Finnish, with a total of 11 items, from released PISA items. The Programme for International Student Assessment (PISA) is funded by the OECD (Organization for Economic Cooperation and Development) and measures key competencies in reading, mathematics, and science, in order to assess educational outcomes in OECD member countries. The current series of tests takes place every 3 years. Reading literacy in the language of instruction was the main focus of the 2000 survey, and then again in 2009.

The PISA Reading Framework (OECD, 2009) describes the construct of the tests, aimed at 15-year-olds in full-time education, in terms of the skills students need to acquire, the processes that need to be formed and the contexts in which knowledge and skills are applied. The 2009 Reading Framework defines reading literacy as *"understanding, using, reflecting on and engaging with written texts, in order to achieve one's goals, to develop one's knowledge and potential, and to participate in society"* (p. 23).

The domain aims to ensure a broad coverage of what students read and for what purposes, and to represent a range of difficulty. Three major text characteristics are identified according to which they are classified:

- *situation* (personal, public, educational, and occupational);
- *text* (medium—print; format—continuous, non-continuous, multiple, and mixed; text type—description, narration, exposition, argumentation, instruction, and transaction)
- *aspect* (access and retrieve, integrate and interpret, reflect, and evaluate).

Response formats differ according to whether they are closed (i.e., selected response), and do not require coding, or constructed response, which may be given partial credits for degrees of accuracy or appropriateness. For further information, see www.oecd.org/document/44/0,3343,en_2649_35845621_44455276_1_1_1_1,00.html

The PISA test tasks used (which are *not* intended to be diagnostic) were as follows, with the main aspect being tested indicated in italics (the item numbers are as in the test booklets; www.oecd.org/pisa):

1. **Telecommuting** (2 short texts, with 3 items)
   - (Item 26) *Integrate and interpret: form a broad understanding, recognize the relationship between two short argumentative texts*
   - (Item 27) *Reflect and evaluate: reflect on and evaluate the content of a text, use prior knowledge to generate an example that fits a category described in a text*
   - (Item 28) *Integrate and interpret: develop an interpretation, recognize a common position expressed in two short argumentative texts*

2. **The Play's the Thing** (the text is an extract from a play, with 4 items)
   - (Item 33) *Integrate and interpret: develop an interpretation, identify an event in the world of the play in relation to other events in the play and an event in the 'real' world.*
   - (Item 34) *Integrate and interpret: develop an interpretation, infer the meaning of a phrase in a play using contextual references*
   - (Item 35) *Integrate and interpret: develop an interpretation, support an opinion by construing a character's motivation in a play*
   - (Item 36) *Integrate and interpret: form a broad understanding, recognize the conceptual theme of a play.*

3. **Mobile Phone Safety** (2 texts, 4 items)
   - (Item 37) *Integrate and interpret: form a broad understanding, recognize the purpose of a section (a table) in an expository text;*
   - (Item 38) *Reflect and evaluate: reflect on and evaluate the content of a text, recognize the relationship between a generalized statement external to the text and a pair of statements in a table;*
   - (Item 39) *Reflect and evaluate: reflect on and evaluate the content of a text, use prior knowledge to reflect on information presented in a text*
   - (Item 40) *Integrate and interpret: develop an interpretation, recognize an assumption in part of an expository text.*

The L1 Russian Primary Group

The primary students took two tasks from the Progress in International Reading Literacy Study (PIRLS) 2006 in Russian, one based on a text about Antarctica, intended to test the ability to read to acquire and use information, and one entitled 'Little Lump of Clay,' intended to test the ability to read for literary experience. There were both multiple-choice and short answer tasks, and the items tested a range of skills:

- Focus on and retrieve explicitly stated information and ideas
- Interpret and integrate ideas and information
- Make straightforward inferences
- Examine and evaluate content, language, and textual elements.

For more details, see Foy and Kennedy (2008, pp. 2–24) at http://timss.bc.edu/pirls2006/user_guide.html.

The L1 Russian Lower Secondary Group

The L1 Russian tests for the lower secondary group were the same PISA tests as described above for Finnish (Telecommuting, The Play's the Thing, and Mobile Phone Safety), but in Russian.

Having described the L1 reading tests used in DIALUKI, we now turn to describe the second or foreign language reading tests used in that project.

Second/Foreign Language Reading Measures

Where these exist, standardized second or foreign language reading tests were used whose properties are well known. As in the case of the L1 reading tests, because learners at different ages are the object of study, different reading tests have to be used, which are as suitable as possible for the particular age group.

Table 4.3 sets out the details of the various SFL reading tests in English (foreign language) and Finnish (second language) used in DIALUKI Studies One and Two.

TABLE 4.3 DIALUKI second or foreign language reading tests

SFL	Target group	Measures
English	Primary school group	Pearson Test of English (PTE) Young Learners Test at A1/A2 on the CEFR
	Lower secondary group	Pearson Test of English (PTE) General A2/B1 + DIALANG English (fixed at intermediate level)
	Upper secondary group	Pearson Test of English (PTE) General B1/B2 + DIALANG English (fixed at advanced level)
Finnish	Primary school group (a) Beginners (b) Advanced	Finnish Certificate reading test, 12 items DIALANG reading 10 items
	Lower secondary group (a) Beginners (b) Advanced	Finnish Certificate reading test, 12 items DIALANG reading (intermediate) 30 items

Primary Fourth Grade FL English Reading Test

The English FL reading test for fourth graders was a version of the *Pearson Test of English for Young Learners*, which Pearson kindly allowed us to access (see www. pearsonpte.com/PTEYOUNGLEARNERS/Pages/home.aspx.)

The description of the Firstwords level is as follows:

This test is designed to motivate and reward young learners who have just started learning English in an academic context. It may be particularly useful for learners who have had to master the use of the Roman alphabet.

The aim is primarily to test the learners' ability to use the language communicatively rather than to test their knowledge of the language system.

The fourth FL English reading grade test was taken from the Firstwords level tests (CEFR Level A1/A2). There was a total of 20 items in three tasks. Task One involved matching pictures of objects to words in English. Task Two involved matching sentences from a short story to pictures of the same story, in the correct order. Task Three involved a gapped six-line text, and words had to be inserted into the gaps from a bank of single words.

Secondary School FL English Reading Test: Person Test of English General

The English FL reading tests for lower secondary and upper secondary were a combination of DIALANG items described in an earlier section of this chapter, and tasks from the *Pearson Test of English* (General). Since the operational Pearson tests are confidential, we can only describe what they are intended to test and how.

PTE General integrates all four skills (Listening, Reading, Speaking, and Writing) and focuses on assessing the ability of communicating in English, rather than test-taking skills. The tasks in the test are "a natural continuation of what happens in the classroom, giving test takers the opportunity to perform at their best." The tasks are described in the Pearson website as follows:

Assessment of Communicative Ability

PTE General is a scenario-based English language test designed to allow students the freedom to express themselves, show what they can do and how well they can use English.

Realistic and Familiar Tasks

The test uses real-life material and tasks, such as writing messages, understanding talks and newspaper articles, or participating in conversation.

Positive Testing Experience

Through a variety of tasks that are relevant and authentic, the test will help students identify their strengths and track improvement and success.
(www.pearsonpte.com/ptegeneral/pages/home.aspx)

The Test of Reading for eighth graders is at A2/B1 level. The description of the A2 level follows:

This test is for test takers with a basic command of English to cope with language needs for social, travel and everyday purposes. Test takers will be expected to understand straightforward information. The written paper is divided into nine tasks, which are linked to a theme. At (A2 level) the theme tends to relate to familiar and routine matters, such as home and shopping.

The description of the B1 level is as follows:

This test is for test takers with intermediate English for practical use in study, work, travel and other everyday purposes. Test takers will be expected to understand . . . information, ideas, feelings, opinions and common functions about everyday situations in straightforward . . . written language. The written paper is divided into nine tasks which are linked to a theme. At Level 2 Intermediate the theme tends to relate to familiar and routine matters, such as home and shopping.

The eighth-grade reading test used in Study One had five reading tasks with a total of 25 items. Task One contained five three-option multiple choice items, each on a separate text, all of which were public notices, with a gap to be filled from the options. The texts ranged from 13 to 24 words in length, total 97 words. Task Two contains one text, which appears to be from a newspaper report, of 292 words, with five three-option multiple choice items. Task Three contains a four-paragraph story about an accident, 199 words long, and four short answer questions. Task Four is an advertisement for a pop concert, containing 71 words, and four short answer questions. Task Five is an e-mail letter, containing 108 words and seven gap-filling items.

The upper secondary school FL English reading test is at the B1/B2 CEFR level. The description for the B1 level was given above. The B2 level description is as follows:

This test is for test takers who use or will use an upper intermediate level of English for their personal, social, educational or working life. Test takers will be expected to understand . . . the purpose, information and points of view in . . . written communication of the kind required in a variety of study, work, everyday and leisure-related contexts in daily life. The written paper is divided into nine tasks which are linked to a theme. At Level 3 the theme tends to be quite abstract, such as global issues like pollution and conservation.

The upper secondary school reading test used in Study One consists of five tasks with a total of 25 items. Task One contains seven texts of adverts or longer public notices. Lengths range from 21 to 33 words, with a total of 197 words. There are seven three-option multiple-choice items, one per text. Task Two is the same as Task Two in the eighth-grade test. Task Three has a text about a football tournament that is 224 words long, and there are four short-answer questions. Task Four has a 216 word text about child poverty, with four short answer questions. Task Five contains a 343 word text about global warming, and five gap-filling questions.

Practice tests for all *Pearson Tests of English* (General) are available at this website: www.pearsonpte.com/PTEGeneral/Pages/resources.aspx

Secondary School FL English Reading Test: DIALANG

The DIALANG component of the reading test contained 30 items per age group. The DIALANG tests are described and exemplified in the section on DIALANG above. Lower secondary eighth graders took 30 DIALANG Intermediate items, as shown in Table 4.4.

Primary level SL Finnish Reading Test

The Russian-speaking learners of Finnish were in two different sorts of classes: regular classes and preparatory classes. The students in regular classes comprise the clear majority of the L2 Finnish participants. Preparatory classes are intended for immigrants who are only starting to learn Finnish and cannot yet cope in

TABLE 4.4 DIALANG Intermediate Items used in DIALUKI Study One by sub-skill

Sub-skill	Items
Identifying main idea	8, 19, 20, 22, 24, 25
Reading for detail	9
Inferencing	1, 2, 3, 4, 5, 6, 7, 10, 11, 12, 13, 14, 15, 16, 17, 18, 21, 23, 26, 27, 28, 29, 30

the regular Finnish-medium classes. The purpose of this educational strand is to build their Finnish skills so that they will be able to join regular Finnish-medium instruction in the future.

With the primary school regular classes, we used a selection of 10 DIALANG Finnish reading items from the easy and intermediate tests. They were selected on the basis of the suitability of item content for young learners and in order to cover a range of proficiency levels (from roughly A1 to B1). This was a paper and pencil test rather than the more usual computer-based test.

Lower Secondary Level SL Finnish Reading Test

In the lower secondary school regular classes, the students took the full 30-item Intermediate DIALANG Finnish reading test administered by computer and using a special platform designed by the project to deliver DIALANG tests to our informants.

Preparatory Class Learners

The students in preparatory classes took a test comprising 12 retired Finnish L2 reading items from the National Certificates (YKI) basic level test. The items were chosen on the basis of their suitability for A1–A2 levels and, in terms of content, for young learners.

Conclusion

In this chapter we have described the construct of SFL reading from a variety of theoretical perspectives and presented descriptions and examples of reading test tasks used in the diagnosis of strengths and weaknesses in reading. In the next three chapters we will present a description of a range of variables potentially relevant to such diagnoses, together with empirical results from DIALUKI of the relationship between measures of L1 and SFL reading and these predictor variables. Chapter Five explores the role of linguistic variables, Chapter Six looks at the influence of cognitive variables on SFL reading, and Chapter Seven investigates what role background and motivational variables might play in affecting performance on SFL reading tests and reading in SFL more generally.

5

THE LINGUISTIC BASIS OF READING IN A SECOND OR FOREIGN LANGUAGE

Reading is thought to include a range of different contributory sub-skills, processes, and elements, as was discussed in Chapter Four. While there is considerable disagreement and uncertainty about the number and nature of these components of reading, it is, however, clear that reading is not just one indivisible and unanalyzable whole. And although the different levels of processing and components of skills and knowledge that reading entails must somehow work in a coordinated, even integrated manner, it is nevertheless useful to try to distinguish some of the components—especially if our intention is to diagnose reading.

One set of components of reading that has long interested both researchers and teachers of reading has to do with the linguistic elements that must somehow be part of reading both in L1 and in SFL. When we talk about the linguistic basis or linguistic elements in reading, we usually mean vocabulary, grammar, and pragmatics. Understanding a written text is severely limited if you do not know a word of the language the text is written in and you have no idea of the grammar either.

Obviously, it is possible to understand something of the text on the basis of the context in which the text appears and the visuals involved. Background knowledge can also help. So, even if you do not have a clue about the vocabulary and grammar of the language, if you happen to see a text with the headline "4–3 xxxx xx Barcelona xxxxx xxxx Manchester United xxx xxxxx" and there is a picture of footballers in action beside the text, you get a pretty good idea of what the text is about. Of course, you need a modicum of background knowledge about major soccer teams in Europe to infer that the story and the picture are not about some local derby between two villages. And you probably need to know the outcome of the match on the previous evening between the two teams in question to be sure who actually won.

The context where the text appears, the names of people and places you can spot, and the pictures, graphs, and so forth that appear with the text can thus help you to figure out something general about the text and even some details. This is, however, very limited and will be even more difficult if you have to deal with a different script from the one(s) that you happen to master. Knowing even a few linguistic elements of the language in question would help you considerably. But which would be more helpful—to know words or to know structures? Or do you have to have a somehow balanced mastery of the two for you to be able to read fluently and also comprehend what you read? And what does it mean to know words or structures in the first place? These are questions that have occupied many researchers interested in SFL reading.

Let us start with a little practical test. Below you can see two pieces of text that have been manipulated in different ways. The first is a text in English from which all words that carry a lot of meaning have been replaced by *x*s; these are so-called content words (i.e., nouns, verbs, adjectives, and adverbs). In the first text only the 'function' words, or words that carry grammatical meaning, are left (i.e., pronouns, prepositions, linking words, prefixes, and suffixes). The second piece of text has all the 'content' in place but all the 'grammar' has been replaced by *x*s. To illustrate how the relationship between 'words' and 'grammar' can differ between languages, we also provide the translations into Finnish of the same texts, manipulated in the same way.

English Text 1: A text that contains only grammatical meanings.

In a xxxxxxxx xxxxxxx, it is xxx xxxxxx xxxxxed how xxxxxxx the xxx of xxxxxing xx. Although xxxxxxx have xx xxxxx to xxxx, xxxx xx so xxxxly and with xxxxxxxxxly xxxxxx xxxxxx. And if the xxx of xxxxxing xx xxxxxx xxxxxx to xxxx xxxxxxxxxxxs and xxxxxxs, then what could be xxxxier than xxxxing the xxxxx to xxxx?

English Text 2: A text that contains only word meanings ('content').

Just take x text, ask x few questionx xxxxx xxx text, xxx you have x valid test xx readxxx! Xxxxxxx, life is not xx simple. Xxxx text xxxxxx xx selectxx? Xxxx xxx text serve xxx purpose, xxxx xxx topic? Handwritxxx xx word-processxx text? Xxx long xxxxx xxx text xx? Xxx familiar xxxxxx xxx wordx xx?

Finnish Text 1: A text that contains only grammatical meanings.

Xxxxxxxxxxxxxssa, xxxssa xxxxxxan xxxxxxxsti xxxxa xx xxxx xxxxxxa, xxxxxx xxxxxxxxxxxxxx xxxxxxxxxxxxxxxx xx. Xxxxxx xxxxxen xxxxxy xxxxa xxxxx- aan, xxxxxn xxx xxxxxy xiihen xxxxxsti xx xxxxxxxxxxsen xxxxxxxxxxxsti. Xx xxx xxxran xxximmilla xxxxxxxilla xx xxxxilla xxxxxxxx xxxxu xxxx xxxxxään, xxxx xxxx xxisi olla xxxxxxpaa xxxx xxxxxxta xxxxxxxxxxa?

Finnish Text 2: A text that contains only word meanings ('content').

Otexxxx vain teksti, kysyxxxx sxxxx muutama kysymys xx mexxxx ox pätevä lukemixxx testi! Elämä ei xxxxxxxxxx oxx xxxx yksinkertaixxx. Xxxx teksti pitäxxx valitx? Käyxx xxxx tahansa teksti, xxxxx tahansa aihexxxx?

Käsixkirjoitxxxx xxx tekstixkäsittelyohjelmaxxx tehxx teksti? Xxxxxx pitkä tekstix pitäxxx xxxx? Xxxxxx tuttuxx pitäxxx sanxxxx oxxx?

An attentive reader may have noticed that the texts above come from the beginning of Chapter Four of this book. We may argue about the details of what exactly in the texts is the meaning conveyed by content words and what counts as grammar. For example, the role of pronouns is debatable. However, it should be sufficiently clear from the examples that removing a bigger part of either word or grammatical meaning of a text affects the fluency with which we can read the text and the degree to which we comprehend it. It is also obvious that if the text only has its grammatical meaning left, it becomes impossible to understand. However, a text stripped of its grammatical meaning also becomes rather difficult to understand but compared to the grammar-only text, it is possible to extract quite a lot of its content, although how the different pieces of content relate to each other becomes hard to deduce—because it is precisely the function of grammar to convey that information. It also appears that the two structurally very different languages chosen as examples, English and Finnish, look very similar in this respect. The fact that grammatical meaning is conveyed more often in word endings in Finnish than in English may not make much of a difference to the comprehensibility of a text.

Ultimately, however, the question of whether the role of grammar versus vocabulary in reading in an SFL varies depending on the language is an empirical question. Later in this chapter we will be reporting on some research that sheds light on this question, among other things.

What Is Grammatical Knowledge?

The definition of grammar and grammatical knowledge has varied over time, and the current conceptualizations are very different from those of the past decades, but it appears that most grammar tests have not changed much and still focus on syntactic knowledge (Alderson & Bachman, 2004). The ability to apply rules in order to produce grammatically correct sentences is often thought to be at the core of grammatical knowledge.

Conceptualizations of grammatical knowledge often make a distinction between grammatical form and grammatical meaning, and attempts may be made to test them separately. Learners might be able to add the *-ed* affix to English verbs, for example, thus demonstrating knowledge of that particular grammatical form, but they may not necessarily know the meaning of past-tense verbs or how to use them (Purpura, 2014a). It appears that much testing of grammar has emphasized the knowledge of grammatical form. For example, Urquhart and Weir (1998) advocate focusing on formal grammar and the exclusion of the 'communicative' elements as far as possible when outlining how the role of grammar in reading could be studied.

The most recent definition of grammar knowledge in the area of language testing (Purpura, 2004a, 2012, 2014a) combines grammatical form and meaning, and links that with language use in context (pragmatics). According to Purpura (2014a, p. 6), grammatical knowledge is defined in terms of "a range of linguistic forms (e.g., "*s*" affix; word order) and semantic meanings associated with these forms, either individually (e.g., plurality with a noun; time reference with a verb) or collectively (e.g., the overall literal meaning of the utterance)."

He further specifies that grammatical forms and meaning occur at different levels ranging from sub-sentential to discourse levels, and can be categorized with regard to (a) phonology/graphology, (b) lexis, (c) morphosyntax, (d) cohesion, (e) information management, and (f) interaction (e.g., meta-discourse markers). Learners' ability to map these grammatical forms and meanings is crucial for their understanding and production of the literal and intended meanings expressed in SFL use situations. Furthermore, they also play an important role in being able to deal with pragmatic meanings that are often expressed implicitly and have to be understood by considering the context in which they are used.

Purpura (2012, 2014a) also provides an operational model of language knowledge that links different grammatical forms with their grammatical (semantic) meanings and possible pragmatic meanings. Such a systematic list of features could be used to design assessments for different purposes; obviously, this includes the provision of information for learners about strengths and weaknesses in their grammatical knowledge (i.e., assessment for diagnostic purposes).

What Is Vocabulary Knowledge?

The most common way to define knowledge of vocabulary is to refer to the number of different words whose meaning a person knows. This means thinking about vocabulary as a list of individual words with their definitions (cf. a monolingual dictionary) or with their translations (cf. a bilingual dictionary). It is very common to say about one's vocabulary that one 'knows a lot of words.'

Such a definition is, however, problematic, as it is somewhat superficial and focuses on only one aspect of vocabulary. First, knowing a word can mean a range of different things. Second, the number of different words one knows tells only half the story, at most. Word knowledge entails several different but related aspects (see Read, 2000; Nation, 2001). Knowing the form of the word, that is, being able to pronounce or spell the word constitutes one dimension of word knowledge. Knowing the meaning of a word is another dimension, but there we are in fact talking not only about its conceptual meaning, but also about its associations and relations with other words (e.g., synonyms, antonyms). Word knowledge also has use-related dimensions: Knowing a word involves knowing which other words it is typically used with, which is called collocational knowledge, and in which contexts it is appropriate to use it, which is knowledge about different registers.

It is common to distinguish two dimensions of vocabulary knowledge: breadth and depth. Breadth relates to the traditional quantitative definition of vocabulary (i.e., to the size of somebody's vocabulary), to how many words one knows. The depth dimension concerns the quality of one's vocabulary knowledge and here it is useful to refer back to the different dimensions of word knowledge discussed above. The better you know the different aspects of a word such as its spelling, pronunciation, meaning, register, collocations, as well as its morphological and syntactical properties, the deeper your knowledge of that word is (see Qian, 2002).

A distinction that is relevant when we consider the role of vocabulary knowledge in diagnosing reading concerns receptive and productive vocabulary. Although the distinction is not a dichotomy, but rather a continuum with reception (understanding) and production occupying the opposite ends of it, reading could be characterized more as a receptive skill and writing as a productive skill. Therefore, it is likely that measures of receptive vocabulary are more relevant in diagnosing reading than productive measures, but there appears little empirical research to back this assumption. Read (2000) warns against confusing two different ways of conceptualizing reception, as it can be either about recognition or comprehension, which are also typically measured with different kinds of vocabulary tests. Recognition tasks are very decontextualized: Learners are typically presented with a word in an SFL and asked to demonstrate that they understand its meaning by, for example, translating it into their L1 or by matching it with one of the definitions presented to them, either in a L1 or SFL, in multiple choice options. In contrast, comprehension tasks are contextualized: Learners have to show their understanding of the words presented to them in some textual context ranging from a sentence to a whole text.

Viewing vocabulary as knowledge of single words is a simplification of reality, however. Not all 'words' consist of one graphological unit, as there are combinations of words that have a joint meaning that can differ significantly from the separate meanings of their parts. Formulaic expressions in general are examples of such multiword units that have their specific meaning and context of use. Examples of formulaic expressions in English include phrases such as 'how do you do?' 'by no means,' and 'as a result of.'

Phrasal verbs in English are a special case of formulaic expressions. 'Words' such as 'look up,' 'look for,' and 'look into' all have their own different meanings that cannot be directly derived from the meaning of their constituent parts.

Grammar and vocabulary are not always conceptualized as separate aspects of language. We have already seen above how some aspects of vocabulary knowledge involve knowledge about the word's syntactic and other grammatical dimensions. Several applied linguists and corpus linguists (e.g., Wilkins, 1972; Halliday, 1973; Purpura, 1997, 2004a; Sinclair, 2004; Römer, 2009) argue that vocabulary and grammar are inseparable and that calling them lexicogrammar or lexicogrammatical knowledge would in fact represent reality far better than continuing the use of the two traditional terms.

Research on the Role of Grammar and Vocabulary in SFL Reading

In order to have a more detailed understanding of reading in an SFL to be able to predict and more fully diagnose reading performance, it is important to discuss what is known about the relative contribution of vocabulary and grammar knowledge to the ability to read in an SFL. To what extent does vocabulary or grammar knowledge predict reading performance in the first place? Would it be more efficient to focus on vocabulary if we wanted to understand and predict reading? Or should we focus on grammar instead? Or do we need both? And if research produces conflicting results, can the findings be explained by taking a better account of the learners' characteristics, for example, their level of proficiency and first language and the way reading and/or grammar and vocabulary have been operationalized in research?

The little exercise at the beginning of this chapter with the grammar-stripped and content-stripped texts seems to suggest that perhaps vocabulary knowledge is more crucial to our ability to understand texts than grammatical knowledge. In everyday talk we also often equate language skills and vocabulary knowledge. 'Do you know German?—Just a few words' or 'I don't understand a word of what you say.' It would be strange indeed to hear somebody say 'I don't understand a single structure of what you say.'

When we look at the research into the contribution of grammar and vocabulary to reading in SFL, several studies indeed seem to confirm our intuition that vocabulary knowledge contributes significantly to reading comprehension, and that it is usually more important for SFL reading than grammar knowledge.

Henning (1975), Koda (1989), and Sternberg (1987) are examples of earlier studies on the role of vocabulary in reading that all came to the conclusion that vocabulary is a highly significant contributor to the ability to read. Similar findings are reported in Schoonen et al. (1998), Alderson (2000), and Qian (2002).

While many studies have established the crucial role of vocabulary in reading, this obviously does not mean that grammatical knowledge plays no part in comprehension. Remember how difficult it was to get a full, detailed understanding of the text that was stripped of its grammatical meaning at the beginning of this chapter.

Alderson (1993) examined the underlying structure of different components of a language test battery, which included tests of grammar, vocabulary, reading, and listening. He found that grammar and reading were closely related. Van Gelderen et al. (2003, 2004) also studied the underlying structure of language abilities among Dutch learners of English as L2 and L3, and found that knowledge of both grammar and vocabulary were significant predictors of reading performance. Also in the Dutch context, Droop and Verhoeven (2003) discovered that grammatical and vocabulary knowledge were both strongly correlated with reading.

Shiotsu and Weir (2007) and Shiotsu (2010) are among the few studies that have come to the conclusion that grammatical knowledge can be a better predictor of the ability to read in SFL than vocabulary knowledge. Shiotsu and Weir (2007) studied three groups of Japanese learners of English whose reading was tested with short passages requiring careful reading. The researchers found that the syntactic knowledge test was slightly more related to reading in English as a foreign language test than the vocabulary knowledge measure (Vocabulary Levels Test). The vocabulary and syntax measures were strongly associated with each other in two of the studies. However, the measure of syntax used in these studies has recently been criticized and this will be described in more detail later in this chapter.

Kremmel (2012) also investigated the contribution of grammar and vocabulary knowledge to reading performance of Austrian learners of English at the end of their secondary education. The study was a partial replication of Shiotsu's (2010) study as he used Shiotsu's test of syntactic knowledge. However, the reading and vocabulary instruments were different in the two studies. As a vocabulary measure, Kremmel used the DIALANG vocabulary test, which will be described later, and as a reading measure he used the reading component of the standardized Austrian school exit examination that targets the B2 level in the Common European Framework of Reference. The reading passages required a broad comprehension of main ideas and supporting details.

Kremmel's findings showed that knowledge of vocabulary was a far better predictor of SFL reading than knowledge of syntax. Kremmel's study, thus, produced different results than Shiotsu's (2010) study in that vocabulary knowledge predicted reading better than syntactic knowledge. However, Kremmel, too, found that vocabulary and grammar knowledge were significantly related to each other.

In addition to the vocabulary and grammar tests described above, Kremmel (2012) used a test measuring the knowledge of phrasal expressions, which combines vocabulary and grammatical knowledge (this test of phrasal expression will be described in detail later in this chapter). The inclusion of phrasal knowledge as the third predictor along with vocabulary and grammar knowledge increased the overall prediction of reading performance slightly. The phrasal knowledge test and the vocabulary size test were very strongly associated with each other, but the relationship of the phrasal test with the grammar test was considerably weaker.

There may be at least two reasons why Shiotsu and Kremmel came to different conclusions about the relative importance of vocabulary and grammatical knowledge in reading in English as a foreign language. First, the reading measures were different. Shiotsu's test was based on short passages with multiple-choice questions whereas Kremmel's texts were longer and both multiple-choice and short-answer questions were employed. Kremmel (2012) proposes that Shiotsu's reading tasks involved more careful reading of short passages and, thus, required more syntactic processing, whereas the Austrian reading passages required broader comprehension of main ideas and supporting details. Second, Kremmel's informants were more advanced learners than in Shiotsu's studies and may have depended less on grammatical knowledge than vocabulary and other components of reading ability. Shiotsu's and Weir's (2007) more detailed analysis of the participants in one of their three studies in fact showed that syntactic knowledge was a more important contributor to reading for the lower proficiency group than for the higher proficiency group.

To summarize thus far, it appears to be the case that both vocabulary knowledge and grammatical (usually syntactic) knowledge relate quite strongly to SFL reading, with vocabulary being a somewhat stronger correlate in most of the studies. It is possible to argue that vocabulary and grammatical knowledge can be used as predictors of reading in an SFL. However, Shiotsu and Weir (2007) and Kremmel (2012) suggest that the nature of the reading tasks and the learners' proficiency level may also affect the relative importance of vocabulary and grammatical knowledge in SFL reading.

The DIALUKI project described in Chapters One, Three, and Four may shed more light on the contribution of grammatical and vocabulary knowledge in SFL reading because the project studied two different linguistic groups, Finnish-speaking learners of English and Russian-speaking learners of Finnish in two somewhat different context (foreign language context for English and second language context for Finnish).

DIALUKI Study 1 provides evidence about the contribution of first and second/foreign language vocabulary knowledge to reading in an SFL, as several aspects of learners' knowledge of vocabulary were measured in it. It also provides a limited amount of information about the contribution of grammatical knowledge.

In comparison with most other studies that have studied the contribution of vocabulary to SFL reading, the DIALUKI study included measures of a range of different aspects of vocabulary knowledge. In addition to an overall measure of SFL vocabulary, there were measures that tapped the speed of retrieval of words from memory (speed of reading aloud of isolated words and of naming simple objects) and measures of a rapid, automatic recognition of words. All these measures were administered both in the first and second or foreign language of the learners. Furthermore, the study included an overall measure of L1 vocabulary and a task testing learners' knowledge of the spelling of L1 words. These are summarized in Table 5.1 below (see also Chapter Six in this book for a more detailed description of some of these measures). As was described in Chapter Four, SFL reading in the DIALUKI study was measured with tasks selected from, for example, the DIALANG tests, the Pearson Test of English General, and the PISA tests.

The DIALUKI study did not include conventional measures of grammatical knowledge, since most previous research had suggested that vocabulary was a better predictor of reading and writing. The fact that the linguistic predictors

TABLE 5.1 Dimensions of vocabulary knowledge and their measures included in the DIALUKI study

Dimension/aspect of vocabulary	Test
Size of SFL vocabulary	Vocabulary Levels Test (Schmitt, Schmitt, & Clapham, 2001) for FL English DIALANG Vocabulary Size Placement Test (for L2 Finnish)
Size of L1 vocabulary	DIALANG Vocabulary Size Placement Test (for L1 Finnish, L1 Russian)
Access to L1 and SFL vocabulary (time and correctness) (reading words aloud)	Reading a list of 105 frequent words in 60 seconds (L1 Finnish, L1 Russian; FL English, L2 Finnish)
Access to L1 and SFL vocabulary (time and correctness) (naming symbols)	Naming a list of colors, numbers, and letters (or objects) (L1 Finnish, L1 Russian; FL English, L2 Finnish)
Rapid recognition of words in L1 and SFL (sight word reading)	Recognition of rapidly presented frequent words (L1 Finnish, L1 Russian; FL English, L2 Finnish)
Spelling of L1 or L2 vocabulary (time and correctness)	Correcting a list of misspelled words (L1 Finnish; L2 Finnish)

of SFL proficiency were not the main focus of the project was also a factor in this decision. Instead the project intended to explore the diagnostic potential of many cognitive/psycholinguistic factors that had been found useful in studies on L1 problems. As a result, we focused on operationalizing those aspects of knowledge, in addition to measuring L1 and SFL reading and writing as comprehensively as possible. This resulted in a very large number of different measures to be administered to the learners. As a result, certain aspects of language proficiency could not be explicitly tested in the study.

Nonetheless, the study did include a measure, both in L1 and SFL, that appears to tap grammatical knowledge, at least to some extent, although it is probably fair to say that the task in question integrates vocabulary and grammatical knowledge. This measure was a segmentation task, where the learner was presented with a few lines of text. Two different segmentation tasks were administered to the learners: one that contained a text in their L1 and another in which the text was in the SFL. All the words in the 'text' were, however, written together in lower case letters without spaces or punctuation marks. The learner's task was to draw lines between the words. Both the time to complete the task and the accuracy of segmentation into words were measured.

Below is the English SFL segmentation task for the fourth graders:

sothenextdaythethreelittlepigslefthomethefirstpigmadeahomefromstraw
thesecondpigmadeahomefromsticksbutthethirdpigwascleverhemadehishome
frombricksonedaythebigbadwolfcametothestrawhouseheknockedonthedoor

Segmentation appears to be a rather unusual instrument in applied linguists' toolkits. A rare exception is the study by Leong et al. (2013) on the construct of reading and writing in Chinese, in which they found that ability to segment Chinese text into phrases predicted reading comprehension in the older learners (Grade 11), but not in Grades 7 and 9. Segmentation, however, predicted ability to write in Chinese across all three age groups.

Our analyses show that general vocabulary knowledge was quite strongly associated with reading in SFL in all three age groups (primary, lower secondary, and upper secondary). Moreover, the two Russian-speaking groups of Finnish L2 learners also revealed an almost as strong relationship between L2 vocabulary knowledge and L2 reading as was found for the Finnish-speaking learners of English as a foreign language. Interestingly, the L1 vocabulary measures were also related with SFL reading test scores, at least for the Finnish learners of English, although rather modestly.

In most cases, the more specific measures of different dimensions of vocabulary knowledge were also significantly correlated with reading in an SFL, but typically much less strongly than the overall vocabulary tests. Interestingly, the rapidly presented words task, where the learner has to recognize a word that is displayed only for 80 milliseconds, had a relatively robust association with reading, especially for the younger learners and for L2 Finnish.

However, the most remarkable result was the strong correlation between reading in SFL and the accuracy of segmenting a string of letters into words in both English as FL and Finnish as L2. In fact, the segmentation task turned out to be almost as good an indicator of reading in English as the more global measure of English vocabulary knowledge. Indeed, for reading in Finnish as L2, the segmentation task outperformed the global measure of Finnish vocabulary as an indicator of reading. The strong relationship of reading with the segmentation task may be due to its integration of vocabulary and grammatical knowledge.

So far, we have found that quite a few vocabulary measures used in DIALUKI correlate with reading in SFL, but the strength of association varies. Overall, it was found that the different vocabulary measures, some of which also measure grammatical knowledge, explained between a third and more than half of learners' performance on the SFL reading measures used. Expressed more technically, variance in learners' vocabulary test scores explained a considerable amount of the variance in the reading test scores. For the fourth-grade learners of English this explained variance was almost 40% and for the other two older groups well over 50%; for the Russian-speaking learners of Finnish it was about 40%. The results of our study are, thus, in line with the research reviewed earlier in this chapter, namely that both vocabulary and grammatical knowledge are strongly related to reading performance in an SFL (see also Purpura, 1997; Liao, 2009). We could even say that it is possible to use vocabulary and grammatical knowledge to 'predict' how well an SFL learner is able to read and understand texts in that language.

What correlated best with reading in an SFL differed to some extent in the foreign and second language groups. For learners of English as FL, general English vocabulary knowledge was the strongest indicator of ability to read in English. For the Finnish as L2 learners, the corresponding general vocabulary knowledge was the second strongest indicator, and only in the younger group of learners.

As we noted earlier, the relationship between segmentation tasks and reading tests in our data were stronger than what we had perhaps expected. In this case, an ability to segment texts into words turned out to be a significant explanatory variable. Thus, it contributes something unique to the prediction that differs from what the general vocabulary measures (or other significant indicators) contribute. Across all five learner groups studied, segmentation was among the two strongest predictors of SFL reading. The foreign language groups differed from the second language groups as far as the strongest indicator of reading in the SFL is concerned. In all three English as FL groups the measure of English vocabulary size related more strongly to reading in English than the segmentation task in English did. In both Finnish as L2 groups the order of the predictors of reading was reversed: Segmentation in Finnish was stronger than vocabulary in Finnish.

To summarize, research on linguistic predictors of reading in SFL has typically focused on examining the extent to which knowledge of vocabulary and grammar relates to reading performance. Sometimes the purpose of the research has been to establish which of these two areas of language is more important in reading. While several studies suggest that vocabulary knowledge is more important in reading it is also clear that grammatical knowledge plays an important role. Thus, it is advisable to consider both vocabulary and grammar in any attempts to predict reading.

Findings from the DIALUKI project suggest that diagnostic information concerning the linguistic basis of SFL reading depends on either the particular SFL studied (English or Finnish in this case) or the context (second or foreign language context) or both. Furthermore, the age of the learners may be important, too. Diagnosis of reading in an SFL may thus be quite sensitive to which particular SFL we are attempting to diagnose and who the learners are.

It is important to remember that the operational definitions (i.e., the tests) of vocabulary and grammatical knowledge are usually somewhat traditional and therefore limited. A more complex or nuanced and thereby more valid construct that includes lexicogrammar and also examines aspects of pragmatics should be investigated in future research to address the limitations of the instruments used to date (see also Purpura, 2004a, pp. 264–270, on the need to reconsider the tasks used in grammar tests).

Examples of Diagnostic Grammar and Vocabulary Tests

In the first half of this chapter we have reviewed research on the linguistic basis of reading in a second or foreign language. We focused on vocabulary and grammatical knowledge, which can also be viewed as lexicogrammatical knowledge in recognition of the fact that words and grammar are in many ways connected with each other. This is not to say that there is no other type of linguistic knowledge that plays a part when we read in an SFL but it reflects the current focus of research into linguistic correlates of reading.

Given this focus, we will next describe selected grammar and vocabulary tests to illustrate how the constructs of grammatical and vocabulary knowledge have been defined and operationalized in practice as concrete tests and test items. Interestingly, some of the tests we will present claim to be diagnostic, which raises some questions such as, What exactly might make them diagnostic? What do they diagnose? How might they be diagnostic of SFL reading?

One feature of tests of linguistic knowledge to consider is whether these tests intend to provide an overall estimate of vocabulary or grammatical knowledge (or a combined estimate of lexicogrammar) or whether they produce a profile for different dimensions of vocabulary or grammar. An overall measure of vocabulary or grammar does not provide much diagnostically useful information about the learner's vocabulary or grammatical knowledge, as it lacks the details that diagnosis requires (see Alderson's 2005 list of characteristics of diagnostic tests). If the intention is to diagnose a macro-language skill such as reading, even overall measures of linguistic knowledge can provide diagnostically relevant information, if linguistic knowledge relates to reading in some systematic way, as has indeed been shown to be the case with the segmentation test, according to the research reviewed in this chapter. Thus, one conclusion that could be drawn from a particularly poor performance on a vocabulary test might be that the learner's poor reading performance is likely to be due to an overall lack of vocabulary knowledge (limited vocabulary size, for example) and, thus, learning more words would likely result in an improved reading performance.

Tests of linguistic knowledge that comprise items intended to tap different aspects of vocabulary and grammatical knowledge have different diagnostic potential than overall measures of vocabulary or grammar. They can help diagnose learners' problems in vocabulary and grammar, and lead to improvement in these areas, which in turn can improve reading and other macro-language skills. It is also possible that more detailed information about vocabulary and grammatical knowledge has more direct diagnostic value for reading in an SFL. For example, poor performance on items testing the knowledge of grammar used in creating cohesion in a text may indicate that the learner has problems in understanding how different parts of the text relate to each other when reading the text. Or poor performance on vocabulary items measuring the depth of word knowledge may suggest problems in understanding details and nuances in SFL texts. There seems to be very little empirical research on how performance on different aspects of vocabulary and grammar relate to reading in an SFL. However, Liao's (2009) study sheds some light on this; she found that items testing grammatical meaning were somewhat more closely related to FL reading test performance than were items testing grammatical forms, which suggests that knowledge of grammatical meaning plays a more important role in reading comprehension than knowledge of grammatical form.

In addition to the level of detail provided by a test of grammatical and vocabulary knowledge, it is important to consider the item types used in the test in order to evaluate its diagnostic potential in SFL reading. To put it simply, the more the vocabulary and grammar knowledge items simulate what happens when we read, and, for example, require comprehension rather than production of words/grammar, the more likely is performance on such items to correlate with performance on reading. This is, however, speculative, as there is very little research into this. Again, Liao's (2009) study provides us with some relevant information. She operationalized SFL reading ability by two item types: one requiring the comprehension of literal meaning that was expressed explicitly in the text and the other requiring the comprehension of pragmatic meaning conveyed implicitly. Lexicogrammatical knowledge was strongly associated with performance on both types of reading items but the relationship was stronger for the literal-explicit items. This suggests that literal-explicit reading comprehension items may rely more on the reader's lexicogrammatical knowledge to decode text than do pragmatic-implicit reading items.

A discussion of the diagnostic potential for SFL reading of various tests of vocabulary and grammatical knowledge presented next will, thus, also be rather speculative. However, we feel it is important to obtain an understanding of the areas of vocabulary and grammatical knowledge that different tests intend to measure and how these areas have been operationalized in test items. Such information and examples can help us understand the diagnostic potential these tests may have and to provide ideas for researchers who want to study the linguistic basis of SFL reading in the future.

While we focus on the DIALANG and DELTA vocabulary and grammar tests in our review of tests below, we also discuss the Martinez (2011) test of multiword expressions, Shiotsu's (2010) test of syntactic knowledge, and the *Birmingham Assessment and Diagnostic Test* (BADT; Johns, 1976) that focuses on grammar. Some research carried out on these tests is also reported to complement our understanding of the contribution of vocabulary and grammar to reading in an SFL.

Grammar Tests With Diagnostic Potential

The oldest references we have found to a test that claims to be diagnostic of SFL abilities are to the BADT grammar tests developed at the University of Birmingham (see Chapter Three). Presumably this is because grammar was long the focus of foreign language teaching and any test that could yield detailed information about the grammar that the learners were having problems with would have a clear diagnostic potential, as an indicator of, and problems in, overall SFL proficiency or one of its main components such as reading.

The Birmingham Assessment and Diagnostic Test

As was described in more detail in Chapter Three, an early example of an English language diagnostic test is the University of Birmingham Assessment and Diagnostic Test (BADT). This test was designed to obtain "a microdiagnostic syntactic profile of all arriving overseas students at the University of Birmingham" (Johns, 1976, p. 2). The original version consisted of 130 items divided into 21 diagnostic areas of syntax (Johns, 1976; see Table 5.2 for details). The areas were selected mainly on the basis of their importance in written academic discourse, and their difficulty for a range of different learners of English.

Each diagnostic area was tested by either 5 or 10 items, and if the student failed to master 80% of the items in a particular area they were considered to have problems with it and were directed to specific lessons.

Later versions of the BADT attempted the diagnosis of 24 areas, as shown in Table 5.3 (BADT, n.d.).

TABLE 5.2 Micro-diagnostic syntactic areas originally tested by the BADT

Diagnostic area	Syntactic description
1.	Present and timeless time reference
2.	Past time reference
3.	Future time reference
4.	Modality: inference and probability
5.	Modality: obligation
6.	Modality: hypothetical
7.	Question tags
8.	Complementation: predicate complementation
9.	Complementation: double-object verbs
10.	Verb + preposition collocations
11.	Adjective + preposition collocations
12.	Prepositions of Space
13.	Prepositions of Time
14.	Genitive constructions
15.	Determiners: Definite vs. indefinite
16.	Determiners: quantifiers
17.	Determiners: specification
18.	Pronominalization
19.	Intensification and down-grading: simplex
20.	Intensification and down-grading: complex
21.	Word order

TABLE 5.3 Areas of grammar tested by the 1991 Version of BADT

Area	Grammar topic
1–2	Continuous vs. non-continuous
3–4	Past time reference
5–6	Probability and Obligation
7–8	Hypotheticality
9–10	Monotransitivity and Intransitivity
11–12	Ditransitivity
13–14	Sentential Complementation
15–16	Number agreement
17–18	Determiners
19–20	Intensifiers and downgraders
21–22	Logical connectors
23–24	Miscellaneous

A few sample items from the 1991 version of the BADT are presented below:

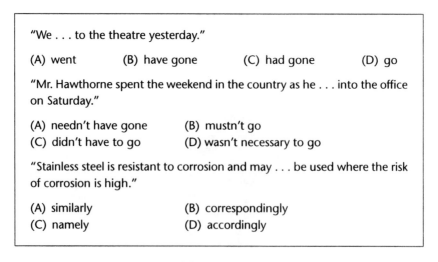

"We . . . to the theatre yesterday."

(A) went   (B) have gone   (C) had gone   (D) go

"Mr. Hawthorne spent the weekend in the country as he . . . into the office on Saturday."

(A) needn't have gone   (B) mustn't go
(C) didn't have to go   (D) wasn't necessary to go

"Stainless steel is resistant to corrosion and may . . . be used where the risk of corrosion is high."

(A) similarly   (B) correspondingly
(C) namely   (D) accordingly

The grammatical categories measured by these sample items are not given, but it is likely that the first item is intended to tap 'Past time reference,' the second 'Probability and obligation,' and the third 'Logical connectors.' Comparison of the grammatical categories in the older and newer versions of the BADT in Table 5.2 and 5.3 suggests that the new test emphasizes grammatical meaning rather than form. However, the test content appears not to have changed significantly, and many items seem to tap both grammatical form and meaning. Unfortunately, there is rather little information available about the way the BADT has been used and, in particular, how it might have been used on courses involving reading.

DIALANG Test of Structures

DIALANG is the first large-scale language test that was designed, in the late 1990s, to be diagnostic from the onset (Alderson, 2005). It is an online assessment system which provides its users with feedback on the strengths and weaknesses in their language proficiency in reading, writing, listening, vocabulary and structures, and in different areas or sub-skills within these five macro skills. DIALANG includes tests in 14 languages: Danish, Dutch, English, Finnish, French, German, Greek, Icelandic, Irish, Italian, Norwegian, Portuguese, Spanish, and Swedish.

Although the Common European Framework (CEFR, Council of Europe, 2001) was used extensively in the design of the content for DIALANG, the CEFR was not used as a source for describing the grammar construct. In fact, the categories selected for the grammar tests were quite traditional. They were not based on a particular theory of grammar; an important selection criterion for the grammatical categories was that they were expected to be familiar to most language teachers and learners. A common set of grammatical categories was defined for all languages (see below) but the test development teams could follow the conventions of the teaching traditions in their particular language in deciding how to categorize their grammar items. In the DIALANG structures test, the items measure the user's knowledge of, and ability to understand and use morphology, as well as knowledge of, and ability to, understand and use syntax.

The teams adapted the 19 grammatical categories listed below to the needs of their own language:

Morphology

NOUNS

> Inflection—cases
> Definite/indefinite—articles
> Proper/common

ADJECTIVES AND ADVERBS

> Inflection
> Comparison

PRONOUNS

> Inflection
> Context (referent)

VERBS

> Inflection: tense, mood, person
> Active/Passive voice

NUMERALS

> Inflection
> Context

OTHER

Syntax

ORGANIZATION/ REALIZATION OF PARTS OF SPEECH

> Word order: statements, questions, exclamations
> Agreement

SIMPLE vs. COMPLEX CLAUSES

> Coordination
> Subordination
> Deixis

PUNCTUATION
OTHER

DIALANG reports the results of the grammar test to its users as both an overall CEFR level (A1–C2) and a profile, where the learners can see how the different grammar items relate to different grammatical categories. As this test was designed from the onset to be used for diagnostic purposes, the learners can review each item and their answers to them, if they wish.

Several DIALANG grammar items in Table 5.4 illustrate how the above-mentioned categories of grammar were operationalized for French and German.

In his analyses of the DIALANG pilot tests of English, Alderson (2005) found that the scores from the grammar tests correlated with scores from the reading tests at the .69 level. A more detailed analysis of the areas of grammatical knowledge showed that the knowledge of specific categories of grammar was significantly if only slightly correlated with reading performance. Below, the categories that were correlated with reading and that included at least four items are listed in the order of the strength of association with reading (the most closely related categories are mentioned first):

- Morphology
- Proper and common nouns
- Verbs (tense, mood, etc.)
- Syntax organization
- Pronouns—context
- Verbs (active vs. passive)

TABLE 5.4 Examples of DIALANG grammar items for French and German

Examples of items, including directions to the test taker	Grammatical category and comments
Quand nous étions en vacances, ____ un accident Options: j'avais / j'ai / j'ai eu	Verbs (appears to measure both form [tense] and meaning [aspect])
J'habite ici _____ Options: il y a un mois / depuis un mois / en un mois	Clauses (a phrase in this example; may only measure the meaning rather than the form)
C'est un film _____ j'ai vu trois fois.	Pronouns (probably measures both form and meaning)
Attention, la chaise sur _____ tu es assis n'est pas solide. Options: lequel / laquelle / lesquels / lesquelles	Pronouns
Die Party war lustig, weil Willy auch da war. Wenn Willy _____, wäre es langweilig gewesen. Options: nicht eingeladen hätte / nicht eingeladen worden ist / nicht eingeladen worden wäre / nicht eingeladen würde	Parts of speech (probably also measures meaning and form [past passive subjunctive; word order is held constant])
Wie lautet die Zahl als ausgeschriebenes Wort? In China feierte letztes Jahr eine Frau ihren 124. Geburtstag. Options: einhundertzwanzigundvierten / einhundertvierundzwanzigste / einhundertvierundzwanzigsten / einhundertzwanzigundvierte	Numerals (more precisely: ordinal number morphology)
Können Sie mir einen _____ Film empfehlen? Options: spannend / spannendem / spannenden / spannender	Adjectives and adverbs (measures morphosyntactic form as lexical meaning is held constant)

- Comparison of adjectives and adverbs
- Morphology—numerals
- Syntax punctuation.

An important purpose of the diagnosis in DIALANG is to give users feedback on their CEFR level in each of the skills tested (reading, listening, writing, vocabulary, structures) and information about the correct and incorrect responses to items measuring different areas within each skill. The CEFR levels were determined on the basis of standard setting procedures that involved experts judging the CEFR level of the test items and considering the results of the pilot testing (see Alderson, 2005, for details). Learners can, thus, see if there is a skill or an area within a skill where they appear to have more problems (incorrect answers) than in others. However, the system does not give explicit advice on what exactly the learners should do if they receive a particular profile of results across skills or areas. Nor does DIALANG give advice on what receiving a particular result from the grammar or vocabulary test implies for reading ability. However, the system does contain advice on how to improve, for example, reading (see Chapter Eight on feedback for more information). It can also be expected that users participating in language courses can consult their language teacher in order to better interpret the results and plan for further action.

DELTA Test of Grammar

DELTA is an online language assessment system developed in Hong Kong in the late 2000s for diagnosing English for academic purposes (see Chapter Three). According to Urmston (2012) the system intends to diagnose students' strengths and weaknesses across language skills, to track and report their language development, and to help them plan their language learning. It is linked to institutional curricula and teaching materials, and it aims at informing curriculum development at the university.

The DELTA Grammar component "was based on several definitions of the construct of grammatical knowledge" (Urmston et al., 2013, p. 66). These include Rea-Dickins's (1991) definition of grammar as 'the single embodiment of syntax, semantics and pragmatics'; Larsen-Freeman's (1991) characterization of grammatical knowledge along three dimensions—linguistic form (accuracy), semantic meaning (meaningfulness), and pragmatic use (appropriacy); Purpura's (2004a) conclusion that grammatical knowledge "embodies two highly related components: grammatical form and grammatical meaning" (p. 61).

Despite differences in definition, all emphasize that "correct formation of grammatical structures and accurate conveyance of meaning are key skills in (the) demonstration of grammatical knowledge" (Urmston et al., 2013, p. 67). Some of the grammatical elements used in the DELTA follow:

- Adjective
- Adverb
- Cohesive device
- Determiner
- Gerund
- Infinitive
- Object pronoun
- Participle (present or past participle used as attributive or adverbial)
- Phrasal verb
- Preposition
- Reflexive pronoun
- Relative pronoun

- Singular/plural (phrases)
- Subject/verb agreement.

Below is an extract from a retired DELTA test that focuses on grammar. The first half of the text, and the first six items, are presented here. In the items, the correct answer is indicated with an asterisk (★), and the words in brackets after the words 'The correct version is' are not presented to the test takers but are shown here simply to indicate which grammatical category each item is intended to measure.

Read the following text written by a student and answer the questions about the underlined parts.

Dear Editor:

I am writing to support the Hong Kong government <u>pull</u> down the old buildings.

First, it is a trend of the world. Many developed countries wanted to have more space to develop so they <u>teared</u> down many historic buildings just like America, Japan, Australia, and so on. When every other <u>countries</u> did so, it is not wrong that Hong Kong government to tear down the old buildings.

Second, if we didn't tear down the old buildings it would bring lots of serious consequence. The living space would be <u>more</u> small, when the population grows it would be no place for us to live. When we do have not enough space, the opportunity of getting sick <u>should</u> also increase.

Third, it is right to tear down the old buildings. Hong Kong Chief Executive Mr. Donald Tsang said it is a compulsory action for Hong Kong to not keep the historic buildings. <u>What he says</u> is important to Hong Kong people. . . .

---

1. The correct version is: (continuous tense)

    A. pulls
    B. pulled
    C. pulling ★
    D. No change

2. The correct version is: (simple past tense)

    A. tore ★
    B. tear
    C. tearing
    D. No change

3. The correct version is: (singular/plural)

   A. country ★
   B. country's
   C. countries'
   D. No change

4. The correct version is: (adverb)

   A. too ★
   B. most
   C. completely
   D. No change

5. The correct version is: (1ˢᵗ conditional)

   A. can
   B. ought
   C. would ★
   D. No change

6. The correct version is: (subject clause)

   A. He says
   B. That he says
   C. That what he says
   D. No change ★

We will discuss the relevance for diagnostic assessment of reading of the DELTA tests later in this chapter, after the description of the DELTA vocabulary test.

Shiotsu's Test of Syntactic Knowledge

An account was given earlier in this chapter of research by Shiotsu (2010) and Shiotsu and Weir (2007) on the role of grammatical knowledge in reading in an SFL. The instrument developed in those studies is known as the Shiotsu Test of Syntactic Knowledge. In fact, the test consists of items that originally came from published versions of the *TOEFL Test of Written English* and the *Test of English for Educational Purposes* (TEEP), but that were slightly modified for Shiotsu's studies. As the name suggests, the test focuses on the syntactic aspects of grammatical knowledge which Shiotsu (2010, p. 61) defines as "knowledge of sentence structures and that of acceptable sequences and forms of words in terms of syntax." Although Shiotsu's intention was to try to measure syntactic knowledge separately from lexico-semantic knowledge, he admitted that it is not possible to fully remove lexical knowledge (i.e., meaning) from any measure of syntax (p. 46).

Sample items:

Sample items:	What the item appears to measure according to Alderson & Kremmel (2013)

(Item 5) We found _____ to understand his lecture.
  difficulty
  difficult
  so difficult
  it difficult
	syntactic knowledge
	given the additional info (so, it), this also gets at meaning

(Item 16) _____ I need is a long holiday.
  What
  That
  Which
  The which
	mostly syntactic knowledge nothing syntactic about this. Just cohesive meaning (cleft sentence) if word order were played with, I could see "syntax"

(Item 3) By the time this course finishes _____ a lot about engineering.
  I will learn
  I learn
  I will have learnt
  I have learnt
	syntactic knowledge

(Item 9) _____ a pity you did not check the figures with your partner.
  What's
  That's
  There's
  It's
	both syntactic and lexico-semantic knowledge

(Item 12) _____ how hard he worked, his tutor never commented on it.
  Of no account
  No matter
  Without regard
  Mindless
	mostly lexico-semantic meaning

As part of refining the test of syntactic knowledge, Shiotsu (2010) had a group of experts judge if the items in the test measured syntactic knowledge or lexical-semantic knowledge. Alderson and Kremmel (2013) reported on a series of replications of these expert judgments to examine the value of such judgments in determining what constructs language tests are measuring and, in particular, to ascertain to what extent this test claiming to tap syntactic knowledge in fact does that. Their conclusion was that, overall, the test is a measure of syntax, but it contains many items whose construct was unclear or was related to lexical knowledge or both lexical and syntactic knowledge. This illustrates the issues that tests of grammar (or vocabulary, for that matter) might have and the importance of ensuring the construct validity of instruments used in research on the relationship between reading and various areas of linguistic knowledge.

Diagnostic Vocabulary Tests

DIALANG Tests of Vocabulary

The DIALANG diagnostic battery contains two different subtests of vocabulary. One, the Vocabulary Size Placement Test (VSPT), is intended to provide an estimate of one's vocabulary size by using the yes-no test format devised by Meara and Buxton (1987). This test includes a mixture of real words of the target language and invented words, which meet the phonological constraints of the language, but do not bear meaning (Huibregtse, Admiraal, & Meara, 2002). The DIALANG VSPT consists only of verbs as they were considered to be easier to sample in the same way across different languages compared with nouns and adjectives (Alderson, 2005). The test taker is presented with a list of these words and asked to indicate which of them are real and which are invented words in the language to be tested. The following list presents the first 10 items in the VSPT and, thus, illustrates both real and invented English verbs in that test:

- to campaign
- to futt
- to bourble
- to fear
- to preyout
- to study
- to savedown
- to compile
- to motivate
- to decite

The main purpose of the VSPT is to enable DIALANG to decide if the test taker is a beginning, intermediate, or advanced learner of the language so that DIALANG can administer to him/her the most appropriate level of test in the skill, such as reading, that the learner wishes to take. The routing of test takers to one of three test levels was made possible by creating a model, based on pilot test data, that allows the VSPT scores to be used as predictors of performance on the main language tests (see Alderson, 2005). In this way the VSPT aims at increasing the accuracy of the subsequent measurement of the learner's reading skills, thereby contributing to the quality of diagnostic feedback about reading that the learner receives. However, learners are also provided with a brief description of what their VSPT scores mean in terms of ability to use the language. The aim of such feedback, together with much other feedback from DIALANG, is to increase learners' awareness of their language skills, as described in Chapter Eight. The following is what a learner scoring relatively low on the VSPT and being placed at the second lowest of the total of six score bands will see:

> This level indicates a very basic knowledge of the language, probably good enough for tourist purposes or 'getting by,' but not for managing easily in many situations.

The second vocabulary test in DIALANG, part of the main battery of tests rather than a placement test, focuses on aspects of vocabulary knowledge in depth, in particular assessing mastery of the meanings of simple word units and combinations. Four dimensions of word meaning are distinguished:

- denotative meaning, including semantic fields, connotation, appropriateness;
- semantic relations, including synonymy/antonymy/converses, hyponymy/ hypernymy, polysemy;
- combinations, including collocation and idiomaticity;
- word formation (compounding and affixation).

Thus, the construct of vocabulary knowledge implemented in DIALANG covers both the breadth (the VSPT) and depth (the main vocabulary test) dimensions that current theory and research consider the main, complementary aspects of vocabulary knowledge.

The following English vocabulary items from DIALANG illustrate the four dimensions of word knowledge that the system was planned to cover:

Items focusing on *denotative meaning* of words:

Choose the best word for the gap (. . .) in the following sentence:

The . . . of this factory is increasing.

title   product   output   aim

What is the best word for the gap in the sentence? Write it in the box. The word begins with an 'a.'

Our ⬚ at the airport was delayed by roadworks

Items focusing on *semantic relations*:

Choose the word that means the same as 'motion.'

movement   watching   reacting   converting

Which word means the opposite of the word written in CAPITALS in the following sentence? Write that word in the box.

But the state should go further to DISCOURAGE impressionable children from smoking, says political activist Steven Brown.

[ ]

Items focusing on *word combinations*:

Choose the best word for the gap (. . .) in the following sentence:

Don't wait any longer, you have to strike while the . . . is hot.

iron   gold   steel   metal

Choose the best word for the gap (. . .) in both sentences.

We built a sandcastle. It . . . when the waves came.

Our plans . . . , when the time allowed for completion was changed.

declined   ruined   collapsed   devastated

Items focusing on *word formation*:

What is the word related to the word 'deep' which can be used in the following sentence? Write it in the box.

The lake was no more than three meters in [   ]

Write the missing part of the word in the box.

My latest novel was [   ] jected by the first publishers, but with the fourth one, I got lucky.

DELTA Test of Vocabulary

The Vocabulary component of the DELTA (Urmston et al., 2013) test "aims to assess students' knowledge of a specific range of vocabulary—their academic vocabulary knowledge" (p. 68). Because the DELTA was designed for tertiary level students, the vocabulary test is based on Coxhead's (2000) Academic Word List (AWL). A further reason for constructing the DELTA vocabulary test with reference to the Academic Word List was that vocabulary exercises have been developed over the years that are linked to the list, thereby providing learners with support in their vocabulary learning, according to Urmston et al. (2013).

The DELTA vocabulary test consists of 20 to 25 multiple choice items, which are administered on computer, as is the DELTA grammar test and its other components (reading and listening). Urmston et al. (2013) report that the format was chosen because it allows immediate computerized marking; responses to each item are marked as either correct or incorrect. Test takers are given a profile across the four skills measured—vocabulary, grammar, reading, and listening—in a way that displays whether the skill in question is above, below, or at the student's mean ability level, which is based on a combined statistical analysis (calibration) of all items across all four skills (Urmston et al., 2013).

The DELTA vocabulary test gives the students an overall score for vocabulary. Similarly, the grammar test described earlier yields only one score. Therefore, the diagnostic information that DELTA provides its users is not very detailed, but the joint calibration of all four skills in the statistical analysis allows the learners to compare how well they do in vocabulary and grammar relative to the other skills (reading and listening). A unique feature of DELTA is its longitudinal dimension: students who choose to use it receive feedback on their progress in the measured skills, typically once a year during their studies.

Martinez's Test of Multiword Expressions

The purpose of the Martinez's Test of Multiword Expressions is to enable the testing of learners' knowledge of formulaic expressions in English. Formulaic expressions are combinations of two or more words whose meaning cannot easily be figured out from the meanings of the words that comprise the expression (e.g., *at once, take for granted*). According to Martinez and Schmitt (2012), "most definitions indicate that individual formulaic sequences behave much the same as individual words, matching a single meaning or function to a form, although that form consists of multiple orthographic or phonological words" (p. 299).

Such formulaic, phraseologic language is central to the way both the L1 and SFL are used, processed and acquired (Martinez & Schmitt, 2012). Martinez's Test of Multiword Expressions is thus an attempt to operationalize the formulaic view of language, and more specifically to develop a more valid measure of receptive vocabulary (Martinez & Schmitt, 2012). Examples of multiword test items in Martinez's test follow:

---

at once: I did it **at once**.
  a. one time
  b. many times
  c. early
  d. immediately

take for granted: She **took** it **for granted**.
  a. kept it
  b. did not give it importance
  c. wanted it a lot
  d. thought about it carefully

as yet: They have not travelled **as yet**.
  a. not now but maybe later
  b. because they don't want to
  c. because they have no time
  d. not now and not ever

happen to: She **happened to** call.
  a. pretended
  b. tried hard to
  c. did not want to
  d. by chance did

The samples illustrate the range of constructions that multiword expressions can take in the English language. For example, verb + preposition and preposition + adverb constructions are very typical formulaic expressions. Most such units have two or three immediately adjacent elements but the 'take for granted' example shows that it is also possible for other words to be inserted into the fixed expression.

Kremmel (2012) discovered that the multiword test correlated with SFL reading somewhat more strongly than the overall vocabulary measure (from DIALANG) that he used, but that these two vocabulary tests were highly related, indicating that they tapped very similar aspects of vocabulary knowledge.

The implication for diagnostic assessment of reading of tests that tap formulaic sequences is at least twofold. First, they expand the notion of linguistic knowledge by adding a new dimension to vocabulary knowledge that is not traditionally considered in vocabulary testing. Tests of formulaic expressions can, thus, increase learners' awareness of the existence and importance of this aspect of linguistic knowledge, which is bound to be involved when we read texts in an SFL. Second, it is possible that some learners are poorer at understanding formulaic expressions than single words, in which case they might benefit from receiving feedback on how their knowledge of individual words compares with their knowledge of multiword expressions. Kremmel's (2012) study suggested that the two kinds of knowledge are strongly correlated, but as the correlation was not perfect there were at least some individuals, even in his study, whose scores in the two kinds of vocabulary measures did not match.

Discussion and Conclusions

Some of the studies on the contribution of lexical and grammatical knowledge to reading in an SFL reviewed in this chapter suggest that vocabulary knowledge may play a somewhat bigger role in reading than grammatical knowledge. However, it is clear that grammatical knowledge also contributes to understanding of written texts, often very considerably.

It is often very difficult, if not impossible, to create pure measures of either vocabulary or grammar, although it appears that this is particularly difficult in the case of measuring grammatical ability. Tests of grammar also involve knowledge of vocabulary and the reverse is also often true. Using measures of both vocabulary and grammar usually improves the prediction of reading in an SFL compared to when only one of the aspects of linguistic knowledge is tested, as some of the studies reviewed above indicate. Moreover, some measures that appear to combine vocabulary and grammatical knowledge such as the segmentation task used in the DIALUKI study and by Leong et al. (2013) have turned out to be rather good indicators of SFL reading. It is therefore more appropriate to think that both vocabulary knowledge and mastery of grammar are good predictors of SFL reading, and thus, have diagnostic potential.

Some of the studies suggest that the nature of the reading tasks (e.g., short vs. long texts) or certain learner characteristics may affect the way grammatical and vocabulary knowledge contribute to reading.

Kremmel (2012) suggested that short passages requiring careful reading may depend more on syntactic processing than on vocabulary. Also, Urquhart and Weir (1998) claim that the role of grammatical vs. vocabulary knowledge may depend on the purpose of reading and contrast scanning (going through the text quickly to find specific information), which appears to require little if any grammatical knowledge, with careful local reading that probably depends on successful syntactic processing. Recent research on machine-analysis of the readability of reading texts in English as a first language (Nelson, Perfetti, Liben, & Liben, 2011) showed that the linguistic and textual characteristics that can be analyzed automatically by various computerized tools did a better job in predicting both text level and students' performance on reading tests when the texts were informational rather than narrative. This suggests that vocabulary and grammatical knowledge may be more important in reading informational than narrative texts.

Kremmel (2012) also suggested that beginning readers may rely more on syntactic knowledge whereas more advanced learners can use a wider range of reading skills. A similar finding was made by Yamashita (1999), who discovered that for Japanese learners of English, knowledge of English vocabulary was a better predictor of reading in English than grammatical knowledge if the learners were stronger readers but the situation was reversed for weaker readers. Findings from the DIALUKI project suggest that the particular language one tries to diagnose and the learners' first language can influence which type of linguistic measures are most strongly related with reading performance. Possibly, the results differ also between second and foreign language contexts.

As mentioned above, the way reading is operationalized can affect the findings about the role of linguistic knowledge in reading. The same applies to the construction of vocabulary and grammar tests: What is included in them and what is left out is bound to affect the relationships between linguistic measures and reading. Thus, when interpreting and comparing different studies, it is important to consider the constructs measured by both the reading tests and their linguistic predictors. Interestingly, there seems to be a trend in the research to use more than one type of vocabulary or grammar test, rather than using only a Vocabulary Size Test or only a test of syntax, which may be due to the fact that grammar and vocabulary are both thought to comprise several different aspects or dimensions of knowledge.

A potentially useful new approach which may contribute to diagnostic assessment of reading in an SFL is the automated analysis of the characteristics of texts. Several automated tools for analyzing texts written in English by both native speakers and learners have been developed by language examination organizations, commercial publishers and universities (see Nelson et al., 2011, for a recent review). These tools analyze a range of features related to vocabulary (e.g., word length, frequency, and concreteness) and grammar (e.g., sentence length and complexity) but also to other characteristics of texts such as paragraph length and complexity, order of information, and within-sentence and between-sentence cohesion (Nelson et al., 2011, pp. 9–16). Research on how such features of texts relate to learners' performances on reading items based on those texts can shed light on which linguistic and textual characteristics relate to performance on reading tests and whether the relationship depends on, for example, the genre of the texts or the characteristics of the learners such as their level of SFL proficiency.

Another—and a rather different approach to studying the relationship between linguistic skills and reading—would be to link the measures more directly with each other in terms of their vocabulary and grammar content. Thus, it might be worth researching the diagnostic value of tests of the specific grammar and vocabulary in texts being read in the reading tests, rather than the more general tests of grammar and vocabulary that may not be relevant to particular texts.

An interesting but to date unanswered question is, to what extent are the various categories of morphology and syntax, or vocabulary, predictive of problems readers experience in reading their SFL? Alderson's (2005) analyses of the DIALANG pilot test data, for instance, lead to the conclusion that it is clear that not only is the relationship between the various categories likely to vary across languages with respect to the prediction of reading problems, but, in a sense more importantly, this will almost certainly vary according to the L1 of the learners of the particular target language.

Generalizations, therefore, are likely to be hard to achieve for the diagnostic potential of specific grammatical or lexical categories or features. It will thus be important in future research to explore the diagnostic potential for SFL reading ability of a multitude of L1s in combination with a range of target languages. This will doubtless be an enormous and complex undertaking, but it is nonetheless important.

6

THE COGNITIVE BASIS OF READING IN A SECOND OR FOREIGN LANGUAGE

We are not born with genes for reading nor are particular parts of our brain devoted to reading. Therefore, we utilize the same cognitive skills for successful reading as we use for many other everyday activities and processes. Actually, in the history of human beings, reading is quite a recent skill. Yet it has become such an important ability that in the modern world people are categorized according to their literacy skills or lack of them, and reading problems have become an important target of psychological and linguistic research in the search for methods of diagnosis and tools for treatment of reading problems. Literacy, the ability to read (and write) and to cope with the written information that constantly surrounds us, is recognized as one of the basic skills one needs to be able to participate in society.

The ultimate purpose of reading is to transform print into meaning. We may study reading from different perspectives, such as what kind of properties a readable text should have or how and for what purposes people read or what their reading habits are. These various perspectives on reading are text based, education-based or even sociologically oriented. In this chapter, however, we are going to focus on readers and what happens in their minds when they are reading. In other words, we will concentrate on the cognitive demands of the reading process and on how the process leads to the reading product, that is, comprehension. The cognitive processes involved in reading have been rather extensively researched, although the target has usually been first language reading. Many of the cognitive skills studied are also considered to be precursors of reading outcomes, the base on which reading ability is firmly built. This is why the cognitive skills related to reading have also become important targets of diagnosis when the focus of investigation is on the causes of reading difficulties and ways to target remediation accurately. In this chapter we introduce cognitive precursors of reading and describe a range of methods to investigate them. We then discuss the use of these methods to explore how these cognitive factors function in first (L1), second, and foreign language (SFL) reading, and what the results imply for the diagnosis of reading.

Cognitive Factors in Reading Processes

Lower-Level Reading Processes

As pointed out in Chapter Four, reading involves cognitive processes on two levels. On the lower level the processes are related to mechanical reading skills such as recognizing symbol-sound correspondences and converting strings of letters or symbols into words, that is, decoding. Higher-level processes lead to comprehension, which involves not only the ideas expressed explicitly in the text, but also the drawing of inferences, and readers making connections between their background knowledge and the text. All these processes involve various cognitive skills.

The lower-level process of decoding is at the core of reading ability and it is based on a knowledge of symbol-sound correspondences. To discover the correspondence between graphemes and phonemes a reader needs well-developed phonological awareness. Phonological awareness is necessary for perceiving and categorizing, for producing, and for manipulating phonological information. An important role is also played by phonological memory, which involves recalling and repeating sounds, words and sentences accurately. In SFL reading, phonological awareness also provides a reader with an analytical framework to segment speech (Kuo & Anderson, 2008), to discover which linguistic units are encoded in the writing system, and how exactly this is done. Although phonological awareness is essential for decoding and reading, the relationship between aware-ness and reading is also reciprocal: Reading gives you more experience of sounds and letters, and therefore the more you read the better your phonological aware-ness becomes. Dyslexia research suggests that difficulties in processing phono-logical information are probably among the main reasons for reading disabilities (Vellutino, Fletcher, Snowling, & Scanlon, 2004).

Another factor influencing decoding is the orthography of the language. In alphabetical writing systems, where sounds are referred to by letters, orthographies differ from each other in transparency. In the shallowest or most transparent orthographies, one letter corresponds to one sound, which obviously makes it relatively easy for a beginning reader to detect the relationship and learn to decode. For example, Finnish and Spanish have shallow orthographies, whereas English and French are at the other end of the continuum, with a deep or opaque orthography (Seymour, Aro, & Erskine, 2003). In English the same sound can be referred to with several different letters. For example, in the words *fish*, *enough* and *philosophy*, there is the sound /f/, but in each word the sound is written differently: with the letter *f* (*fish*) or with the combinations *gh* (*enough*) and *ph* (*philosophy*). In addition, the same letter or letter combination does not necessarily always refer to the same sound. For example the combination *gh* at the end of the word *although* does not refer to the sound /f/, but is left unpronounced. This kind of bidirectional inconsistency obviously makes it more challenging for a beginning reader to discover the symbol-sound correspondences. Ziegler and Goswami's (2005) psycholinguistic grain size theory describes how beginning readers have to adjust their decoding strategies to the orthography. In languages with a shallow orthography readers can concentrate on only one grain size, phonemes, because of the very high consistency in symbol-sound correspondence. In deep orthographies, however, larger grain sizes such as syllables, rhymes, and whole words are more consistent units for decoding than phonemes. This leads to differences in reading accuracy and speed in beginning readers, since the larger and more varied the grain size, the more units there are to be learned. In any language, there are more syllables than phonemes, more rimes than syllables, and finally, more words than rimes. In Finnish, readers have to deal with only one grain size, but for English readers they have to deal not only with one of the largest grain sizes (words), but also with at least three different grain sizes: syllables, rimes, and whole words. They also have to decide which grain size is most useful at any given moment. It is obvious that orthographic factors also affect SFL reading, especially if the system of the new language differs greatly from a reader's L1 system. For example, at least in the beginning stages, learners with a transparent L1 orthography read an opaque SFL writing by using the one-symbol-to-sound-approach learned in their L1 (Perfetti & Dunlap, 2008), which may prevent them from recognizing even familiar words when encountering them in the written form for the first time.

To become a more fluent reader, one must be efficient in recognizing words. Word recognition skills play a fundamental role in rapid and accurate reading, which is needed to ensure that enough cognitive space remains for comprehension. In addition to decoding, readers use different methods to recognize words, especially if the reader is encountering the written form of the word for the first time. In skilled readers, word recognition processes differ in different orthographic systems (Frost, 2005). For example, in transparent orthographies like Finnish, decoding is a rather efficient way of reading unknown words—even those which are not yet in the reader's own lexicon—whereas in English a decoding strategy does not always work, due to the complex relationship between sounds and letters in both directions (one sound can correspond to several letters or letter clusters and one letter can correspond to several sounds). A much more efficient strategy in English is analogy, to take advantage of the similarity between the unknown written form and a word already familiar to the reader. Syllables can be broken into onset and rime (the initial consonant and the vowel-consonant blend; *f-ight, n-ight*), and the shared rimes in words function as a key to analogy

(Ehri & Snowling, 2004). Use of analogy such as reading *fight* with the help of *night* helps readers to discover the accurate pronunciation of the written form, and further connect it to the spoken equivalent in the lexicon.

Another strategy to attack unknown words in print is prediction. When predicting a word, a reader can use many cues provided by the text such as the initial letter of the word and the words that precede the unknown one (and that thus gives syntactic and semantic cues). The pictures in the text can also be very useful for prediction. However, the kind of prediction which is either based on wrong cues or is not based on any clear cues at all and is close to random guessing is not a very efficient way of recognizing words, and it often produces inaccurate results. If the word in question is not in the reader's lexicon, prediction has no chance of producing an accurate answer to the problem.

As experience in reading increases, the number of unknown words encountered in texts decreases and the skills of word recognition become more rapid and accurate, and eventually become automatic. In other words, reading fluency increases. Similarly, comprehension increases as the number of unknown words decreases, as shown by Schmitt, Jiang, and Grabe (2011). A skilled reader can use sight reading (also called memory reading) to read words previously encountered in texts. Seeing a familiar word automatically triggers the connections that the form has to pronunciation and meaning. Therefore, the sight reading process does not interrupt ongoing comprehension processes in the way that decoding, analogy, or prediction strategies would do, and the reader can concentrate on the meaning of a text.

Word recognition depends partly on vocabulary size. It has been argued that vocabulary size and comprehension are likely to have a reciprocal relationship (see also Chapter Five for a discussion of the relationship between vocabulary knowledge and reading). Vocabulary growth promotes comprehension, but comprehension helps a reader to learn new words when the meaning of an unfamiliar word can be inferred from the text context (Perfetti, Landi, & Oakhill, 2005). Another factor affecting word recognition is the speed of access to vocabulary entries. Not all words or concepts are equal in terms of fast access. For example, frequently used words as well as concrete words are accessed more rapidly than infrequent or abstract ones. The most frequent words are likely to become automatized and thus very quickly processed bits of language. This automatization decreases the cost of cognitive processing in word recognition and thus frees up resources for fluent reading, writing, or speaking. The speed of lexical access has an important role in the reading skill because slow naming and word retrieval have been found to be strongly connected to later reading outcomes (see, e.g., Bowey, 2005). Naming things requires a well-organized store of concepts and their meanings in long term memory, but also fast access to this store.

SFL readers almost constantly face challenges in word recognition. Word recognition skills are closely related to vocabulary size, speed of lexical access, and automatization. In other words, this is largely a question of language proficiency. According to Cheung and Lin's (2005) study, word recognition can be automatized as SFL proficiency develops, but word frequency also contributes to automatization. The more a reader encounters the same word, the quicker it becomes an automatically recognized word, and, therefore, reading experience in an SFL is crucial. Clearly, more experienced SFL readers recognize SFL words faster and more accurately than inexperienced ones.

Higher-Level Reading Processes

Hoover and Gough's (1990) "Simple View of Reading" distinguishes two equally important components of reading: decoding and comprehension. According to their theory reading is not possible without both these skills. For Hoover and Gough, reading comprehension approximates general language comprehension (including listening comprehension), the skill we learn while acquiring our first language.

Not all theories see reading comprehension in as simplistic a way as Hoover and Gough do. Many linguists think that reading comprehension is based on both the microstructure and the macrostructure of the text. The microstructure consists of all the propositions in a text, that is, the semantic information written in the sentences. On the other hand, all the sentences and the information in them create a macrostructure for the text, for example, in what order and how the things are presented in the text. Together the micro- and macrostructure form a text base, which is the meaning of the text as it is actually expressed by the text (Kintsch & Rawson, 2005). While the text has at least two overlapping structures, reading comprehension also has at least two levels. Comprehension remains rather shallow if the reader understands only those meanings that are explicitly expressed in the text. For example, if readers understand only what is explicitly written, the sentence *John gave Mary some beautiful red roses and a box of delicious chocolates on Valentine's Day* tells us about John, who gave flowers and chocolate to Mary on a day which is for some reason called Valentine's Day. For a deeper comprehension, readers must integrate the meaning of the text base with their prior knowledge to create a situational model, which is a reader's mental model of the situation described by the text (as discussed in Chapter Four). If readers know what Valentine's Day is and what can be expressed with flowers, and integrate the sentence with this prior knowledge, the sentence is not merely understood as a description of John's actions but as a description of how John expresses his deep affection for Mary on a day which is dedicated to friendship and love. For adequate comprehension a reader must make inferences based on explicit text and prior knowledge as well as make logical, causal, and referential connections between propositions.

Reading comprehension, in fact, is a cyclical process in which readers constantly also monitor their comprehension to check if the interpretation seems logical and accurate. If readers are not satisfied with their interpretation, they have to go back to the text and make repairs or modifications to their interpretation. Another factor promoting deeper understanding of texts is readers' familiarity with the text genre. When they know the genre, they have expectations about the text structure, the linguistic features, and even exact expressions. When we see a text starting with *Once upon a time* we immediately know we are reading a fairy tale, which is very different from a scientific article, newspaper text, or an e-mail message from a friend. Sensitivity to different genres helps the reader to see the overall structural patterns of the text and thus aids comprehension (Perfetti et al., 2005).

Working memory plays an important role in all reading processes, but in comprehension it is crucial. Working memory capacity is limited, and therefore it is important that the lower-level processes of reading such as decoding and word recognition in general are automatic and fluent. Otherwise, they can take up much cognitive capacity and thus slow down or even hinder higher-level processes (Bowey, 2005; Perfetti et al., 2005). Impairments in working memory itself may explain problems in comprehension (Paris & Hamilton, 2009), as in the case of less-skilled L1 readers, who have problems with processing syntax and morphology in reading although they have similar linguistic knowledge to that of good readers (Perfetti et al., 2005).

What is working memory like and how does it work? According to the latest, widely accepted theories on working memory, it consists of four different components (see Figure 6.1). The central executive is the most important component, and it has three slave components, namely, the phonological loop, the visuospatial sketchpad, and the episodic buffer. The phonological loop has evolved to store and manipulate verbal material, whereas the visuospatial sketchpad processes and stores visual and spatial material. The most recently proposed component of working memory is the episodic buffer, which is a linking system between the other components and which integrates the units of visual, spatial, and verbal information. It also has links to long-term memory. The input from these slave systems is coordinated by the central executive, which is also connected to long-term memory (Baddeley, 2003).

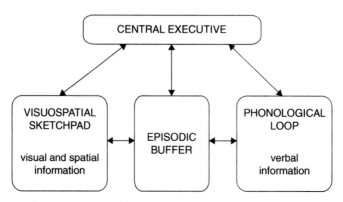

FIGURE 6.1 The components of working memory according to Baddeley (2003)

Thus, working memory is not just storage but also an active processing system. It is not called *working* memory for nothing. Its importance for reading comprehension lies in storing—for a few moments, as the reader is moving forward in the text—the meaning of words, phrases, and sentences of a text in order to create an integrated meaning, in making connections with relevant previous knowledge stored in long-term memory, in storing the resulting interpretation for constant monitoring—and for correction, if needed—and in taking advantage of the genre patterns familiar to a reader. Without properly functioning working memory, reading would not lead to comprehension of a text.

It is obvious that reading comprehension in SFL is even more challenging than in the L1. Becoming a skilled reader and comprehender in an SFL is slowed down by several cognitive obstacles, often related to language proficiency (e.g., knowledge of SFL vocabulary) and motivation. Successful and fast reading in SFL requires at least a partial automatization of lower-level processes in order to free up space for higher-level processes in working memory. However, even highly proficient bilinguals are known to read more slowly in their SFL than in their L1 (Segalowitz, 2000), thus probably bringing some extra challenge to the comprehension processes in working memory. However, whether their comprehension of SFL texts is affected by this speed difference at these high levels of language proficiency is not known. Walter (2004) has observed that at lower levels of proficiency, SFL reading comprehension skills seem to fall behind learners' ability to understand texts sentence by sentence, which means that creating the whole picture of the text, making inferences, and monitoring comprehension are not yet functioning properly, possibly due to the lack of capacity available for these processes in working memory. However, dual-language involvement is still implicated since a reader's L1 is never totally 'switched off,' although it may be short-circuited. In fact, SFL readers can draw on their prior literacy experience, and this may help them in learning to read in the SFL. This brings us to the issue of transfer effects.

Traditionally, transfer has been defined as reliance on L1 knowledge while processing an SFL, and sometimes this has been interpreted rather negatively as the L1 interfering with SFL processes. More recently, transfer has been seen more broadly as involving additional resources: not only might linguistic structures transfer but also cognitive abilities and skills, which may enable readers of SFL to utilize the skills they have developed while learning to read in their L1 (Koda, 2008). Transfer has been an important target of investigation in SFL studies, but in the study of SFL reading, the focus has been on the transfer of phonological awareness from L1 to SFL. It seems that the connection between phonological skills in the two languages is rather close, and this relates particularly to SFL decoding skills (Koda, 2008).

Another area of research has been the transfer of reading comprehension skills. Walter (2004) found support for the idea that SFL reading comprehension is dependent on how well text structure building skills are transferred from L1 to

SFL, which is linked to working memory development in SFL. Walter also suggests that such results give support to the threshold hypothesis: the idea that a given skill can only be learned after a certain level in SFL proficiency has been reached (for the threshold hypothesis, see Chapter Four and Grabe, 2009, pp. 146–148).

How to Measure Cognitive Skills Relevant to Reading?

Many kinds of tests are used to assess whether people can read or not, or whether they understand what they are reading. But if we want to go deeper into understanding the different cognitive components of reading skills, asking somebody simply to read a text and answer some questions based on it is not enough. In modern society, various reading disabilities, such as dyslexia, are recognized as plausible reasons for a cycle of failure, not only in education but in life in general. Therefore, it is not surprising that many methods and procedures have been developed to assess especially those cognitive skills that have been found to be precursors of dyslexia. In this section we describe how different cognitive skills relevant especially to the lower-level skills of reading can be assessed. As pointed out earlier, good reading comprehension requires well-developed lower-level skills (mechanical reading skills). Many of the different methods we introduce were originally developed for neuropsychological purposes, and their use has only relatively recently expanded to the assessment of reading skills as well.

Tasks to Measure Phonological Awareness

There are several ways to assess the different aspects of phonological awareness, or phonological sensitivity, as it is sometimes called. It is common to use non-words (i.e., invented words) as stimuli in such measures to ensure that no participant is familiar with the verbal material to be processed in the task. The non-words can either follow the phonotactic rules (language-specific rules of how sounds can be combined into words) of a real language or they may resemble no particular language. The purpose of phonological awareness tasks is to assess what kind of phonological material the participant can perceive, produce, and manipulate, and how well these processes are carried out. This, in turn, is strongly related to the ability to recognize and utilize symbol-sound correspondences while decoding words. Thus, assessing phonological awareness is one way to diagnose abilities essential for word recognition.

In a repetition task, participants hear a non-word and immediately after hearing each word have to repeat it aloud. Usually, the initial stimuli are short words (e.g. *skey, bassim*) which are considered simpler than longer words (e.g. *beenodoofop*; examples from Gupta, Lipinski, Abbs, & Lin, 2005), which appear toward the end of the task. Including different stress patterns can add to the complexity of the stimuli because participants must then pay attention not only to the phonemic level but also to the prosodic level of the stimuli. Non-word repetition tasks focus on the accurate perception and production of novel phonological information. It has been found that accurate repetition of non-words is specifically related to vocabulary acquisition (Gathercole, 2006), which in turn benefits word recognition and comprehension.

Another task assessing phonological awareness is the phoneme deletion task, which was used, for example, in the Jyväskylä Longitudinal Study of Dyslexia (JLD). This task taps the ability to manipulate phonological information but, in addition, it is also a repetition task. First, a participant is asked to repeat aloud a non-word after hearing it ("Say, *kisp*"). Next, the participant is asked to repeat the non-word without a given phoneme ("Now, say *kisp* without saying /p/"). The correctness of repetition and the resulting non-word after the target phoneme has been deleted is assessed. The non-words become longer as the task progresses, and the phoneme to be deleted may be in an initial, middle, or final position.

Yet another way to assess phonological awareness is a task which involves detecting the phonological unit common to a pair of non-words. This task requires the abilities to perceive, segment, and categorize phonemes in order to identify the one that is present in both non-words. Participants hear each non-word pair only once and are then given enough time to figure out their response. The common phoneme is presented in different positions in the stimuli as in the words *mip* and *pank* in an English-based task and *vaaso* and *leikua* in a Finnish-based task. The idea of this task is simple, but it has been found to be a rather demanding task.

Knowledge of symbol-sound correspondences is measured with non-word reading (decoding) and spelling (recoding) tasks. Because decoding is also a word recognition strategy, the non-word reading task could be considered to assess word recognition skills as well. The idea of both tasks is very simple: read aloud the non-words which you see on a computer screen or paper, or write down the non-words you hear. In the decoding task the assessment usually focuses on both speed and accuracy, whereas in the recoding task only accuracy counts (this obviously depends on how exactly the task and the scoring of responses are designed). Just as in non-word repetition tasks, the stimuli may or may not resemble some particular language. However, if the purpose of the tasks is to detect learners with specific reading problems such as dyslexia, it is possible to incorporate sequences in the stimuli which are known to be difficult for reading-disabled people. For example, in a Finnish non-word spelling task, there are consonant clusters and long vowels (*kimpuraali*) as well as diphthongs and geminates (*paunitteri*) in the non-words, because getting these letter sequences right in writing has been found to be challenging for Finnish dyslexics (Lyytinen, Leinonen, Nikula, & Leiwo, 1995).

The connection of L1 reading and phonological awareness is well established in research. However, it seems that the same connection can be found in L2 reading as well. Frederickson and Frith (1998) found that both monolingual and bilingual disabled readers showed similar deficiencies in phonological processing. These findings have been confirmed in several more recent studies (e.g., Everatt, Smythe, Adams, & Ocampo, 2000; Jongejan, Verhoeven, & Siegel, 2007).

Although all the tasks mentioned above are designed to tap phonological awareness in particular, they also require other cognitive abilities, especially an adequate phonological memory capacity to restore a stimulus from the very moment a participant hears it all the way to responding. Without restoring a stimulus, it is not possible to repeat non-words or write them down. Manipulating a stimulus or comparing non-words in order to detect the phonological unit they have in common is not possible without adequate working memory capacity, which makes it possible to keep the stimulus items in mind for a sufficient time to solve the task. Working memory is in one way or another involved in almost every cognitive process, and therefore, it is difficult to create a task where it does not have a role. Thus, difficulties in these phonological tasks may not only imply a lack of phonological awareness but also a shortage of working memory capacity, both of which crucially affect reading. Therefore, to make a more accurate diagnosis of possible cognitive causes of reading difficulties, special tasks are used for studying working memory capacity alone, and some of these will be introduced next.

Tasks to Assess Working Memory Capacity

In the field of neuropsychological assessment, there is a wide range of different memory tests and test batteries, such as the *Wechsler Memory Scale* (1945; the latest version, WMS-IV, 2009). Individual memory tests measure the capacity of short-term memory, verbal memory, visual memory, or working memory, whereas test batteries try to cover all or many of these aspects of memory. Such tests and test batteries are used for research as well as for clinical purposes to diagnose and examine, for example, brain injuries or memory diseases such as Alzheimer's and dementia.

Probably the most commonly administered memory task is the Forward Digit Span, which is part of the *Wechsler Memory Scale* test batteries (WMS-Revised, 1987; WMS-III, 1997). In a Forward Digit Span task a participant hears a random series of numbers (e.g. 9-3-7) and has to recall them in the same order. The test starts with a two-digit series and the number of digits increases gradually up to eight digits. Another task tapping the storage capacity of the phonological loop is a word span test, where either real but unrelated words, or non-words are used in the same way as numbers in the Forward Digit Span task as lists with gradually lengthening stimuli, which the participant hears and then repeats. However, neither of these tasks is a *working* memory task because they do not require manipulation or other processing of the stimulus. The only requirement for memory is to hold the numbers or words in mind during the task.

In *working* memory tests, both the material storing and material processing capacities are combined. The Backward Digit Span task is an example of this. The basic idea of recalling number sequences is the same as in the Forward Digit Span task, but this time the participant has to recall the digits in reverse order: the correct response to stimulus 3-7-1 is 1-7-3. Simultaneously storing the stimulus in memory and reversing the order of the numbers is an effortful activity and requires interaction between at least two components of working memory: the phonological loop (storage of verbal material) and the central executive (processing the material).

Another working memory task that is quite widely used for research purposes is Daneman and Carpenter's (1980) Reading Span Test. In this task, a participant first reads aloud two unrelated sentences, 13 to 16 words long, and is then asked to recall the final word of each sentence. Next, a participant reads three sentences and is again asked to recall the final words. This goes on up to six sentences. Each sentence ends in a different word, and the words must be recalled in the correct order from the first sentence onward.

In this book we focus on verbal activity, and therefore the memory and working memory tasks just introduced also concentrate on verbal memory (phonological loop). However, there are also tests, not covered in detail here, which tap visual and spatial working memory, which use visual images, such as pictures of faces or family members in the *Wechsler Memory Scale* test battery or, for example, movable cubes as in the Corsi Block-Tapping Test (Milner, 1971), which is a kind of spatial equivalent to the Forward Digit Span test.

Assessing working memory capacity and function relates to diagnosis of reading in more than one way. First, low working memory capacity may show in inadequate reading comprehension because a reader has not enough resources to make inferences or connect his or her background knowledge to what is read. Second, low working memory capacity may strengthen the effect of deficient phonological processes: while decoding and word recognition are slow, the reader forgets what was said in the beginning of the sentence when finally reaching the last word. And third, low working memory capacity together with normal reading comprehension may indicate a reader's successful use of strategies to compensate for the problems caused by insufficient working memory. All these situations require feedback and remediation, which we will discuss in more detail in Chapter Eight.

Tasks to Assess Word Recognition

Word recognition skills are among the low-level reading processes that create a firm base for comprehension. If these skills are impeded, they greatly hinder reading comprehension by taking over the majority of the cognitive capacity available for reading processes.

Theories of the core causes of dyslexia make different proposals as to what processes of reading actually belong to word recognition and thus what kind of tests should be administered to tap word recognition skills. According to the Core-Deficit Hypothesis (e.g., Stanovich, 1988; see also Vellutino et al., 2004), which is largely accepted in dyslexia studies, it is the phonological processing skills (i.e., phonological awareness, phonological coding in lexical access, and phonological coding in working memory) that underlie word recognition. The supporters of this hypothesis suggest that to assess word recognition the focus should be on tasks assessing phonological processing. Therefore, the tests introduced in the above section on phonological awareness tasks could just as well be placed in this section. A different view, the Double-Deficit Hypothesis (Wolf & Bowers, 1999), claims that the core reason for impeded word recognition lies in lexical retrieval, which is most often assessed with naming tasks such as Rapid Automatized Naming (RAN; Roth, 2004). However, in this chapter, although recognizing the problem of drawing clear boundaries between the processes and what underlies them, we introduce tests of phonological awareness and lexical access in separate sections.

Traditional approaches to word recognition are typically diagnostic: They try to identify learners with problems in word recognition. Usually such tests are standardized, which makes age- and grade-related comparisons relatively easy in principle, although they are reported to frequently over- or under-estimate a test taker's need for treatment in reading problems (Roth, 2004). Traditional word recognition tests measure phonological processing but also spelling of both non-words and real words, and oral reading at either a passage or word level. In passage level oral reading a set of graded passages is used and both word recognition (errors) and fluency (time spent in reading) are measured. In the single-word reading task, a test taker reads a list of words that gradually increase in length and complexity and at the same time decrease in frequency. The list-reading task is often considered more difficult than reading a text passage because it lacks all the contextual cues that a connected text may provide to the reader. Some list-reading tasks are untimed, for example, in the *Woodcock-Johnson Psycho-Educational Battery* (Woodcock & Johnson, 1989), whereas others are timed, for example, the Finnish standardized list-reading task in the Lukilasse test battery (Häyrinen, Serenius-Sirve, & Korkman, 1999), where test takers have 60 seconds to read aloud 105 Finnish words as accurately and as quickly as they can.

Sight word reading, which is the most advanced level of word recognition and requires automatization, can be tested with rapidly presented words. In this task a test taker must recognize a word (e.g., *good*) that flashes on the screen for only 80 milliseconds and is then masked with non-letter characters (e.g. #&:¤). Typically a test taker either immediately knows the word in question or doesn't have a clue what it is. Therefore, either a correct response is given or no response at all; incorrect answers are not very common, and they are based on guessing. As in many other word tasks, the stimuli get longer toward the end of the test.

However, it is questionable whether a longer stimulus is actually more difficult, because longer words may provide more clues than do short words and thus be more recognizable. Short three-letter-words do not have as many possibilities for different letter combinations as words with, for example, eight letters, and they indisputably resemble each other (e.g., *sad* and *sat* or *bat* and *bet*): they are visual 'neighbors.' There is evidence that words with large neighborhoods (a relatively large number of similar looking words) are processed more rapidly, but the situation is not always so simple, because word frequency affects recognition as well. High frequency of a word usually helps in recognition and short words very often have this advantage, but high frequency combined with short words may be a disadvantage as well. It is not always easy to keep similar-looking short words apart if they are all very frequently encountered words. Some studies provide evidence that words with high-frequency neighbors are not processed as rapidly as words without such neighbors (Lupker, 2005).

Well-developed word recognition strategies are essential for fluent reading and facilitate comprehension. In Geva's (2000) study on L2 narrative comprehension of young English language learners, 22% of the variance in reading comprehension was accounted for by listening comprehension, but when word recognition was also taken into account, the variance accounted for became as large as 82%. Thus, word recognition is a valuable target for the diagnosis of comprehension, and as noted earlier, it in turn is affected by efficiency of phonological processes and skills in lexical access.

Tasks to Assess Speed of Lexical Access

Two very similar tests are used to assess automatization and speed of lexical access. In 1974, Denckla and Rudel published a study in which they introduced a test of Rapid Automatized Naming (RAN). In RAN the stimuli are colors (black, red, yellow, green, and blue), numbers (2, 6, 9, 4, and 7), letters (A, D, S, L, and R), or pictures of very familiar objects (a comb, a key, a watch, scissors, and an umbrella). In each test section, there are 50 stimuli in a random order representing only one of these categories (i.e., only colors or only numbers). A participant's task is to name the stimuli one by one as fast and as accurately as possible.

A slightly different way to assess the speed of lexical access is an addition to the RAN test set, a new task introduced by Maryanne Wolf in 1986. In this task, called the Rapid Alternating Stimulus (RAS), the same categories of stimuli are used as in RAN tasks, but this time the focus is on investigating how the constant change of category affects lexical access. In one task version there are numbers and letters and in another colors, numbers, and letters, mixed in a random order. Again, the test taker has to name the stimuli one by one as fast and as accurately as possible. In RAN and RAS tasks, the result is based on both the time spent in naming and the errors made.

Slow naming is often a good indicator of poor reading both at a technical level and in comprehension. Kirby, Parrila, and Pfeiffer (2003) found that the connection between naming speed and reading became stronger with age. In their study, speed of lexical access together with phonological awareness proved to be the best predictors of later reading disability: Children who had problems with both abilities in kindergarten were most likely to show difficulties in reading in the fifth grade. Thus, measuring the speed of lexical access has become an important diagnostic tool for detecting problems in reading in L1, and in Geva's (2000) study it proved to be a good predictor of L2 reading skills as well. Young English language learners, who were clearly worse than their peers in reading comprehension, word recognition, and non-word reading, and thus showed a typical profile of reading disability, were also slower than their peers in a letter naming task already in the first grade. The gap between normal and disabled readers continued to grow in the second grade.

Cognitive Skills and Reading Outcomes in Different Linguistic Contexts

In one of the sub-studies in the DIALUKI project we examined the contribution of cognitive skills to our informants' SFL reading comprehension. We report on the results of that study; as it covered different age groups and two different languages and linguistic contexts, we feel it contributes to the existing literature on the relationship between the cognitive skills discussed in this chapter and reading in an SFL.

The study involved three different age groups of monolingual Finnish-speaking pupils learning English at school as a foreign language (the FIN-ENG groups) and Russian-speaking pupils with an immigrant background learning Finnish as a second language both at school and elsewhere in the environment and who over time had become bilinguals (the RUS-FIN group). All the members of the RUS-FIN group are integrated in regular Finnish-speaking classes. (For more details of the DIALUKI project and the participants, see Chapters One, Three, and Four.)

Monolingual speakers such as the learners of English in the FIN-ENG group have a clear L1, which is also recognized as their mother tongue. In contrast to the fairly homogeneous FIN-ENG group, the members of the RUS-FIN group are very different from each other in many aspects. Some were born in Finland and had attended only a Finnish school whereas others had moved to Finland only 1 year before the study and had thus begun their education in the Russian language. For all the children in the RUS-FIN group, Russian is a heritage language, which is used at home with a parent, during visits to the former home country, when surfing Russian pages on the Internet, or in Russian lessons at school. According to Montrul (2012, p. 2) "*heritage speakers* are the children of immigrants born in the host country or immigrant children who arrived in the host country some time in childhood." Some of the children in the RUS–FIN group have home language instruction at school, some do not. Also their degree of bilingualism varies considerably, some being simultaneous bilinguals (they acquired both Russian and Finnish simultaneously from birth) and others are sequential bilinguals, that is, they first acquired Russian and only after that started to learn Finnish. Some have special instruction in Finnish at school and some of them do not. In bilingual speakers one of their languages may be stronger and the speakers themselves may consider it as their mother tongue. However, this language is not necessarily the one they learned first at home—if their homes were monolingual. What such children have in common is that their level of Russian is less developed than that of children in Russian-speaking countries (for incomplete acquisition, see, e.g., Montrul, 2008, 2012), and by the time they reach adulthood the heritage language has become their weaker language (Montrul, 2012). In fact, according to the background questionnaire administered to the learners in our study (see Chapter Seven), some of the children in the RUS–FIN group already felt that for them, Finnish was more their mother tongue than was Russian.

To see if cognitive skills contributed similarly to L1 and SFL reading in monolingual and bilingual children in the FIN–ENG and RUS–FIN groups, we tested their working memory, phonological awareness, word recognition, and speed of lexical access. The tasks measuring these skills are shown in Table 6.1.

TABLE 6.1 Tasks that measure working memory, phonological awareness, word recognition, and speed of lexical access (G4 = fourth grade; G8 = eighth grade; GYM = second year in gymnasium (upper secondary school); Prim = primary school; LowS = lower secondary school)

Cognitive skills and measures	Groups				
	FIN-ENG			RUS-FIN	
	G4	G8	GYM	Prim	LowS
Working memory capacity: Backward digit span in L1 + SFL	X	X	X	X	X
Phonological awareness:					
Non-word repetition in L1 + SFL	X	X	X	X	X
Phoneme deletion in L1 + SFL	X	X	X	X	X
Common unit L1	X	X	X	X	X
Common unit SFL		X	X		X
Non-word spelling in L1	X	X	X	X	X
Non-word reading in L1	X	X	X	X	X
Non-word reading in SFL		X	X		X
Word recognition:					
Rapidly presented words in L1 + SFL	X	X	X	X	X
Word list reading in L1 + SFL	X	X	X	X	X
Speed of lexical access:					
RAS in L1 + SFL	X	X	X	X	X

We also administered age-appropriate reading tasks in both the first and the second or foreign language. The reading comprehension tasks are described in more detail in Chapter Four.

It is commonly argued that, to avoid inaccurate results due to a low level of language proficiency, neuropsychological abilities should be assessed by only using measures in the first or the dominant language (Lezak, Howieson, Loring, Hannay, & Fischer 2004, p. 313). However, we wanted to explore the predictive and diagnostic potential of cognitive tasks presented in both L1 and SFL, and we wanted to find out how performances on L1 and SFL cognitive tasks are related. Therefore, with only a few exceptions, we administered the tasks in two languages in each group: in Finnish and English in the FIN-ENG groups and in Russian and Finnish in the RUS-FIN groups. Furthermore, for the participants in the RUS-FIN groups, it would have been very difficult to define their mother tongue or their stronger language.

The results from a stepwise multiple regression analysis (see Table 6.2) in our monolingual FIN-ENG groups showed that the cognitive skills we measured no longer play a substantial role in L1 reading comprehension, or their role is no longer identifiable in pupils' performances. Among the 10-year-old fourth graders, the cognitive skills we measured accounted for only 10.8% of the variance in Finnish L1 reading comprehension, and in the older groups (G8 and GYM) the level of prediction was even lower. The cognitive skills that explained some variation (even if it was a small amount) in reading results changed as the participants grew older. For the fourth graders word recognition, working memory capacity and phonological awareness all predicted about the same amount of the variance in reading in L1 Finnish, but for the eighth graders, working memory capacity was the best predictor, and finally, for the gymnasium students working memory was the only cognitive predictor of the reading comprehension outcome in L1.

TABLE 6.2 Summary of the results of the regression analysis: how much the cognitive skills accounted for the variance in reading comprehension in mother tongue (L1), foreign language (FL), heritage language (HL), and second language (SL)

Grade	Monolingual FIN-ENG group		Bilingual RUS-FIN group	
	Reading FIN (L1)	Reading ENG (FL)	Reading RUS (HL)	Reading FIN (SL)
G4	10.8%	26.4%		
G8	8.6%	26.0%		
GYM	3.9%	24.5%		
Primary (Grades 3–6)			44.9%	32.0%
LowSec (Grades 7–9)			27.3%	27.9%

The above finding that cognitive measures accounted for only a rather modest amount of variance in L1 reading, which diminished even further as learners' age increased, corresponds to our expectations, based on earlier research and also on the nature of Finnish orthography. In the FIN-ENG groups the participants were no longer beginners in L1 reading. Even the 10-year-old fourth graders were already fluent readers, mainly because Finnish orthography is very transparent and regular. The fact that working memory capacity ended up as the sole predictor in the oldest group was also as expected, since working memory is involved in almost all reading processes and especially in reading comprehension.

In the bilingual RUS-FIN groups the situation was very different (see Table 6.2). The cognitive skills accounted for over 40% of the variance in reading outcome in their heritage language (Russian) in the primary school group and almost 30% in the lower secondary school group. In both groups the cognitive ability that explained most variance in reading outcomes was phonological awareness. It is highly likely that both in Finnish schools and in the Finnish environment in general, these children have only very little experience reading in Russian. This is why their Russian reading skills often do not progress beyond the basic level.

In second or foreign language reading, the role of cognitive skills is likely to be different from that in L1 or heritage language reading. The members of the monolingual FIN-ENG groups started to learn English as a foreign language at school in the third grade, and thus our different age groups had studied it formally in the school for one (G4), five (G8), or eight (GYM) academic years, respectively. However, the English language is also very much present in the Finnish environment and media outside school, and thus everyday exposure to written and spoken English may unconsciously prepare Finnish students for reading it.

As could be expected, the cognitive skills accounted for considerably more (approximately 25%) of the variance in the FL than in L1 reading test scores. In addition to this, the results differed in many respects from those in L1 reading. First, the amount of explained variance in the reading scores did not diminish with age as it did in L1 reading. A possible reason for this is the reading tasks were designed for each age group to be at the upper limit of their language proficiency. Thus, even the more advanced students would encounter unfamiliar words, new expressions, and idioms as well as new syntactic or morphological forms in the text. Therefore, in all age and proficiency groups, comprehending the texts called for very basic, mechanical reading abilities, and the unfamiliar parts of the text required more processing capacity than the familiar linguistic elements. Second, the cognitive skills that correlated with reading comprehension were not the same as in L1 reading. In all age groups the best predictor of FL reading was phonological awareness, accompanied by speed of lexical access in the two older groups. This strengthens the finding that FL reading involves similar basic cognitive processes in all age and proficiency groups.

Finally, the third difference compared to the L1 results was that this time it was the English cognitive tasks that correlated most strongly with the reading outcome. The results imply that language is a cognitive ability, and the cognitive tasks are at least partly linguistic tasks. The lower the proficiency in the task language, the more linguistic the task becomes for the test taker. It appears that in many tasks a certain level of proficiency in the target language helped participants to perform better. For example, in the Backward Digit Span task, if one knows numbers well in the task language (regardless of whether it is L1 or SFL), one does not have to use up cognitive capacity in processing the words which refer to numbers; instead, one can concentrate fully on recalling and manipulating the order of the numbers. In word-list reading one can read the words faster and more accurately if one knows the words and does not have to figure out their pronunciation or read letter by letter. In some tasks, knowledge of the language is essential: one will not perform well on the Rapidly Presented Words task if one does not recognize the stimuli immediately. In the SFL versions of this task we used only very basic words that could be assumed to be known by everybody precisely in order to avoid the task turning into a test of vocabulary knowledge, but it is entirely possible that the learners' command of even these very frequent words varied to some extent.

Thus the results showed that the Finnish monolingual informants who we studied differed in which cognitive skills were involved in their L1 and FL reading comprehension and how much they correlated with the reading test scores. Therefore, we expected that the bilingual Russian-Finnish readers would differ in which cognitive variables best correlate with their reading performance in their two different languages, but our results did not fully bear this out. In the primary school group, different cognitive skills accounted for reading performance in the two languages but the amount of explained variance was much smaller in their second language (Finnish; 32.0%) than in their heritage language (Russian; 44.9%). This suggests that the pupils had progressed further in reading Finnish than in reading Russian, if it is the case, as previous research suggests, that the importance of lower-level cognitive skills diminishes with increasing language proficiency. In the lower secondary group there was no difference between the languages and the prediction was on the same level both in heritage language reading (27.3%) and in second language reading (27.9%).

What these results suggest is that for monolingual learners, the importance of the cognitive skills essential for learning to read differs depending on whether one reads in L1 or in a foreign language. They also show that monolinguals and bilinguals are different in terms of the role that cognitive skills play in reading either in their second/foreign language or in their first/heritage language. Those who design diagnostic tests or diagnose pupils' reading skills in a classroom should be aware of all the aspects discussed above—a pupil's linguistic background is indeed important for interpreting the results.

What Differentiates Weak FL Readers From Good Readers in Terms of Cognitive Skills?

Being aware of the differences in how cognitive skills are involved in reading in different linguistic contexts is important for diagnosis. What is even more important, however, from the practical point of view is knowing how weak readers differ from medium and strong readers: What kinds of differences in cognitive skills are typical for struggling FL readers and what do the results suggest for remediation? In the DIALUKI project we investigated this in the FIN-ENG groups.

Based on their scores in reading comprehension tests in L1 and FL, we first separated the strong, medium, and weak readers. The strong readers were those who scored one standard deviation or more above the average and the weak readers those who scored one standard deviation or more below the average. Table 6.3 shows how many of the students who were categorized as strong, medium, or weak readers in L1 (Finnish) turned out to be weak readers in FL (English) (Alderson, Huhta, Nieminen, Ullakonoja, & Haapakangas, 2012).

As Table 6.3 shows, a total of 23 to 29 pupils in each age group were categorized as weak readers of English as a foreign language. This equals slightly over 10% of the population tested in the study. It is not surprising that those who are weak readers in L1 turn out to be weak readers in FL as well. Severe reading difficulties may not be language specific. However, what was interesting is that most of the weak foreign language readers were, in fact, medium or even strong L1 readers (i.e., those who do not seem to have any particular problems in reading as long as the texts are in their first language). These results suggest that a foreign language may cause reading difficulties to surface. Pupils may have used reading strategies that help them to cope with difficulties in L1 but that are of no use in reading FL. To cope with a new language and a new type of orthography, new strategies must be created in order to become an average or even a strong reader in a foreign language. All this suggests that those who are average or good in L1 reading should not be excluded from diagnosis, and difficulties they show in foreign language reading must be taken

TABLE 6.3 Strong, medium, and weak readers of Finnish (L1) as weak readers of English (FL) (Alderson et al., 2012)

Reading status in L1 Finnish	Weak readers in English as a foreign language			
	G4 (n = 211)	G8 (n = 207)	GYM (n = 218)	Total
Strong	4	0	4	8
Medium	11	13	16	40
Weak	12	10	9	31
Total	27	23	29	79

TABLE 6.4 Relationship between reading ability and cognitive measures: Cognitive tasks resulting in statistically significant differences between weak and strong readers in English as a foreign language (Alderson et al. 2012)

Grade	Cognitive tasks differing significantly between strong and weak readers	
	English cognitive tasks	Finnish cognitive tasks
G4	Backward Digit Span	Rapidly Presented Words
	Rapidly Presented Words	Word list reading
	Word list reading	Non-word repetition
	RAS	
	Phoneme deletion	
G8	Backward digit span	Backward Digit Span
	Rapidly Presented Words	Rapidly Presented Words
	Word list reading	
	RAS	
	Non-word reading	
	Non-word repetition	
	Phoneme deletion	
GYM	Backward Digit Span	Backward digit span
	Rapidly Presented Words	Phoneme deletion
	Word list reading	Common unit
	RAS	
	Non-word reading	
	Non-word repetition	
	Phoneme deletion	

seriously because they might be signs of some deeper cause whose effects the pupil has managed to compensate through the use of efficient reading strategies in L1.

In which cognitive skills do weak and strong foreign language readers differ most from each other? Table 6.4 shows those tasks in which the results differed significantly between the weak and strong FL readers.

Even a quick glance at the table reveals that it is the English tasks that most clearly differentiate the weak from the strong readers. Another easily noticeable point is that in every age group the English tasks represent working memory, word recognition, speed of lexical access, and phonological awareness, in other words, all the cognitive skills we have focused on in this chapter. From the point of view of diagnosing reading in a foreign language this means at least two things. First, by using simple target language tasks tapping these skills it is possible to identify possibly struggling readers, and second, practicing these skills with target language tasks might help the struggling foreign language readers, if not to overcome but at least to cope with their reading problems in the foreign language.

Summary

It is sometimes said that to become a better reader you just have to read more. For many people this is indeed an efficient way to improve their reading skills. For example, in the bilingual group of Russian immigrant children studied in the DIALUKI Project who learn Finnish as a second language the lack of experience of and exposure to written Russian appeared to affect performance in reading in their heritage language. However, sometimes more reading is not enough. Difficulties in reading may originate somewhere in the background such as in dyslexia, in skills that themselves are not reading skills but are closely connected with reading. In that case, practicing the cognitive skills known to be essential for reading may lead to progress in both the basic technical reading skills and in comprehension. Doing, for example, phonological awareness tasks, that is, other things than pure reading, might be refreshing especially for those who have already started to avoid or even hate reading, because of their difficulties.

What we have learned in this chapter is that one's linguistic situation may be connected with reading performance. The first language of a monolingual person may be different from the first or heritage language of a bilingual person in terms of reading and cognitive skills. Also, a second language may differ from a foreign language as far as reading and its cognitive correlates are concerned. Hence diagnosing the SFL reading skills of a monolingual learner appears to differ from that of a bilingual learner. Furthermore, diagnosing with cognitive measures using the L1 of the learner differs from diagnosing with SFL measures even if the measures in the different languages appear to be the same or very similar. The results from different linguistic contexts or from measurements using different languages should always be compared with an appropriate baseline. We need standards for each linguistic situation and possibly for measures administered in the L1 vs SFL of the learner.

When comparing weak and strong foreign language readers other important issues came up. Strong or medium readers in L1 may turn out to be weak readers in a foreign language. This may be caused by some underlying problems in the cognitive skills related to reading but this may be successfully compensated in L1 reading by efficient reading strategies. However, in foreign language reading, the strategies alone prove to be insufficient, and the difficulties show up. In our study, weak readers in English as a foreign language differed significantly from strong readers in all the cognitive skill areas discussed in this chapter. This does not mean that being deficient in cognitive skills is the only thing that affects foreign language reading, but it may be that this contributes significantly to SFL reading difficulties.

The relationship between language, cognitive abilities, and reading cannot be expressed in a mathematical formula which gives exact results. Obviously, the people involved in the learning process decide how they use their capacity for learning. Other things affecting learning are factors related to learners' background, attitudes and how motivated they are to learn. Do they think that learning a new language is useful for them? Do they feel that they are supported by their parents or friends? Are they interested in languages? Do they like to read, in any language? What benefits, if any, do they hope to achieve through learning languages? These questions arise when language learners' motivation is studied. The next chapter focuses on SFL learners' motivation and on the connections between SFL reading and learners' background characteristics, including their motivation for learning and using a second or foreign language.

7

BACKGROUND FACTORS OF READING IN A SECOND OR FOREIGN LANGUAGE

As we saw in Chapter Six, in addition to linguistic elements, cognitive factors are important in reading in a second or foreign language (SFL). It was shown that such factors are able to explain some variation in reading comprehension results. However, there are other factors that can be explored for the prediction of reading performance in SFL, namely those related to the learner's background and motivation toward learning the language. The focus of this chapter is on the role of different background influences on reading, with a particular emphasis on motivational factors.

The background factors include both the individual characteristics of the learner and of the learning environment. These factors can also affect motivation and SFL reading performance through motivation. Background factors include the reading and writing habits of the learner, the use of the SFL in free time, learners' attitudes to reading and writing and learners' motivation toward learning the SFL. As far as motivation is concerned, a distinction is usually made between motivation to begin an action and motivation to make a continued effort in doing something. This chapter focuses on the latter (i.e., motivation to continue making an effort when studying an SFL).

We first discuss the role of learners' background in reading in L1 and SFL and then focus on motivation. An interesting topic to be covered in this chapter is the applicability of background factors for diagnosing SFL skills.

Research on the Role of Learners' Background in Reading

A multitude of factors can affect learners' SFL proficiency and learning. These include factors that are external to the learner, such as the learning opportunities offered by the school, country, and home as well as internal characteristics of the learners such as their age, gender, attitudes, and motivation. As the role of background factors varies in different countries, we will focus on Finland as an example, because it is the context of our DIALUKI study and because of its success in international L1 reading studies such as *Progress in International Reading Literacy Study* (PIRLS), the *Programme for International Student Assessment* (PISA), and the *Programme for the International Assessment of Adult Competencies* (PIAAC). PIRLS 2011 (Mullis, Martin, Foy, & Drucker, 2012) measured fourth graders, PISA 2009 (OECD, 2010) 15-year olds, and PIAAC 2012 (OECD, 2013) adults on their performance in L1 reading comprehension tests. Only one larger scale international study has been conducted on L2 literacy skills in recent decades. The *First European Survey on Language Competences* (ESLC) was carried out in 14 European countries in 2011 for 14- to 15-year-olds (European Commission, 2012).

All the studies mentioned above included a comprehensive background questionnaire to the participants. The results show that location (region or country) is an important external background factor. For example, there are enormous differences in pupils' L1 reading comprehension between the participating countries (OECD, 2010; Mullis et al., 2012). FL English reading comprehension skills also varied in 14- to 15-year-olds in different countries (European Commission, 2012). Regional differences are also evident within a country, such that pupils in urban schools perform on average better than in rural schools. This can perhaps be explained by the fact that the urban schools may have easier access to libraries, museums, etc. as compared with rural schools, which may be rather isolated (Mullis et al., 2012). Furthermore, parents in urban schools may have a higher socioeconomic status, on average, than those in rural schools. Countries, however, differ in how much their regions vary. For example, in Finland, significant regional differences were not found at primary or lower secondary school level, but, for example, in Italy and Spain regional differences were observed in lower secondary schools (OECD, 2010; Sulkunen et al., 2010; Kupari, Sulkunen, Vettenranta, & Nissinen, 2012).

Another learner external factor is socioeconomic background. Educational research (Chiu & Khoo, 2005; Sirin, 2005) has shown, for example, that the socioeconomic status of the family and especially the mother's educational level correlate with the child's achievement at school. Thus, the better educated the parents are and the wealthier the home is, the better the child's results are in tests measuring achievement across a range of school subjects. The socioeconomic background of the pupils has also been shown to influence performance in reading comprehension tests (OECD, 2010; Mullis et al., 2012). This influence was also seen in adults (OECD, 2013). In PISA 2009, the socioeconomic background of the pupils was measured using the so called ESCS-index (PISA Index of Economic, Social and Cultural Status), which took into account the parents' occupation, parents' education, and home resources such as books in the home and wealth (OECD, 2010). Both the international results in all countries, as well as the results of Finland only, showed that there is a link between the socioeconomic background of the school and reading performance, in that in affluent schools the reading achievement is higher than average. However, in PISA 2009, the socioeconomic background variable was only able to explain 8% of the variance in the reading results in Finland, which was less than the average in OECD countries (Sulkunen et al., 2010). Home resources, such as books and study support at home, parents' education and occupation, have also been shown to be important in reading achievement for primary school pupils (Mullis et al., 2012). Parents' education was also important for reading achievement in the adult population in some countries (including Finland), but not in others (OECD, 2013). It is possible that if a parent has higher education, it creates an atmosphere in the family that favors education and information processing (Malin, Sulkunen, & Laine, 2013).

Apart from pupils' socioeconomic background and location, schools also differ in their facilities in some countries more than in others, and a shortage of resources can influence reading achievement since the facilities also often influence teachers' working conditions. The learning environment offered by the school can also vary in terms of discipline and safety as well as the incidence of bullying, which, in turn, is linked with reading achievement (Mullis et al., 2012). When it comes to the FL, European schools differ in how 'language-friendly' they are (European Commission, 2012), for example, how many lessons they have in foreign languages, how many foreign languages are offered, whether Content and Language Integrated Learning (CLIL) is offered in some subjects, or whether students participate in intercultural exchange programs.

Learners' individual characteristics can also influence the learning environment. Age is known to influence reading comprehension in L1, in that in the international adults' literacy study (PIAAC 2012), the strongest L1 readers are between 20 and 34 years old, the average reading achievement slowly decreasing after that (OECD, 2013). Finnish adults were the second best in the world in reading comprehension, but Finnish adults' reading skills also varied a great deal: Over 20% of the population were strong readers, but more than 10% were categorized as poor readers (Malin et al., 2013). Eight percent of Finnish 15-year-olds were poor readers (Sulkunen et al. 2010), which is less than in the adult population, but still considerable considering the literacy demands of today's society.

Gender is often seen as a factor contributing to reading proficiency in L1, because girls are known to outperform boys (e.g., Mullis et al., 2012) in most countries. This is also the case in Finland for primary school pupils, where the difference between boys and girls is more pronounced in reading fiction than nonfiction (Kupari et al., 2012). In lower secondary school pupils the difference between genders was the greatest in Finland out of all the OECD countries (Sulkunen et al., 2010). For adults, the differences between the two genders were not so clear and not even significant in some countries (such as Finland; Malin et al., 2013; OECD, 2013). Some previous studies (Csizér & Dörnyei, 2005; Kissau,

2006) have found girls to be more motivated toward SFL learning than boys. For immigrant adults, there was a significant difference in literacy proficiency in the host country's majority language (which in most cases is different from the immigrant's L1), depending on the length of time they had lived in the host country, 5 years being an important borderline in terms of L1 reading proficiency (OECD, 2013). From the diagnostic point of view, family background, age, and gender may be useful predictors of good versus poor achievement in some cases, but they are not factors that the teacher or the school can change, and they are therefore of somewhat limited diagnostic value, even if the school and the teachers certainly have to consider these factors, too, when deciding what may be a feasible way forward for a particular learner.

Factors that relate to the learners themselves are more likely to be diagnostically useful, as they can at least potentially be modified. Examples are how often the learners use the SFL in their free time, what kind of literacy activities the parents have engaged in with their children, or what parents' attitudes toward reading are. It is reasonable to assume that learners who spend time using a foreign language outside school hours should make more rapid progress in the language than their peers who only use the language during school lessons.

Early literacy activities prior to school age as well as attending preschool education have been shown to support learning to read in L1 (Mullis et al., 2012). However, compared to other countries, Finnish children had relatively little reading-related experience prior to starting school (Kupari et al., 2012), yet the children still performed well. It is likely but not necessarily certain that a positive attitude to the subject studied and higher achievement in it go hand in hand. Conversely, low achievement and more negative attitudes are linked. Previous international studies have shown a strong connection between attitudes toward reading and reading achievement in L1 in primary school internationally. Parental attitudes have also been shown to be linked with reading achievement (Mullis et al., 2012). Such a clear connection was not found for teenagers in all countries, but for some countries, such as Finland, a strong link was found (OECD, 2010). Only a quarter of Finnish primary school children enjoyed reading and their motivation toward reading in L1 was one of the lowest, but Finnish parents' attitudes to reading were quite positive (Kupari et al., 2012).

In what follows, we give an account of findings from the DIALUKI study concerning the relationship between learners' background and their performance on SFL reading tests.

Background Factors in Diagnosing SFL Reading

In DIALUKI, we surveyed both pupils and guardians in order to explore the potential of a wide range of background variables (see Table 7.1) to influence SFL reading comprehension. One parent or guardian was asked to report about the socioeconomic status of the family, reading and writing practices at home,

TABLE 7.1 Examples of background factors used in the DIALUKI study

Parent's background	Pupil's background
parents' education	mother tongue
parent's occupation	languages used at home
total household income	languages known
reading difficulties	amount of reading and writing in free time
reading and writing done at home	attitudes to reading and writing
self-assessment of SFL (in our case English or Finnish) skills	special education
engagement in pre-reading activities with the child	use of SFL in free-time
	amount of homework
	age when they learned to read

and engagement in pre-reading activities with the child. The pupils were asked to report on their language knowledge and use and their attitudes to reading and writing. All pupils also completed a motivational questionnaire as described later in this chapter.

A total of 188 Finnish EFL learners from the fourth grade (10 years old), 189 from the eighth grade (14 years old), and 177 from gymnasium (17 years old) responded to the motivational and background questionnaires. The number of boys versus girls was approximately the same at each grade level. These pupils were recruited from 14 primary schools, 15 lower secondary schools, and 9 upper secondary (gymnasiums) from around Finland.

The Russian-Finnish bilingual pupils constituted a more heterogeneous group. The primary school pupils' ($n = 173$) age varied between 8 and 15 years (median 11 years) and lower secondary school pupils' ($n = 74$) age ranged from 13 to 17 (median 15 years). Both groups had an almost equal number of boys and girls. In the primary school group, girls outnumbered boys by 5%, but in the lower secondary school group, there was an equal number of both sexes. The distribution of their mother tongues was also very similar: 11% of both groups defined Finnish to be their mother tongue, whereas 66% of primary school pupils and 70% lower secondary school pupils said their mother tongue was Russian. In the primary school group 18% and in the lower secondary school group 15% reported being bilingual and named both Finnish and Russian as their mother tongues.

Overall, for the Finnish learners of English, the background factors were more strongly associated with English reading comprehension in the two older age groups (eighth graders and gymnasium students) than in the younger fourth-grade group. As for the parents' background, there was a clear relationship between the parent's self-assessed English proficiency and the child's proficiency in FL English reading in all the age groups: the better the parent's English skills, the better the child's proficiency, too. In the eighth grade and gymnasium groups there was a strong link between the pupil's socioeconomic background (consisting of the mother's and father's education and income) and reading. As for the learner characteristics, the earlier the children had learned to read in L1, and the more they used English overall in their free time, the better their performance was on EFL reading tests in all age groups. In the two older age groups there was a link between the number of different languages the pupil reported knowing (to any degree) and their English reading performance. In other words, knowledge of several languages indicated better performance on EFL reading comprehension tests (Nieminen, Huhta, Ullakonoja, Haapakangas, & Alderson, 2012). The number and frequency of parents' pre-literacy activities in L1 with the child at the time when the child was learning to read showed no relationship with English reading comprehension in any of the three age groups. There were no differences in the English reading test scores between the two genders in the youngest and oldest age groups, but in the eighth grade group, boys outperformed girls.

The background questionnaires included several questions that are potential indicators of problems in reading in either L1 or SFL. These questions asked if the parents had noticed or were aware of any reading problems in the child's family (parents themselves, the child's siblings, grandparents), whether the child had attended special or remedial education in previous years, and whether the child had learned to read in L1 at the same time as his/her peers or more slowly. Interestingly, a positive reply even to one of the above-mentioned questions was a significant indicator of lower performance on the English FL reading tests. In other words, when we divided the learners into 'risk' and 'no risk' groups based on their responses to these questions, the 'risk' group performed significantly worse on the English reading tests. The findings remained the same across all three age groups (fourth and eighth graders and gymnasium), irrespective of whether we defined the 'risk' group as those who gave several positive replies to the questions charting the potential indicators of risk factors or as those who only gave one such answer. In the latter case, if the parent or child reported that s/he had a sibling with some reading problem, but had not attended special education, and had learned to read at the same time as his/her peers, the child was categorized as an 'at risk' learner.

In the Russian-Finnish bilingual pupils groups, we found a link between reading comprehension in Finnish and the length of the pupils' stay in Finland, the age when they learned to read in Finnish, the number of languages they reported knowing, and their use of Russian. In other words, the longer the pupils had lived in Finland, the earlier they learned to read in Finnish, the more languages they knew, and the less they used Russian, the better their Finnish reading comprehension skills were (Nieminen et al., 2012; Ullakonoja, Nieminen, & Huhta, 2013). The background variables were able to explain 9% of the variance in the Finnish reading comprehension results for primary school, and 25% for lower secondary school. The predictors that emerged in the primary school analysis were the mean use of Russian, the number of known languages, and the age when they learnt to read in Russian. For the lower secondary school pupils, the significant predictors were the number of languages known and the time spent on homework (Nieminen et al., 2012). We found no significant differences in boys' and girls' performances on the Finnish L2 reading tests (Ullakonoja et al., 2013). Pre-literacy activities showed a strong link with Russian reading comprehension results, but not with Finnish reading comprehension.

What Is Motivation?

In this book, we are interested in the diagnosis of individual differences in SFL reading performance, and thus in addition to background factors we explore whether motivation can predict SFL reading performance. Previous research has shown that motivation is connected with reading performance in both L1 and L2 (e.g., Netten, Droop, & Verhoeven, 2011). For example, PISA 2009 measured interest toward reading by asking the subjects to report on their motivation and engagement to learn, their attitudes toward reading, and their beliefs about themselves. Previous research has also shown, for example, that motivation is connected with individual differences in second language learning (e.g., Skehan, 1991). Language learning motivation is seen as an important factor in SFL learning, in that stronger motivation toward learning the SFL leads to better results in learning the SFL (e.g., Gardner & Lambert, 1959; Gardner, 1985; Dörnyei, 2005; Dörnyei & Ushioda, 2011). These are potentially more interesting factors for diagnosis because they may not only explain strong vs. weak performance in reading in an SFL, but the educational system can try to do something about them. For example, teachers can encourage learners to engage in different kinds of activities in the SFL in their free time. Teachers can also try to change learners' negative attitudes and persuade them to see learning in a more positive light, and thus become more motivated learners.

A number of previous studies have attempted to develop a model of language learning motivation, but it is difficult, if not impossible, to create a model that would suit all possible language learning contexts and learners. Based on recent findings by Kormos and Csizér (2008) we suggest that learners' age plays a role in the importance of different motivational constructs. Thus, it is difficult to define what motivational constructs would be the most appropriate for our study of motivation toward SFL learning across the different age groups involved in our study. Our goal was an exploratory investigation of how some motivational constructs, used in previous research, relate to SFL reading performance. We used the following constructs: Instrumentality, Intrinsic Interest, Motivational Intensity, Parental Encouragement, Anxiety, Self-Regulation, and SFL Self-Concept. Examples of the statements on these scales are presented in Table 7.3 below. Previous research focusing on the relationship between motivation and linguistic performance has often relied on self-evaluated or teacher-evaluated proficiency. In our study, we tested the pupils' reading comprehension skills using the tests described in Chapter Five.

There is a huge literature on motivation and multiple theories have emerged in different fields, such as psychology, education, and applied linguistics. It needs to be said from the outset that researchers also differ in their use of the term 'motivation.' Most researchers would say that motivation is about the 'direction and magnitude of human behavior' influencing

- why people decide to do something,
- how long they are willing to sustain the activity, and
- how hard they are going to pursue it (Dörnyei & Ushioda, 2011, p. 4).

However, researchers have disagreed about the relationship between learning and motivation, debating whether motivation is the cause or the effect of learning. Currently the research community has settled for a cyclical model, where high/low motivation results in high/low achievement, which again results in high/low motivation. Gardner (1985) describes motivation from four aspects, namely: goal (why the learner is learning the language), effort (toward achieving the goal), desire (to achieve the goal), and attitudes toward the activity to achieve the goal. As will be described in Chapter Eight, goals are also important for feedback, which usually improves learning only if it relates to goals that are known and shared by learners and specific enough so that learners believe they can achieve them.

It is important to understand that motivation is not something static, but that it can change over time. Some researchers emphasize the process nature of motivation, defining motivation as "dynamically changing cumulative arousal in a person that initiates, directs, coordinates, amplifies, terminates, and evaluates the cognitive and motor processes whereby initial wishes and desires are selected, prioritized, operationalized and (successfully or unsuccessfully) acted out" (Dörnyei & Ottó, 1998, p. 64).

Previous studies on language learning motivation have identified a number of motivational dimensions. In this book and the studies therein, we limit ourselves to only the seven above-mentioned motivational dimensions. Our choice of motivational constructs can be justified by describing the language motivation model put forward by Csizér, Kormos, and Sarkadi (2010), where language learning motivation consists of nested, partly overlapping systems. At the core of the model are learner-related factors, such as goals (Instrumentality in our study), attitudes (Intrinsic Interest), strength of motivated behavior (Motivational Intensity), perceptions of oneself (SFL Self-Concept) and affective factors (Anxiety). The learner is surrounded by the learning milieu (in our study this is represented only by Parental Encouragement) and the social context, which are both part of the instructional setting.

Traditionally, research on language learning motivation introduced a dichotomy of language learning goals: instrumental and integrative. *Instrumentality* means that learning a language is seen as a tool for something, for example, getting a good job in the future (Gardner, 1985; Taguchi, Magid, & Papi, 2009). By *integrative* goals, researchers mean the language learner's wish to become a part of the language community (Gardner, 1985). An integrative goal was left out of the DIALUKI study (see Chapter One for a description of the study), because of its controversial nature (see Yashima, 2009) when it comes to motivation to learn English: for example, it is not clear with which particular English-speaking country the learners would identify themselves.

Language learning attitudes of the model discussed above were limited to *Intrinsic Interest* (Gardner, 1985). By Intrinsic Interest we mean that the learners feel that language itself is interesting or learning a language brings them pleasure. Despite the fact that studying English/Finnish is compulsory for our subjects, it is interesting to know if the pupils' Intrinsic Interest or positive attitudes are linked to SFL reading performance. Usually, Intrinsic Interest is related to positive attitudes and feelings, which may lead to the voluntary study of language (Noels, 2001). In our study we use the term Intrinsic Interest to mean attitudes of the learner toward learning the SFL and his or her SFL learning goals.

Motivational Intensity means the strength of motivation: how much effort the learner is ready to put into learning the SFL and how important he or she considers learning the SFL to be. Strong motivation is one of the most important prerequisites for learning an SFL, and it is often mentioned as a dimension influenced by other motivational dimensions (Gardner, 1985; Dörnyei, 2005; Csizér & Kormos, 2009).

SFL Self-Concept refers to the perceptions of the learner of him- or herself as a language learner (Laine & Pihko, 1991), developed on the basis of one's language learning history (Bong & Skaalvik, 2003). It is also very likely influenced by the feedback given by the learners' teacher, peers, and parents (Laine & Pihko, 1991). A somewhat related concept to the SFL Self-Concept, that was not part of Csizér et al.'s (2010) model, is that of *Self-Regulation* of learning, which refers to "the degree to which individuals are metacognitively, motivationally, and behaviorally active participants in their own learning process" (Zimmerman, 1989; see also Chapter Eight on feedback that aims at influencing learners' Self-Regulation). In the DIALUKI study Self-Regulation covers all these three aspects (metacognition, motivation, behavior), not only that of motivation, and thus differs from the concepts described above.

Researchers do not agree whether *Anxiety* should be considered as a component of motivation or as a separate component influencing language learning outcomes. However, we see it as a component of motivation, because there is evidence that low anxiety, for example not feeling nervous or embarrassed in the English classroom, correlates with good learning outcomes (Horwitz, 1986; Purpura, 2004b).

Parents, peers, and teachers are part of the language learning environment, but in our study we measured only Parental Encouragement, which covers parents' attitudes and views toward language learning (e.g., Gardner, 1985; Kormos & Csizér, 2008; Csizér & Kormos, 2009; Taguchi et al., 2009).

Measuring Motivation Toward Language Learning

There are a number of empirical approaches to investigating motivation, depending on the theoretical framework. Qualitative studies (e.g., an ethnographically oriented study by Gao, 2010) have collected data through learner or teacher interviews, regular conversations, checklists, observations, field notes, and e-mail correspondence. Furthermore, qualitative research approaches have also used learners' self-reports in diaries or written or spoken narratives and through think-aloud-protocols. Some (e.g., Ryan, 2008) have combined quantitative and qualitative approaches by using extensive questionnaires as well as interview techniques.

Even though motivational research can certainly gain new insights through qualitative approaches, quantitative techniques remain the most popular methods in L2 motivational research. The most common method of data collection is the questionnaire, which the DIALUKI study also used to investigate learners' motivation. In L2 motivation research, questionnaires have frequently been used, for example in Canadian (Gardner, Masgoret, Tennant, & Mihic, 2004) Hungarian (Kormos & Csizér, 2008), Chilean (Kormos, Kiddle, & Csizér, 2011), Japanese, Chinese, Iranian (Taguchi et al., 2009) and Polish (Iwaniec, 2014b) contexts. Most questionnaires have included statements with which respondents have to express their degree of agreement or disagreement, often on a Likert scale.

Earlier motivational research relied a great deal on Gardner's (1985) Attitude/ Motivation Test Battery (AMTB), the later (Gardner et al., 2004) version of which used 11 scales to measure motivational intensity, desire, and attitudes toward learning the language (see a modified version in Table 7.2).

TABLE 7.2 Example of Gardner's (Gardner et al., 2004) dimensions of motivation

Motivation
- motivational intensity
- desire to learn the foreign language
- attitudes toward learning the foreign language

Integrativeness
- attitudes toward the foreign languag e community
- integrative orientation
- interest in foreign languages

Instrumental orientation
- instrumental interest

Attitudes toward the learning situation
- teacher evaluation
- course evaluation

Language anxiety
- language class anxiety
- language use anxiety

TABLE 7.3 Dimensions of motivation and examples of the statements used in the DIALUKI study

Dimension	Examples of statements
Instrumentality	I study English because it will be useful to get a job. I study English as it will help me to earn good money.
Intrinsic Interest/Motivation	I find learning English enjoyable. I study English because I'd really like to be good at it.
Motivational Intensity/Behavior	When studying English, I try to do so with my best effort. I try to speak English as much as possible.
Parental Encouragement	My parents consider English an important subject. My parents encourage me to practice my English as much as possible.
Anxiety	I feel more tense and nervous in my English class than in my other classes. I'm afraid other students will laugh at me when I speak English.
Self-Regulation of Motivation	I have my own special techniques to make even the most boring activities more interesting. If there is something I don't understand in English, I do my best to find the answer in a variety of resources (course books, dictionaries, online resources).
SFL Self-Concept (or L2 self)	I have always done well in English. I learn English quickly.

Table 7.3 presents the dimensions and examples of the motivation questionnaire used in DIALUKI. The original questionnaire was created by Janina Iwaniec, from Lancaster University, for the purposes of studying Polish pupils' motivation toward learning English as a foreign language (Iwaniec, 2014a). In her questionnaire, the Anxiety statements were taken mainly from Horwitz, Horwitz, and Cope (1986) which focused on language anxiety only. The English/Finnish Self-Concept statements originated from Lau, Yeung, Jin, and Low (1999), which was based on Marsh's (1990) questionnaire. Instrumentality statements came from Gardner and Lambert (1972), whereas statements on Intrinsic Interest were developed by Iwaniec. Both Motivational Intensity and Parental Encouragement statements were influenced by Csizér and Kormos (2009). Finally, Self-Regulation statements came from Iwaniec, who was influenced by Zimmerman (1989) and Tseng, Dörnyei, and Schmitt (2006).

The questionnaire was translated by the DIALUKI team into Finnish and Russian and adapted to the Finnish context. Each concept was covered by several statements. Some items were dropped from the primary school questionnaire because they involved working life or future career plans, which were thought to be too unfamiliar to primary school pupils. In addition, the language in the primary school version was closer to spoken language, and it was simplified in order to make sure that the statements were understood by pupils. Pupils rated each statement on a 5-point Likert-type scale ranging from *not true at all* (1) to *completely true* (5).

The concepts and approaches described above are taken from mainstream language learning motivation theories which have typically taken a quantitative approach to characterize learner motivation in general and with large numbers of learners. We have followed this tradition. There are, however, other approaches to motivational research, which are more interested in qualitatively describing motivation in a particular context or in a smaller number of individual learners. For example, Ushioda (2011) describes learner motivation in terms of autonomy theory, focusing on the *agency* of individual learners. By using the term agency Ushioda implies a move away from a teacher-centered view (the teacher is responsible for the learner's motivation) toward seeing learners as individuals who have different identities and can themselves be responsible for their motivation and learning. Involving learners, making them feel that they have agency in what and how they learn is an important way of motivating them (see, e.g., Murphey, 2010). Such qualitative approaches remain to be explored in research studies like the DIALUKI one.

Motivational Results in DIALUKI

In what follows we summarize the results of the DIALUKI study on SFL learning motivation and we begin by describing the results of Finnish learners of English.

The fourth graders were, on average, more motivated toward learning English than the older age groups of our study, having a higher mean on all motivational constructs. However, they also had a slightly higher mean on Anxiety, which means that they were also more anxious about their language learning. It is possible that as they were beginner learners of English and English has a rather high status as a school subject, they were excited, but also anxious about learning it. The three age groups also differed in Parental Encouragement, with this being highest for fourth graders, but the eighth grade and gymnasium pupils both rated Instrumentality items to be more important than Parental Encouragement. In Finland, parents are not necessarily very involved in their teenagers' school life, as it is considered important that children learn to become independent and take care of their own business. Also, of course, teenagers are not as dependent on their parents as younger children are. The mean for English Self-Concept decreased from lower secondary school to gymnasium which is likely to reflect the more academically oriented nature of gymnasium, whose learners' English proficiency is higher on average. There was no significant difference in the strength of the motivational constructs between the eighth graders and the gymnasium groups (Alderson, 2012).

In all three age groups lower Anxiety and higher English Self-Concept had a significant link with good performance in English reading comprehension tests.

In the fourth graders' group, in addition to Anxiety and English Self-Concept, Parental Encouragement correlated (but negatively) with the reading comprehension measures, indicating that the better readers reported not getting much parental support. In the eighth graders' group, apart from Anxiety and English Self-Concept, higher Instrumental motivation and Intrinsic Interest was related to better scores in English reading comprehension. In the more academically oriented gymnasium group Intrinsic Interest played an important role in reading comprehension together with Anxiety and English Self-Concept.

When examining how much variance in English reading comprehension the motivational dimensions explained, we found that these aspects of motivation accounted for more variance in the oldest (gymnasium) age group than in the other groups. This group is also the most advanced group in English. The explained variance increased with age from 18% in the fourth graders' group, through 29% for the eighth graders to 35% for the gymnasium students. In all three age groups, English Self-Concept emerged as the most significant predictor, followed by Motivational Intensity, Self-Regulation, and Anxiety when analyzed by regression analysis.

We also examined the relationship between motivational dimensions and SFL reading comprehension in the Russian-Finnish bilingual pupils, and found that there was a strong link between their SFL Self-Concept, Anxiety, and Parental Encouragement and Finnish L2 reading comprehension when analyzed by regression analysis. In other words, the better the Self-Concept, the better the reading comprehension skills. Less anxious pupils scored better in the Finnish L2 reading comprehension test than more anxious ones. The relationship between Parental Encouragement and reading comprehension was negative (i.e., those pupils whose parents did not apparently support them very much, performed better on the Finnish L2 reading comprehension tests). A possible reason for this is that weaker readers need and get more support from their parents, whereas the pupils who already perform quite well do not receive (and do not need) extra support from their parents (Ullakonoja et al., 2013).

Motivational dimensions, more precisely Anxiety and SFL Self-Concept, were able to explain 11% of the variance in the Finnish L2 reading comprehension results. In other words, pupils who see themselves as proficient L2 users and do not experience much language anxiety succeeded in the Finnish reading comprehension tests (Ullakonoja et al., 2013).

The Role of Background Variables and Motivation in Diagnosis

Background Variables

Overall, the selected background characteristics had at best only a relatively modest relationship with reading in an SFL. Especially for the youngest learners, very few significant correlations were found. For the older students in both language groups, some association between language use or attitudes and SFL reading existed. Perhaps the most expected correlations were those between the frequency of reading in the SFL and the reading test result. Indeed, those eighth grade and gymnasium students who reported reading in English in their free time more often usually did better on the English reading tests. Also free time writing in English correlated positively with the ability to read in English. Interestingly, for the Russian-background learners of Finnish, there were no corresponding correlations between free time reading in Finnish as L2 and performance on tests of reading in Finnish as L2. The number of languages that learners reported knowing at least to some degree was linked with a better SFL reading score in three of the five sub-groups studied. In particular, the older Russian-speaking learners of Finnish did considerably better on the Finnish L2 reading tests if they knew several other languages. The number of languages known by the learner may indicate that there is a common underlying factor, such as a general interest in learning languages, which results in the learner choosing to study more than the minimum number of languages at school and also results in higher achievement in any of those languages. Or it may be that the knowledge of several languages in itself helps the learner to perform better on a test of any one of the languages.

The overall time or frequency of reading or writing in any language (L1 or SFL) in learners' free time explained reading in an SFL in some of the groups studied, but only at a very modest level. The correlations were in the expected direction only in the English learners' groups (i.e., that more frequent reading or writing was associated with better test performance). For the Russian-speaking learners of Finnish, there was no correlation between frequency of reading (in general) and reading test performance in L2 Finnish. It is possible that since such learners live in a Finnish-speaking environment, they learn the language mainly through oral interaction and, thus, the amount of reading they do does not influence their L2 skills much. A somewhat surprising finding was that the more often the learners reported writing in general (in any language), the less well they did on the Finnish L2 reading test. The reason for this rather counter-intuitive finding might be that these students write mostly in their stronger language (i.e., L1 Russian; the majority of the students in the study did not have a very high level of Finnish, which obviously makes writing in Finnish harder).

From a diagnostic perspective an important finding was that only one reported difficulty, or a potential risk factor, in reading (i.e., reading problems in the family, slow learning to read in L1, or attendance in special education classes) was enough to distinguish between weaker and stronger SFL readers in all age groups, at least in the group level analyses. This finding suggests that some such simple background information may be sufficient to identify, at least initially, learners who are likely to perform less well on SFL reading tasks, although more information and further investigation is likely to be needed to ascertain if these learners have really serious reading problems—and importantly, what the nature of such problems might be and how they might be best addressed.

We also found that the learners' self-rated attitude to reading in their free time tended to correlate with their SFL reading performance in the two older learner groups, but only for the learners of English. The association was clearest in the oldest, gymnasium group. An obvious implication for English as a foreign language teachers is to encourage their students to read in their free time. This can be done, for example, through extensive reading interventions that will be described in Chapter Ten.

Motivational Dimensions

As far as the motivational dimensions are concerned, it was found that, for example, Anxiety correlated negatively with reading comprehension in all the groups investigated. This means that the less anxious the learners are the better they perform. Anxiety was also an important predictor in the Finnish-English gymnasium group and in the Russian-Finnish group. A clear positive correlation was also found between SFL Self-Concept and reading comprehension in all the groups. Self-Concept and reading performance are likely to influence each other in that if the learners perform well in reading comprehension tests, they are likely to start perceiving themselves as good language learners. Parental Encouragement correlated significantly in both Finnish-English and the Russian-Finnish primary school groups in the way that strong encouragement was correlated with poor performance. This might be due to parents trying to encourage the weak learners more than the strong ones.

Even though we used motivation as a predictor of reading performance and found some correlations between language use, reading attitudes, and reading, it is hard to pinpoint which is the cause and which is the effect. As mentioned earlier, motivation and performance have a reciprocal relationship: The more motivated the learners are, the more they are likely to study or read books in the SFL, which enhances both their motivation and learning, and so on. However, the relationship between motivational constructs and reading comprehension can be more clearly reciprocal for some constructs than others. For example, SFL Self-Concept and reading performance in SFL clearly have a two-way relationship: success in reading comprehension enhances or depresses SFL Self-Concept. Anxiety, on the other hand, is likely to be increased by poor reading performance and diminished by good performance. However, beginning language learners should not automatically be considered as anxious about learning an SFL simply because they do not yet know the language well. There must be something else, such as experiences of difficulties in learning the language or unfavorable comparisons of one's performance against better peers that starts the cycle of increasing anxiety and weak performance.

Reading attitudes and motivation should be distinguished from each other. A student who does not like to read in general can be highly motivated extrinsically to learn a particular language, for example, in order to get a job, and can also do well in reading comprehension tests. In other words, students who are not interested in studying languages can still be good at them (see Chapter Eight). Age can also have an effect on motivation, as our results showed that the eighth graders were not as strongly motivated to learn English as an FL as the other age groups across most of the motivational dimensions measured.

How then to make sure that learners are motivated enough to learn or to read and how can we increase their motivation? What teachers can do is to encourage learners to read more in their spare time. One way to encourage free time reading is to use graded readers, which are particularly useful, if they are available, for beginning learners for whom most authentic reading materials are still too demanding.

Reid (2007) and Dörnyei (2001) offer interesting ideas for increasing motivation toward learning a language in classroom contexts. For example, Reid (2007) emphasizes the importance of the visual layout of the classroom, careful attention to the arrangement of the furniture in the classroom, and the colors and lighting in order to create a stimulating learning environment that is free of stress and pressure. The teacher can motivate pupils by choosing tasks that are not too demanding and that reward the learner when they succeed (see Chapter Eight on feedback). The teacher should encourage the learners to be creative and to use different learning styles. The teacher should also try to break tasks into small achievable steps (again, see Chapter Eight on concrete, achievable goals). Teachers also play a crucial role in enhancing the learner's SFL Self-Concept, which can be done, for example, through constructive feedback. In short, the teacher plays an important role in motivating the learner to read (see also Guthrie & Wigfield, 1997).

In addition to the class atmosphere, Dörnyei (2001) talks about teacher behavior, for example, helping the learners to create language learning goals, promoting cooperation among learners, and self-motivating learner strategies. Having said that, motivating pupils is not useful, if the teaching itself is not clear and of high instructional quality. Motivational teaching practices consist of the following interrelated components: creating the basic motivational conditions, generating initial motivation, maintaining and protecting motivation, and encouraging positive retrospective self-evaluation. In order to create basic motivational conditions, it is essential to create a pleasant and supportive atmosphere in class and to build good relationships between the teacher and the pupils and among the pupils. Generating initial motivation might be more difficult, as adolescents might not find schoolwork enjoyable to begin with. The challenge for the teacher is to be able to promote the learning goals of the tasks and generate positive attitudes toward learning. Once the first two motivational strategies are in place, motivation maintenance is crucial; it can be achieved by creating a stimulating, interesting, enjoyable, and non-monotonous learning environment and by involving the students in learning, for example, by teaching learning strategies and promoting both learner autonomy and cooperation among learners. Finally, encouraging learners to look back on their achievements and failures in language learning in a constructive way can be done, for example, through effective feedback and by increasing learner satisfaction. Thus, it is important to remember that feedback can influence motivation, an issue which we will explore in the next chapter.

In addition to using these motivational strategies, it is important that the teacher evaluates the learning context in question to see whether, and if so, which motivational strategies are the most effective in that environment. However, the teacher alone is not responsible for motivating the pupils. The classroom, their peers, the school ethos and atmosphere also influence motivation. Given that our study showed a link between Anxiety and SFL reading performance, it is important to diminish anxiety in the classroom, which is something the teacher can influence.

Overall, measuring language learning motivation is more useful for diagnostic purposes than measuring or gathering information about most other background variables, since only a few of the background variables can be changed. Teachers cannot influence learners' socioeconomic background, age, gender, or family risk of dyslexia, but they can possibly take them into account when thinking about their teaching and motivational strategies. What teachers can do, as has been described above, is to encourage learners to read more in their spare time and try various ways to create a motivating atmosphere in the classroom. The discussion above has also made it clear that the feedback that learners get is of crucial importance not only for their motivation, but also, directly and indirectly, for their learning and performance on different SFL tasks. The next chapter will focus on how feedback might help learners improve their reading and other SFL skills.

8

FEEDBACK FROM TESTS AND ASSESSMENTS

The usefulness of diagnosis depends on the success of the entire diagnostic process that starts with a problem in a learner's second and foreign language (SFL) skills becoming apparent in some way; for example, the learner's replies to reading exercises suggest possible problems. Ideally, the teacher or whoever makes diagnostic conclusions about the learner has a solid, theory-based understanding on which to base their conclusions about what reasons might underlie the learner's problems. However, diagnosis does not end with noticing problems and having some understanding of their reasons. The diagnoser must also be able to communicate the results in an appropriate way to the learner or other stakeholders and to propose a course of action that addresses the problem. Knowing that something is a problem and even knowing why the problem arises is not enough. Something must be done about the problem, and the entire diagnostic chain must be followed through for diagnosis to have the desired effect. A key phase in ensuring that diagnosis has an effect on any aspect of learning is the communication of information about the problem and, in the case of diagnostic assessment, also about its diagnosis. Such information is called feedback, which is why it is important for anybody interested in diagnostic assessment to have an understanding of what feedback is, how and when it should be given, and what it should focus on. In this chapter, we first review definitions of feedback and discuss what characterizes feedback from diagnostic assessments and how that might differ from feedback from other types of assessments. We will give a brief overview of feedback research in applied linguistics, and then discuss in more detail recent advances in feedback theory that appear particularly relevant for diagnostic assessment in general, but also for reading in an SFL. We will also present and discuss concrete examples of different types of feedback and report on relevant research and developments in the area of SFL.

Feedback is a core element of formal and informal learning. Indeed, the iconic sequence in classroom interaction, according to many studies, is question–answer–response (Martin & Miller, 2003), where the teacher first asks a question, which is answered by a learner, and to which the teacher then responds. Although the response has other functions, it often includes feedback about the correctness or adequacy of the learner's reply. It is usually assumed that feedback results in some change in its recipients, such as learning or changes in their behavior. That is, after all, the purpose of most feedback given in educational settings. It is clear, however, that feedback is a complex phenomenon, and the way it affects learning is far from simple.

Many things can be regarded as feedback, and they probably affect learners differently. Learners also get feedback from many sources, not just from the teacher, as is the case with a language that one uses outside the classroom. A grade on a certificate, a teacher's remark after an oral presentation, a peer's gesture, and a shopkeeper's comment on something said when shopping abroad can all provide feedback on one's ability to use another language, but they are likely to affect the learner differently. Do the learners understand what the particular feedback means? Is the feedback about them or about their performance on the task? Whose feedback do they believe in—the teacher's, a peer's, a foreigner's? Whose feedback affects their views of themselves as learners of the language? Also, the role of feedback in the wider educational setting and the feedback process itself can affect the usefulness of feedback. When should feedback be given, immediately or after some time? What should it focus on? How much feedback should be given? And what should happen after feedback has been given?

What Is Feedback?

We pointed out that many different things can be considered as feedback, and this view is also reflected in the definitions of feedback:

> In the purely instructional sense, feedback can be said to describe any communication or procedure given to inform a learner of the accuracy of a response, usually to an instructional question. . . . More broadly, feedback allows the comparison of actual performance with some set standard of performance.
>
> (Mory, 1996, p. 919)

> Feedback is information with which a learner can confirm, add to, overwrite, tune, or restructure information in memory, whether that information is domain knowledge, metacognitive knowledge, beliefs about self and tasks, or cognitive tactics and strategies.
>
> (Butler & Winne, 1995, p. 275)

> Feedback is . . . information provided by an agent (e.g., teacher, peer, book, parent, self, experience) regarding aspects of one's performance or understanding.
>
> (Hattie & Timperley, 2007, p. 81)

Importantly, according to these definitions, feedback is more than information about learners' errors, although this probably comes to mind first when we hear the word 'feedback' in the context of SFL education. Clearly, feedback on errors, or error correction, is part of the information that we may decide to give learners, but the concept covers much more. What is also worth noting is the range of sources feedback can come from. Furthermore, feedback need not be limited to knowledge (e.g., of an SFL); it can also focus on metacognition, such as consciously monitoring one's comprehension while reading a text. Feedback need not be limited to external sources, either, but may be generated by the learners themselves.

Feedback vs. Diagnostic Feedback?

What makes feedback diagnostic? Should feedback from diagnostic assessments differ from feedback from other kinds of assessments? As we reported earlier, there is no commonly accepted view in the language testing literature about what diagnostic tests are. This is even more the case when it comes to diagnostic feedback. The only attempt at defining it that we have found in applied linguistics is in a recent paper by Jang and Wagner (2014). According to their research, diagnostic feedback (feedback from diagnostic language tests) differs from typical test feedback. Whereas traditional feedback consists of test scores and other such general information, diagnostic feedback is more specific and targets particular cognitive skills or language processes, and provides learners with descriptions of their cognitive strengths, weaknesses, and strategies (see Jang, 2009a, for an example of diagnostic feedback on an SFL reading test). Such feedback not only corrects learners' errors but addresses the cognitive gap between current performance and a goal. As we shall see later in this chapter, Jang and Wagner's view on the characteristics of diagnostic feedback is very similar to the characteristics of effective feedback as defined in the general educational literature by Sadler (1989) and by Hattie and Timperley (2007).

We might want to add to the above-mentioned definition that diagnostic feedback can also contain hints or explicit proposals about the action the learners should take to remedy the problem that is identified in their performance. We argue that it is typical of diagnostic feedback to tie together the different phases of the entire diagnostic process by referring back to the error, problem, or deficiency that was identified (and its likely reasons) and by referring forward to the action that should address the problem. Thus, the key characteristics of diagnostic feedback appear to be that

- it is much more detailed than, for example, a reading test score;
- it is not limited to the actual errors that the learner makes;
- it is based on an understanding of what probably underlies those errors; and, finally,
- it is not limited to errors but also addresses what the learner could do to improve the skill involved.

We will revisit the definition of diagnostic feedback after a discussion of how effective feedback can be modeled (see Hattie & Timperley, 2007).

General Characteristics of Feedback Research

Most feedback given to learners focuses on what they produce, such as responses to teachers' questions or to test items. Prototypical feedback informs the learners about the correctness of their answers. Not surprisingly, therefore, most research on feedback in SFL education and second language acquisition (SLA) has focused on corrective feedback (e.g., Lyster & Ranta, 1997; Li, 2010; Lyster, Saito, & Sato, 2013). An emphasis on products is apparent also in research into feedback: most feedback studies, both in SFL and more generally, have focused on learners' final products rather than, for example, their cognitive processing or the strategies they use for speaking, writing, and comprehending (Jang & Wagner, 2014; see also general reviews on feedback research by Mory, 1996, 2004).

Research has usually ignored the learner's role in the feedback process, so rather little is known about how learners receive and integrate feedback into their learning process (i.e., into how learners set and modify their goals or how they select strategies). Little is also known about how learners integrate external feedback into their previous knowledge or how feedback affects the way learners monitor their learning. Jang and Wagner (2014) argue that product-oriented feedback, which does not take the learner into account, is of very limited diagnostic relevance.

From the perspective of understanding what feedback on comprehension is about and what kind of feedback is particularly useful to improve SFL reading, it is unfortunate that most studies on SFL feedback focus on speaking and writing (see, e.g., review by Li, 2010)—feedback on comprehension is rarely investigated. As a result, very little is known about the effectiveness of feedback in SFL reading specifically. Therefore, in most cases, we have to infer from research on the other language skills and in other skill and knowledge areas than language what useful and effective feedback on SFL reading might be like.

Recent Advances in Feedback Theory

The feedback model developed by Hattie and Timperley (2007), which will be discussed next, takes a broad view of feedback and covers not only the products of learning but also the processes and strategies that learners engage in. Importantly, it gives the learner a central role and attempts to describe how feedback relates to learners' personal characteristics, such as their ability to regulate their learning and performance. The Hattie and Timperley model has its origins in a synthesis of over 500 meta-analyses of factors that might affect learning (Hattie, 1999), which showed that different forms of feedback were often among the strongest influences on achievement. A meta-analysis is a study that summarizes the findings of many single studies, thereby providing aggregated evidence about a phenomenon of interest than any one study can. Hattie's study thus provides powerful evidence for the argument that feedback significantly improves learning. The model developed from Hattie's synthesis tries to explain in more detail why and how feedback is likely to work (see Figure 8.1).

According to Hattie and Timperley (2007), feedback should not be considered as an isolated action; rather, it needs to be seen as part of the entire learning and teaching process. Their conceptualization of feedback as an important part of a larger entity agrees very much with the view expressed at the beginning of this chapter—that, as far as diagnostic assessment is concerned, we need to consider the entire diagnostic chain, including feedback, before we can judge if diagnosis has been successful. It is the comprehensiveness of the Hattie and Timperley model, the central role of the learner in it, and the fact that the model goes beyond the task level (i.e., corrective feedback, knowledge of results) that

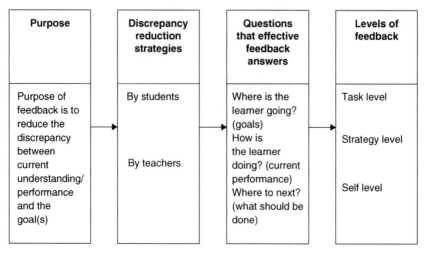

FIGURE 8.1 A modified version of Hattie and Timperley's (2007) model of how feedback enhances learning

makes it useful in understanding feedback and its role in learning. The levels of feedback postulated by the model, however, are somewhat problematic, particularly when it comes to defining the levels beyond the task level. Therefore, when we discuss the different levels of feedback below, we will use concepts and terminology that are probably more familiar to the readers and more in line with the most recent research and theorizing in applied linguistics.

According to the Hattie and Timperley (2007) model, effective feedback must address three kinds of questions that span the entire learning process. Both the teacher and the learner must be aware of all these aspects of the feedback process in order for the feedback to have a real impact on learning: Where is the learner going? (What are the goals?), How is the learner doing? (What is the learner's current knowledge or performance?), What should the learner do next? (What activities would cause learning to happen given the current state of knowledge?).

We will next elaborate the central role of goals in learning and in feedback, and then describe different levels of feedback and why the level matters.

Why Are Goals So Important in Feedback?

Goals are a key component of the feedback process, since feedback is useful only if it relates to the goals of learning and moves the learner toward those goals. The main purpose of feedback is to narrow the gap between the learners' current state of knowledge and the goal toward which they are moving (see also Sadler, 1989).

The nature of goals matters. They must be clear and specific enough, and the learners have to believe that they can attain them. Such goals help focus learners' attention and may also lead to an increase in learners' efforts to do more but also to tackle more challenging tasks (Hattie & Timperley, 2007).

If the goal is poorly defined, the learners will not only fail to understand the direction in which they should be going, but they will also not be able to see clearly if they are making any progress toward that goal (Hattie & Timperley, 2007).

However, the existence of clear learning goals is not enough. The learners should be aware of them and understand them. Teachers and learners should share an understanding of the goals, as well as other essential elements of learning, such as the criteria for success and for assessment (Sadler, 1989). Second, learners need to be committed to achieving the goals. A major challenge here is that not all learners have clear goals because they may not be very goal oriented in the first place—they are studying certain subjects just because they have to. Their goal may simply be to do the homework and tests given by the teacher. Some learners may have only performance goals—that is, they want to do well in order to excel but are not interested in learning. Feedback that reveals problems in such performance-oriented learners' proficiency may actually be unwelcome as it threatens their self-concept, whereas learners with real learning goals not only welcome such feedback but might also actively seek it (Hattie & Timperley, 2007; see also Jang & Wagner, 2014).

Fortunately, commitment to goals can be improved by using incentives and role models. Earley and Kanfer (1985) showed that learners who observed high-performing students developed a stronger commitment to goals than those who observed low-performing students. Thus, using skilled performers as a model can serve as an exemplification of the performance that is a goal for learning and also strengthen learners' desire to achieve that goal.

Levels of Feedback

Relevance to clearly defined goals is an essential starting point for feedback that improves learning. However, not all feedback is equally effective. One of the central elements in Hattie and Timperley's (2007) model, the concept of the levels of feedback, aims to clarify why and how feedback affects learning. The original model distinguishes four levels at which feedback operates: task (product), process, self-regulation, and self. However, the 'process' and 'self-regulation' levels are problematic. The definition of 'process' in the model appears to be quite unusual, even in the context of the general educational research from which the model emerges, let alone in applied linguistics. Therefore, it makes sense to use concepts and terminology that are more familiar to the readers and more directly based on research and theorizing in applied linguistics. Since Hattie and Timperley (2007) consider strategies as the key feature of both the process and self-regulation levels, we will make use of the work on the learner strategies done by applied linguists to discuss those two feedback levels. In fact, in this book we have decided to merge those two original levels into one that we have named the 'strategy level.' Although we depart here from the original model, we believe the discussion about feedback becomes clearer and, importantly, one of the main points argued for by Hattie and Timperley, namely that feedback focusing on the strategies that learners use is a powerful way to improve learning, remains essentially unchanged.

Currently in applied linguistics, strategy use is seen as part of learners' strategic competence (Purpura, 2014b, 2014c). Purpura (2014c) defines a strategy as a thought or behavior used by learners to regulate their SFL learning or use. A distinction has traditionally been made between metacognitive and cognitive strategies. Cognitive strategies have to do with action ('doing'), such as attending to information, comprehending, remembering, retrieving from memory, and using new information. Broadly speaking, metacognitive strategies refer to what Hattie and Timpley (2007) call self-regulation. They involve mental regulation ('thinking') of action and traditionally include planning, monitoring, and evaluation activities. Metacognition can be seen to regulate which cognitive activities or strategies to use in any given situation. An example from reading illustrates the difference between metacognitive and cognitive activities or strategies: "Reading a particular section of a text is a cognitive activity in itself, but the decision to select only that particular section to read is of a metacognitive nature" (Schellings, van Hout-Wolters, Veenman, & Meijer, 2013, p. 965).

Besides metacognitive and cognitive strategies, current theories (Oxford, 2011; Purpura, 2014c) on strategic competence include social (or socio-cultural–interactional) strategies that refer to collaboration between SFL learners and users (i.e., helping each other) and affective strategies that enable the learners to identify and adjust their feelings and beliefs related to an SFL (e.g., overcoming disappointments in learning/ using the SFL).

As was mentioned above, we combined the Hattie and Timperley's (2007) 'process' and 'self-regulation' levels into one 'strategy' level (see Figure 8.1). In light of the recent theorization on learner strategies in applied linguistics, which were briefly reviewed above, the strategy level could in fact be divided into four types: cognitive, metacognitive, social, and affective (Oxford, 2011; Purpura, 2014c). Cognitive strategies bear some resemblance to the 'process' level in the Hattie and Timperley model, and metacognitive strategies cover almost the same ground as the self-regulation level, except that Hattie and Timperley's self-regulation also includes certain types of affective (or meta-affective) strategies. In contrast, the Hattie and Timperley model largely ignores social strategies and covers affective strategies only indirectly. However, it is logical to assume that feedback focusing on social and affective strategies might also be beneficial for learning. Therefore, although we discuss feedback that mainly targets metacognitive and cognitive strategies (see below), we should keep in mind that feedback on learners' social and affective strategies can also potentially improve their learning or be useful for them in other ways.

What do we know about the effectiveness of different types (levels) of feedback? A large number of empirical studies from different areas of education as summarized by Hattie (1999) and Hattie and Timperley (2007) suggests that feedback about task performance (e.g., correctness) can be quite effective, but its usefulness is greatly enhanced if it leads to better ways of doing the task (or a similar task) by applying different, more effective, and appropriate strategies in the future. Therefore, feedback that targets strategy use appears to be particularly useful for developing deeper processing and mastery of tasks. Feedback directed at the self of the learner (such as "Good!" or "Well done") is the least effective of all.

Table 8.1 gives concrete examples of feedback on a reading task. The examples are roughly categorized along a continuum that ranges from the provision of information to the learners about the correctness of their response to providing advice on the use of cognitive and metacognitive strategies to feedback that lacks any specific information but simply serves to encourage the learner. In some respects the categorization follows the levels of feedback proposed in the Hattie and Timperley (2007) model but uses terminology that is likely to be more familiar to readers whose background is in applied linguistics.

TABLE 8.1 Overview of different types of feedback on a reading task

Focus of feedback	Examples of feedback
A. Correctness or adequacy of the response/product (cf. 'Task feedback')	(a) Your answer was incorrect. (b) Your answer was incorrect. The correct answer is X. (c) Your answer was incorrect because [+ explanation] (d) Your answer was incorrect. The correct answer is X because [+ explanation] (e) Your answer was in the correct direction but too general. Try to give a more specific answer.
B. Strategy use with the text that is being read (feedback on the correctness of response plus advice to use a [particular, usually a cognitive] strategy)	(a) Your answer was incorrect. Reread the last two sentences of the third paragraph. (b) Your answer was incorrect. What do you think the words X and Y tell you about the writer's attitude? (c) Your answer was incorrect. Read the text again and try to remember how we figured out the writer's attitude to the topic in the text about global warming we read last week. (d) Your answer was incorrect. Try to use the strategies we have studied on how to figure out the writer's attitude. (e) Tell me why you think that is the correct answer. (+ Ask what your pair thinks is the correct answer and why. Compare your answers and reasons.)
C. More general strategy use when reading any text (mainly meta-cognitive strategies; information about correctness not necessary; cf. 'Self-regulation feedback')	(a) Look at the title of the text and try to predict what the text will be about. After you complete reading it, think about whether your prediction was correct or not, and why. (b) Read texts X, Y, and Z and pay attention to how the writers convey whether they are for or against something. (c) When you read a text, stop at regular intervals to assess what you have understood. If something remains unclear, decide if it matters and if you need to check with the teacher or a peer or consult a dictionary. (d) When you answer questions about a text, consider how certain you are about your responses. For each question, consider why you are certain/uncertain about your answer. (e) When you select a text to read, think about your goals for learning. Try to choose a text that you think helps you to achieve your goal. Also try to read in a way that is relevant to your goal (e.g., quickly searching for specific information or getting an overall idea).
D. Self	Good! Well done. Good job!

Table 8.2 provides further examples of task-level feedback that allows learners to figure out if their answer was correct or not and provides them with an explanation for the correct answer. The examples come from an English as a foreign language reading test designed in Hungary. Feedback relates to

TABLE 8.2 Examples of task-level feedback on short-answer reading questions

Question and answer	Feedback/explanation related to the item
1. How heavy are they at the most? **Answer**: 22 pounds	**Item 1:** The words 'at the most' in the question imply that you need to give an exact figure in response, and the word 'heavy' indicates that you need to look for words like 'weight' or 'weigh' in the text
3. What is the difference between males and females? **Answer**: nothing/they are identical	**Item 3:** This is a slightly tricky question, because there is no difference between the males and females. The question suggests that there is a difference, but you do not have to believe this!
7. Where do they lay their eggs? **Answer**: on bare ground/caves/ (and) (rock) crevices	**Item 7:** Common sense might suggest that birds lay their eggs in a nest, but the text explicitly contradicts this, so you need to read rather carefully the last paragraph of the text to be sure you have the correct answer.

short-answer questions on a text that deals with Californian condors (Alderson & Csereznyés, 2003, pp. 32–34).

We will next describe in more detail the characteristics of different types of feedback that were illustrated in Table 8.1. The description is partly based on the levels of feedback proposed in the Hattie and Timperley model but differs from it when it comes to feedback that concerns strategies.

Task Feedback

The first level of feedback in Hattie and Timperley's (2007) model focuses on the outcome or results of the task that the learner took or was somehow engaged with. Thus, it focuses on the product and typically tells the learners if their answers were correct. The term 'task' covers both single items and more extensive tasks. In the Hattie and Timperley model, task feedback can also be more detailed and explain why the response was correct versus incorrect, as illustrated in Tables 8.1 and 8.2. However, task feedback can also include directions to seek more or different information (e.g., "Your reply was in the correct direction but too general. Try to give more details in your answer."). Feedback on task outcomes is extremely common in classrooms. As mentioned earlier, it can be very effective for learning (Hattie & Timperley, 2007). However, task feedback does not work in the same way across all tasks and all learners. Task characteristics such as task complexity can influence how well feedback functions (Kulhavy, White, Topp, Chan, & Adams, 1985; Balzer, Doherty, & O'Conner, 1989). In fact, research suggests that task feedback is more useful with simple rather than complex tasks. In other words, simple task feedback may be more effective than more complex task feedback, especially when the task at hand is rather simple (Kulhavy et al., 1985).

Two general issues with task feedback are worth mentioning. First, task feedback often generalizes rather poorly to other tasks (Thompson, 1998). In other words, feedback on one task does not automatically help the learner to perform better on other tasks. This is why it is useful if task feedback is followed by feedback that focuses learners' attention on the strategies they use to process the task and to regulate their behavior (e.g., monitor comprehension while reading a text). However, some recent research employing a new approach to studying the effect of different amounts of feedback suggests that task-level feedback can lead to transfer across tasks if the feedback not only informs the learners about the correct answer but also provides an explanation why the answer is correct (Butler, Godbole, & Marsh, 2013). The reason for this is not clear, but the researchers speculate that the explanation may help learners to better apply skills from one task to the next. Alternatively, an explanation may help learners to create a better situation model from the first text (if the task involves reading a text) that helps to understand a new, related text better.

The second issue with task-level feedback refers to the fact that too much task-level feedback is not ideal. Very detailed task-level feedback can maintain learners' attention at that level only and inhibit them from moving toward the other levels (i.e., toward strategy use), which are needed in high-level task performance, especially on complex tasks (Kluger & DeNisi, 1996).

Feedback About Strategies

The second level of feedback in our modified version of Hattie and Timperley's (2007) model concerns strategies that learners use. The original model states that feedback can target either process strategies or self-regulation strategies. As explained earlier in our discussion and exemplification of strategies, we have adopted a view of strategy use based on applied linguistic research in this area. Therefore, Table 8.1 refers to metacognitive and cognitive strategies by providing examples of feedback that encourages readers to engage in particular strategies. When the feedback focuses on a particular text/task combination that the learner had just taken, the feedback can, for example, encourage cognitive strategy use that most likely suits that particular text and task (e.g., feedback points out where in the text the learner can find the expected answer to a question). Metacognitively oriented feedback, for its part, typically encourages the learners to reflect on the text/task before (planning), during (monitoring), or after reading a text and completing a task (evaluating).

As mentioned earlier, when it comes to strategies, we focus on metacognitive and cognitive strategies. The reason for this is that they are the most studied types of strategies in applied linguistics and also because the strategy part of the Hattie and Timperley model focuses on them. However, recent theories on learner strategies (Oxford, 2011; Purpura, 2014c) cover additional types of strategies, such as social strategies (also referred to as socio-cultural–interactional strategies because of their theoretical underpinnings in socio-cultural approaches to language learning and use). A small number of examples presented in Table 8.1 seem to relate to such socially oriented strategies and illustrate what these strategies might be like in practice. For example, feedback that encourages learners to consult their peers for help or for comparing and justifying their own, possibly different, answers to reading items clearly involves the social dimension in strategy use.

Some feedback aims at developing strategies that improve learners' awareness of the characteristics of the task, such as the features of the text (e.g., that it has a particular rhetorical structure) or of the task itself (e.g., what steps to take when one has to write a summary of a text). As a result, learners may learn to check if the new texts they encounter have a similar or different rhetorical structure compared with the one on which they were given feedback. Task feature feedback may encourage the learners, for example, to start underlining key points in a text as a first step in a summary writing task (a cognitive strategy). Hattie and Timperley (2007) argue that feedback that encourages this kind of strategy use helps learners to understand the key characteristics of different tasks. Such understandings can help them better analyze the characteristics of new tasks that they encounter. They further argue that such understanding of task characteristics helps learners to transfer skills from one task to new, different, and possibly more demanding tasks. This transferability across tasks explains the effectiveness of feedback that goes beyond the task (outcome, correctness) and focuses on strategies that learners could use, for example, in reading tasks.

An important group of strategies that feedback on strategies can target are those that learners can use to detect errors in their performance. These are important because they provide the learners with self-initiated feedback (Hattie & Timperley, 2007) and thus can potentially significantly increase the amount of feedback available to them. When learners detect an error in their performance, a reassessment of the situation in terms of their knowledge and skills is triggered (Carver & Scheier, 1990), and they have to decide whether to engage in some error-correction strategies, to seek help, or to simply ignore the problem. Learners' decisions probably depend on their consideration of the seriousness of the error (with reference to their goals) and their overall motivation to achieve the goals. Leung and Mohan (2004) give examples of learner-generated feedback in a setting where learners were asked to justify their answers to reading tasks and to compare their reasons with those of the other students.

The inclusion of feedback on strategies in the Hattie and Timperley (2007) model gives the learner a prominent place in modeling the role and effects of feedback in the learning process. The factors in the model related to such aspects of self-regulation as commitment, control, and confidence (these come under affective or meta-affective strategies in Oxford's, 2011, and Purpura's, 2014c, models) especially have to do with learners' characteristics that are partly independent of teaching and feedback but that can, in fact, be influenced by feedback, at least to a degree. The effectiveness of self–regulation feedback is mediated by several factors that relate to effort, confidence, attribution of success or failure, and generation of internal feedback.

The learners' willingness to make the effort required to seek and utilize feedback influences the way feedback is used. Seeking feedback requires time and effort, and it can also be face threatening, which explains why learners vary in this respect. Not all students seek feedback or other help because of the threat to their self-esteem and their face (Karabenick & Knapp, 1991). Learners' confidence in their responses is a further factor. When learners are confident that their response is correct, and they are right, they spend little time on feedback. However, when the learners are certain of the correctness of their answer, but it turns out not to be so, feedback can become very effective (Kulhavy & Stock, 1989), probably because the surprise the learners encounter increases the salience of the issue at hand and leads them to process it more carefully. The reasons that learners believe are behind their success or failure on a task also affect how they receive feedback. Such attributions may in fact be more important than how successful their performance actually is (Hattie & Timperley, 2007). The implication of this for effective feedback is that it should give learners a reasonable idea of the reasons for their success or failure. Otherwise, they can develop ineffective and distracting ideas about why they succeeded or failed. Effort, ability, and luck are typical attributions that learners give to their success or failure. However, some explanations about success (e.g., effort) are likely to be more beneficial for learning than others (e.g., luck). Research suggests that feedback on the amount of work that learners invest in studying is particularly effective in the early stages of learning, when learners have to make an effort to be successful (Hattie & Timperley, 2007).

Finally, the learners' ability to generate their own feedback while monitoring how they perform a task or when evaluating their performance after task completion is an important aspect of self-regulation (or metacognition, depending on whose model we are talking about). Learners who are good at that are obviously more self-sufficient when it comes to feedback of any type. Learners who cannot easily produce such feedback have to rely on external feedback from the teacher (Butler & Winne, 1995; Hattie & Timperley, 2007). Thus, feedback aimed at developing learners' ability to plan, monitor, and evaluate their performance is likely to improve this useful aspect of self-regulation/metacognition.

Feedback About the Self as a Person

This type or level of feedback in the Hattie and Timperley (2007) model is very different from the feedback covered so far because unlike all previous feedback, it is detached from the tasks that learners perform. This feedback expresses positive or sometimes negative evaluations of the learner as a person and even about his or her mental abilities and is very common in classrooms. Learners like to be praised. Considering how common feedback is that focuses on the person as opposed to his or her performance, it is unfortunate that, according to Hattie and Timperley (2007), feedback that can be classified as praise had quite a small effect on learning outcomes (the effect of punishment and rewards was also small).The reason for the modest effect on learning of feedback on the self seems to be that it does not contain much information about task performance and is not related to learning goals (Kluger & DeNisi, 1998). However, praise that does not just reward, but intends to reinforce something such as effort or self-regulation can be quite effective in raising self-esteem (e.g. "You were very good since you used the strategy we practiced"; see Hattie & Timperley, 2007, p. 97). The effects of feedback on oneself can be quite unpredictable, however. For example, students may or may not want to be seen as 'good' students depending on the attitudes of their peers. If the learners' friends do not value somebody being a good, hard-working student, they probably do not want to hear the teacher praising them in public. It should be added, however, that reflections on the self are seen here rather narrowly—the above concerns only the effects of the kind of minimalist feedback that is simply intended to encourage. More extensive reflection that the learners themselves might engage with (and in which the teacher, too, may participate) are a different matter altogether and can be highly beneficial for improving the learners' motivation, agency, and knowledge of themselves, which in their turn is likely to improve performance.

Implications of the Levels of Feedback for Research on Feedback

At the beginning of this chapter, we listed some questions about feedback, such as what feedback should focus on, whether it is better to give feedback immediately or after some delay, and whether positive or negative feedback better closes the gap between the goal and the current skill level. Research has often produced conflicting results on these and other similar questions. The Hattie and Timperley feedback model helps to provide explanations for some of these issues. The proper timing of feedback has long been debated in the feedback literature. Considering the level of feedback helps us understand when immediate feedback is likely to work. In general, immediate feedback is more effective when it focuses on task outcomes, and delayed feedback works better at the strategies level (Hattie & Timperley, 2007). When the goal of learning is to improve accuracy, in particular, immediate feedback on errors in performance (task-level feedback) is usually effective. However, when the goal is more process oriented (i.e., the aim is to improve fluency), immediate feedback—which also typically focuses on errors—can distract the learners from the goal of the task.

Some research suggests that task difficulty affects the effectiveness of delayed feedback such that delayed feedback improves performance on difficult reading items more than on easier items. The reason for this is presumably that difficult items require more processing of the task, which is possible when feedback is delayed (Clariana, Wagner, & Roher Murphy, 2000).

Another issue that the Hattie and Timperley model can help to interpret are the conflicting findings about the effectiveness of positive and negative feedback. It appears that negative task-level feedback (i.e., information that there was an error) is not effective unless it is accompanied by information about the correct answer (Hattie & Timperley, 2007). The situation is more complex for self-regulation (metacognitive or even meta-affective) feedback as its effectiveness is mediated by several factors such as commitment and perceptions of self-efficacy. Positive feedback benefits learners more who are committed to achieving their goals, but learners who do something simply because they have to are influenced more by negative feedback—but such an effect is unlikely to last. Moreover, it has been found that negative feedback can decrease the motivation of learners who have low self-efficacy.

Levels of Feedback—Conclusions

Combining different levels of feedback is often a very good strategy. For example, it has been found that task feedback that contains cues about where and how to search for information in order to arrive at the correct answer improves the effectiveness of feedback. Such combined feedback is likely to lead to the use of better strategies as it directs the learners' attention to how the task is processed (e.g., the use of cognitive strategies), and it can also improve their self-regulation (e.g., their metacognitive skills). Although typical self-oriented feedback is not normally very effective for learning, it makes sense not to forget such feedback as it has other beneficial effects on learners and can indirectly improve learning outcomes. Levels of feedback and types of feedback questions (see Table 8.1) appear to relate in specific ways. Task-level feedback seems to relate most closely to conveying information about the learners' current knowledge and performance (how is the learner doing?). Feedback on strategy use, in contrast, spans all three aspects of feedback: goals, current state, and needed action. It seems particularly important for planning future action because learning activities should be selected on the basis of the assessment of (and feedback about) the current state of knowledge and with reference to the goals of learning.

Despite its limitations as regards current thinking about learner strategies in particular, a theory of different levels of feedback such as the one proposed by Hattie and Timperley appears to be useful for understanding certain contradictory research findings. Questions regarding the best timing of feedback and the efficacy of positive versus negative feedback are complex, but they appear to be answerable at least partly with reference to the level of feedback whose effectiveness is being studied.

We will next take a closer look at the feedback that tests and teachers typically provide with reference to the feedback model discussed above.

Analysis of the Most Common Forms of Feedback in Terms of Their Level

In the educational context, the teacher is the main source of all kinds of feedback. Teachers' feedback is usually informal, and it is presented orally or even non-verbally in the interactions during lessons. Teachers also give written feedback on open-ended tasks. As far as feedback on reading is concerned, teachers mark and sometimes comment on students' answers to teacher-made tests, or they publicly review the most common problems in answers to test questions when giving the test papers back to students (Tarnanen & Huhta, 2011).The most common feedback from tests is the total score, although sometimes section scores are also reported, for example, for different skills (e.g. reading, listening; see Kunnan & Jang, 2009). In the school context, the students often get their tests back and can thus examine how they did in each task or item.

Table 8.3 presents a classification of common forms of feedback in language education contexts together with a classification of their level in terms of our modified version of the Hattie and Timperley (2007) model. Because DIALANG is a feedback-rich SFL assessment system, the feedback it provides is also included in the table for comparison's sake. This also serves as a reference point for the discussion of DIALANG feedback later in this chapter.

The list in Table 8.3 is not intended to be exhaustive, but it presents a range of feedback that teachers, tests, and other feedback-generating systems can potentially deliver. We can see, for example, that many common forms of feedback given by teachers and tests focus on the task level at most, if not on the overall test result.

Feedback focusing on learners' strategy use often concerns giving advice that leads learners to use specific or different strategies when doing tasks such as reading a text. Feedback on broader strategies (self-regulation or metacognition) relates to engaging learners in self-assessment and in comparing self-assessment with an external measure of their proficiency. Interestingly, it is possible to provide learners with such process-related factors as speed of completing the task (and changes in speed over time), number of pauses, and number of attempts (see, e.g., DIALANG Experimental Items, at www.lancs.ac.uk/fss/projects/linguistics/experimental/start.htm). This is obviously only possible if learners' performances can be observed or captured by some means. Writing performance in, for example, a summary writing task could be recorded and analyzed with keystroke-logging software.

TABLE 8.3 Classification of forms of feedback that could be given in reading in an SFL in terms of a modified Hattie and Timperley (2007) model

Type of feedback	General examples	DIALANG examples	Level of feedback
Total test score	B in a A–F grading system, 5 on a scale of 1-10, C1 on the CEFR scale A1–C2, 75% out of 100%		task (product)
Rank/percentile	5th, 70th percentile		task (product)
Brief verbal statement	Fair, excellent		task (product)
Sub-test score	Reading: A; Speaking B	CEFR level A1–C2 for reading, writing, listening, vocabulary, structures	task (product)
Task or item score/ Teacher's evaluation of the correctness of a learner's response	Item 1: correct, item 2: incorrect, . . . 'Correct', 'no, that's wrong'	Two types: immediately and after the test	task (product)
Profile	Several sub-test, task or item scores reported in the same score report	Profile of correct/ incorrect responses across reading sub-skills given after the test	task (product)
Task or item score (or teacher's evaluation) + explanation	Item 1 incorrect because . . .		task (product) (& strategies)
Task or item score (or teacher's evaluation) + cues or questions	Item 1 incorrect; look at the first two sentences in the second paragraph	Experimental DIALANG items	task (product) & strategies
Markings on learners' written products	Teacher, e.g., marks incorrect points in students' open-ended responses		task (product) (& strategies)
Descriptor of a communicative activity	A sentence describing the activity, e.g., 'You can read simple notes, cards, and personal letters.'		task (product) (& strategies)
Proficiency level (set of descriptors)	Reporting the test result as a description of a level in a scale	Two types (CEFR scale): (1) briefly with the test score, (2) elaborated version	task (product) (& strategies)
Result of self-assessment (SA)	Reporting the result of SA based on 'I can do' statements as a score or a level	Reported as CEFR levels	strategies (self-regulation/ metacognition)

Type of feedback	General examples	DIALANG examples	Level of feedback
Comparison of SA and test result	Reporting SA and test results side by side	Reports and compares SA and test result in terms of CEFR levels	strategies (self-regulation/ metacognition)
Explanations for discrepancies between SA and test result	Explanations why SA and test result may not match (a list of possible reasons or a series of questions that encourage the learner to reflect)	A range of potential reasons described	strategies (self-regulation/ metacognition)
Advice for improvement	Try to learn how new words are typically formed in language X.	Advice specific to skill (read, write, listen) and CEFR level	strategies (self-regulation/ metacognition)
Information about the time spent on task	You spent 35 seconds in Task 1/You did Task 2 five seconds faster than last time		strategies (process/self-regulation/ metacognition)
Information about the number of trials	You tried three times before you found the correct answer	Experimental DIALANG items	strategies (process/self-regulation/ metacognition)
Information about change	In your first draft of the summary, you did X, but in the final version you did Y.		strategies (process/self-regulation/ metacognition)
Use of assistance/ help devices	You looked up three words when reading the text	Experimental DIALANG items	strategies (process/self-regulation/ metacogntion)
Praise	Good/well done/good job		self (& task/outcome)

DIALANG as an Example of Feedback in a Diagnostic Language Assessment System

Table 8.3 shows that the feedback offered by the DIALANG assessment system is quite unusual compared to feedback delivered by most other language tests. It is, therefore, appropriate to discuss DIALANG feedback in some detail. We also report on research that sheds light on how learners view that wide range of feedback. DIALANG was designed to be a diagnostic language assessment system. Feedback research related to DIALANG nicely complements other feedback studies in SFL that have typically concerned speaking and writing. In contrast, the skills tested in DIALANG include reading and listening. Furthermore, DIALANG is a computerized system and, thus, its feedback is also automatically generated, whereas the focus in SFL contexts has been on feedback provided by teachers.

Because the assessment procedure of DIALANG is described in Chapter Three, we focus here on describing feedback given by the system (see also Alderson, 2005; Alderson & Huhta, 2005). To summarize, DIALANG feedback includes the following:

1. Test results as a CEFR level along with a description of the CEFR level
2. Immediate item feedback on the correctness and acceptability of the responses
3. Post-test item feedback on the correctness and acceptability of the responses plus information about the sub-skill of each item
4. Comparison between self-assessment (SA) and test result
5. Information about reasons why SA and test result may not match
6. Extended descriptions of CEFR levels in terms of texts, nature of comprehension, and limitations at each level
7. Advice on improving proficiency
8. Vocabulary Size Placement Test result as a score and brief description of the meaning of the score.

DIALANG provides both traditional test and item-related feedback and innovative types of feedback that concern strategies that relate to self-regulation as defined in the Hattie and Timperley (2007) model or to metacognition as defined by Oxford (2011) and Purpura (2014b).

Test and Task-Level Feedback in DIALANG

DIALANG reports to the learner his/her level in the skill tested in terms of the CEFR level A1–C2 (see Chapter Three for a screenshot). Learners also receive the Vocabulary Size Placement Test result as a score band with a brief description of its meaning. Item-level feedback comes in two forms. During the test itself, the users can turn immediate feedback on, if they want to know immediately if their answer was correct (see Figure 8.2 for an example). If it was incorrect, they are shown the correct answer, or for open-ended items, a list of acceptable answers.

After the test, the users can also review the items they took, irrespective of whether they had used the immediate item-level feedback or not. The post-test item review presents the items in the form of a table and displays which items were answered correctly and which incorrectly. The items are grouped according to the sub-skill of reading that they aim at testing, to give the user an idea of their stronger and weaker sub-skills (see Chapter Four for a description of the sub-skills). Users can click on an item in the table to make it appear on the screen, in exactly the same format as if they were taking the test with immediate

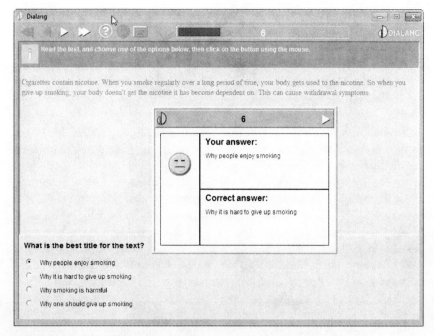

FIGURE 8.2 Sample DIALANG reading item with immediate feedback

feedback enabled. We illustrate below with the sample English reading item shown in Figure 8.2 how the feedback from a regular multiple choice item could be enriched. Real DIALANG items do not come with such detailed feedback; only the correct option is indicated for multiple-choice items, so this item is simply used as an illustration to discuss possibilities in detailed item-level feedback. A tentative rationale follows for the feedback that could be given to learners who choose the first, second, third, or fourth option in the previous reading item:

1. Unless the learner has made a blind guess, selecting this option seems to indicate that the learner's proficiency is well below what the item requires. The learner probably has difficulties in understanding many of the words in the text. Therefore, the advice given to the learner could be rather general and suggest that the learner increases his or her effort (i.e., reads more in the language).
2. This is the correct option.
3. Selecting this option may indicate undue reliance on background knowledge about the harmfulness of smoking, which may lead to superficial or selective reading of the text to confirm the expectation. The learner could be reminded to read the text to the very end, as this option is a good title for

the first two sentences but not for the whole text. The learner could also be warned against relying too much on general knowledge.

4. A possible reason for choosing this option is a failure to understand the meaning of 'give up' or some other key expression in the text, such as 'withdrawal symptoms.' The advice to the learner could be to check the meaning of those expressions.

In addition to, or instead of, the above kinds of feedback, it is possible to use an item such as this to generate other types and levels of feedback. If such an item is discussed in a language classroom, the teacher could ask learners who responded incorrectly to explain their choice, followed by further discussion about the item. The reasons for a correct answer could also be discussed in the same way. Such interaction would allow different interpretations of the text to be aired and turn the assessment and feedback task into a learning task (as happened in the Leung & Mohan, 2004, study).

In addition to item level feedback and the overall test result, DIALANG users are shown detailed descriptions of the level they were assigned to, and the level just above and below the performance level. These CEFR-based descriptions focus on the texts, nature of comprehension and conditions and limitations of comprehension (see Table 8.4). The aim of this is to encourage learners to reflect on what language learning involves, and whether they can recognize themselves in the descriptions.

Feedback Focusing on Strategy Use in DIALANG

Some DIALANG feedback goes beyond the task and focuses self-regulation; this is the case, in particular, with self-assessment feedback. In addition to giving users an opportunity to self-assess (which in itself probably involves self-regulation/ metacognition), the system provides learners with direct feedback on their self-assessment responses. After completing the language test, the learners can see their self-assessment-based CEFR level and compare it with the CEFR level based on their test performance. If there is a discrepancy between the two, the learner is also given a brief comment.

TABLE 8.4 Sample detailed level descriptions (for A2) from DIALANG

	Types of text and speech (I can read/ understand)	What I can do (understand)	Conditions and Limitations
A2	Texts on familiar, concrete matters. Short, simple texts (e.g., routine personal and business letters and faxes, most everyday signs and notices, Yellow Pages, advertisements).	Understand short simple texts. Find specific information in simple everyday material.	Restricted mainly to common everyday language and language related to my job.

Sample feedback about self-assessment in DIALANG (the wording of this feedback is the same for all skills tested in the system):

In the self-assessment task you gave responses that we would normally expect from a learner at level B2. However, your test result suggests that you are at level B1.

If you have a tendency to over-estimate your own proficiency, this could prevent you from setting meaningful and realistic goals for your language learning.

DIALANG feedback also includes further information about the match between the self-assessment and test results. DIALANG does not diagnose the reason for a mismatch in any individual learner's case; instead, it encourages the user to consider various reasons for it by reading 'information about self-assessment.' This part of feedback also contains information about the nature of language proficiency, and describes, for example, the kind of information (i.e., feedback) about language proficiency that different tests can or cannot provide.

Sample explanation of why self-assessment and test results may differ:

You compare yourself with other learners of the same language.

We often compare our abilities with those of other people. How we see our language level may be affected by other learners of the same language in the workplace, classroom, or elsewhere. The more learners at different stages of language learning we know, the better chances we have of obtaining a realistic idea of where we stand in relation to them and whether we can do something better than them.

If you come across only a few learners of the language you are studying, it may be difficult to see the full range of skills and proficiency levels that exist. If you were in class with the weakest language learners at school or if you mainly meet learners who are clearly better than yourself, this might lead you to underestimate your skills. On the other hand, if you were among the best learners at school or you come across only less advanced learners, this might give you the impression that you are more advanced than you really are.

Finally, DIALANG also provides learners with suggestions that aim at helping them to move from their current level to the next one, which aims at improving learners' ability to regulate their actions in this area.

Sample advice: Advice for making progress in reading from level B1 toward B2

- Try to read with active understanding a wider range of texts such as: more difficult texts within your field; specialized texts from other fields; news reports in English that express particular points of view or lines of argument.
- Ask yourself the reasons for reading a text (for enjoyment, for general or particular information, to complete a task) and analyze how you can adjust your reading style (scanning quickly through a text to get the gist, searching rapidly for a specific piece of information, reading in detail for the details of a particular procedure).
- Concentrate from time to time on intensive detailed reading of a text, perhaps with the aid of a dictionary. It is likely that you can cope quite well with most routine texts at this level already, and it will require conscious effort on your part to move to the next level.

Two general characteristics of DIALANG feedback are worth mentioning. First, feedback is fully user-controlled: learners can decide themselves which feedback they attend to and for how long. Second, the feedback is available in many languages, which aims at making it as easily understandable as possible since many users can receive it in a language that they can easily comprehend.

Research Into DIALANG Feedback

Next, we report on studies on the use of, and reactions to, DIALANG feedback. The most comprehensive study (Huhta, 2010) was a survey of 557 tertiary and secondary level students in Finland and Germany who were attending courses in which DIALANG was used as part of the instruction.

The study examined whether the learners read the different DIALANG feedback and how interesting and useful they considered it to be. It did not investigate the effect of feedback on learning, nor the extent to which learners followed the advice given by the system. The following three Likert-scale questions were asked of each type of feedback:

- Do you usually read this part of DIALANG feedback?
- How interesting is this part of feedback in your view?
- How useful is this part of feedback for you?

The respondents could choose from four options. In the first question they were: (almost) always/often/seldom/never, and in the second and third questions: very—somewhat—only a little—not at all (interesting/useful).

The results showed that the learners thought the best feedback was the traditional overall test result. The average rating for it was close to 'very interesting/ useful' on the response scale. The ratings of the other forms of feedback were somewhat lower and equaled 'somewhat interesting/useful.' The exception was the information about self-assessment (reasons for possible mismatch), which was typically rated as 'only a little' interesting or useful. In an additional task the learners had to state which types of feedback were the most or least useful for them by ranking them. The rankings confirm the above findings: almost all students ranked the overall test result among the top three types of feedback in terms of perceived usefulness, whereas the reasons for self-assessment/test mismatch were regarded as one of the three least useful parts of feedback.

The informants' responses to the question on how often they read the feedback give a partly different picture from their evaluations of the interest and usefulness of feedback. Again, the overall test result dominated as the most often read part of feedback. Interestingly, however, two thirds of the learners reported reading feedback on self-assessment (comparison of SA and test result) almost every time they used DIALANG, even though only a third of them considered that feedback as very useful. Perhaps many learners who do not consider this feedback very useful nevertheless wanted to read it after each test just in case they might learn something from it. Also, reading item level feedback was reported to be somewhat more frequent than its rating of usefulness might lead us to expect. Again, learners perhaps hoped to learn by reading such feedback.

Some of the learners were administered a version of the questionnaire that asked them to evaluate not only how useful they considered different types of feedback to be but also to state how strong (certain) their view about the usefulness was (cf. Krosnick et al., 2002). They indicated whether their opinion on the usefulness was 'not at all certain' or 'quite certain.' Most learners had a firm positive opinion on the usefulness of the overall test result and item level feedback. In contrast, one third of the respondents indicated they were not sure about their opinion on the usefulness of either type of feedback concerning self-assessment, whatever their opinion happened to be.

The survey also asked the users to state their preferred item-level feedback: 58% of learners preferred the immediate feedback and 30% the post-test item review; 9% thought they were equally good. Learners' preferences may relate to how they want to interact with the test. Some users reported that immediate feedback interrupted their test-taking and even depressed them when they got items wrong. Others, however, specifically wanted to know right away if they had replied correctly or not. Since the opinions were divided, a reasonable conclusion is that in a system like DIALANG both types of item level feedback should be offered.

Another question concerned the usefulness of the categorization of the test items into sub-skills for post-test item review. In reading, these sub-skills were understanding main points, understanding details, and making inferences. A clear majority (78%) considered it very or somewhat useful to have access to such information.

The users were also given the opportunity to describe in their own words the most or least useful aspects of DIALANG. The most often mentioned benefit of DIALANG was that it gives the learners a chance to see what their proficiency level or language skill is. Many learners valued the possibility of spotting errors given in item-level feedback. The comprehensiveness of the system was also appreciated.

The most often mentioned drawback of DIALANG feedback was its generality. It was criticized for being too general and self-evident. This concerned, in particular, the test result (just a level/the user already knew his/her level), the SA and test comparison (too vague to be of use) and advice (too self-evident). Thus, the most common wish was to get more detailed, extensive and personalized feedback.

Other studies on the usefulness of DIALANG feedback include those by Floropoulou (2002) and Yang (2003). Floropoulou (2002) investigated the reactions to DIALANG of five Greek and five Chinese students at Lancaster University. Her findings indicated that informants' culture was related to their opinions. The Chinese were more positively disposed to DIALANG than the Greeks who tended to be indifferent or even negative toward the system. Some students reported changing the way they viewed their proficiency (in English), because they could identify their strengths and weaknesses. Thus, the system appeared to increase some users' awareness of their language proficiency, and also of how proficiency is conceptualized in the CEFR.

Floropoulou (2002) also asked the students to rank several aspects of DIALANG in terms of their helpfulness. The most helpful part was reported to be the 'advisory feedback,' which consists of extended descriptions of the CEFR levels and advice on how to make progress in the skill in question. Immediate feedback on items was considered the next most helpful type of feedback followed by explanations of why one's SA and test result may not match, and the test result. By far the least helpful was the Vocabulary Size Placement Test result.

Finally, Floropoulou (2002) noted that the students tended to compare DIALANG with the proficiency tests they had already taken such as TOEFL and IELTS, which seemed to prevent them from fully understanding why, for example, self-assessment was included in DIALANG.

Yang (2003) also investigated how test takers used DIALANG feedback. By interviewing 12 postgraduate students at Lancaster University, after taking the English reading test, she found that most learners reacted positively to the feedback. However, their study goals appeared to have an effect on whether they were willing to make efforts to follow DIALANG's advice. Students whose main aim was to get a degree from the university rather than to improve their English were less likely to pay attention to the advice.

Many participants in Yang's study failed to recognize the aims and functions of DIALANG (Yang, 2003). Their prior beliefs based on experience with proficiency tests like TOEFL and IELTS seemed to prevent them from fully understanding the difference between DIALANG and other tests. In particular those learners who were doubtful about the test and its feedback tended to compare it with high-stakes examinations (see also Floropoulou, 2002, above). For example, the role of the vocabulary placement test and self-assessment did not seem clear to them, nor did the need to have information in the test about the explanations of the reasons for possible mismatch between self-assessment and overall test result.

The informants seemed to consider that the main purpose of feedback is error correction, which is a very commonly held view (Kulhavy, 1977). According to Yang (2003), this led them to pay special attention to item review feedback where they can see their errors and ignore those parts of feedback that describe what learners can do.

Yang also found that the explanatory and advisory feedback encouraged her informants to reflect upon their learning process and helped them realize the factors involved in their self-assessment. The comparison of their current level with the next higher level in the extended-level descriptions seemed to provide some learners with goals for learning, and the suggestions for improvement appeared to motivate them to make efforts by providing them with strategies with which to reach the goals. Yang argued that this reflection by the learners shows how feedback can function as a catalyst for self-regulated learning (Butler & Winne, 1995).

The studies reviewed above concerned learners' reactions to computerized DIALANG feedback such as its perceived usefulness and level of interest. Huhta (2010) also covered the frequency of the use of different types of feedback during the period that the learners were using DIALANG. None of the studies focused specifically on feedback from the reading tests, but since reading is one of the skills tested in DIALANG the results are relevant to building our understanding of the nature and potential effectiveness of diagnostic feedback on SFL reading.

Two main conclusions from the DIALANG studies can be drawn. First, learners clearly preferred traditional test feedback—overall test result and item level results. Second, there was also considerable interest in the more innovative feedback that attempts to improve learners' strategy use and increase their ability to regulate their learning and language use. Given the novelty of such feedback for almost all learners involved in the studies, it is not surprising that many appeared to be unsure what to think about this type of feedback. Findings from a study on feedback on SFL reading from another diagnostic test (Jang, 2009a) suggest that learners' level of language proficiency may influence their perception of the usefulness of detailed feedback on the strengths and weakness in proficiency: It appears that especially low-performing learners also need concrete advice on how to utilize such feedback.

An important limitation in the above studies is that they did not follow learners longitudinally to see how learners utilized different kinds of feedback and if they followed the advice they got from the system. Thus, we do not know much, yet, about how effective such automated feedback is in closing the gap between learners' current state of language knowledge and skill and their goals.

Why Research on Feedback on Reading Is So Rare

Most of the feedback studies reviewed in this chapter do not concern reading in either L1 or SFL (Leung & Mohan, 2004, and, partly, the studies on DIALANG are rare exceptions to this). The vast majority of SFL feedback research has focused on speaking and writing at the expense of reading and listening and also most SFL feedback at school focuses on the productive skills. We believe the main reason for this is the hidden and complex nature of reading (reading comprehension, in particular). As was elaborated in Chapter Four, the reading process is usually hidden: it is internal to the reader, it is private and not easily examined. This probably explains the focus on speaking and writing in most feedback research. It is not easy to spot problems in comprehension, although some of them become apparent via incorrect answers to questions in reading tasks. In Chapter Nine we will see that tests are indeed important for language teachers as a source of information about learners' skills, especially in reading.

If incorrect comprehension is not always evident, the process of comprehension such as the chain of reasoning that led to a wrong conclusion or its multiple possible causes (a misunderstood word, false background knowledge) are even more challenging to discover. Knowing the outcome of a comprehension task does not help us to say anything for certain about the process that led to the outcome. Thus, little meaningful feedback can be given to the learner about the process. In the classroom it is possible to ask the learners to explain their answers and thus get an idea of the underlying process (see Leung & Mohan, 2004), but when it comes to answers to a reading test we can only speculate about their reasons and possibly ask the learner to do the task again possibly by applying a somewhat different reading strategy.

A serious attempt to provide a reader with feedback that targets how the learner processes the task assumes that the designer of the feedback knows enough of the comprehension process to have a fairly good idea of what goes wrong if the outcome of the process is a certain kind of answer. Considering the opaque and complex nature of the comprehension process, it may be in fact be better to consider types of feedback that engage the person who has the most intimate and detailed knowledge about this process, namely the learner him/herself. One potentially useful approach to providing feedback on comprehension in general, and on the comprehension process in particular, is to ask the learners questions that encourage them to analyze what they did when reading a text and replying to the task.

Implications of Recent Research and Theories on Feedback

In this chapter we have reviewed a comprehensive model of feedback that places feedback in the larger context of learning (Hattie & Timperley, 2007). To understand why and how feedback works it is necessary to consider the goals of learning and the level of feedback (task, different types of strategies such as metacognitive and cognitive ones, and self). Interestingly, despite its shortcomings when it comes to defining strategies the Hattie and Timperley model is quite compatible with recent views of what makes feedback diagnostic. Jang and Wagner (2014) argue that diagnostic feedback both goes beyond, and is more specific than, mere test scores. It targets particular cognitive skills or language processes and provides learners with descriptions of their cognitive strengths, weaknesses, and strategies. It addresses the gap between current performance and a goal. We think that diagnostic feedback can also contain hints or explicit proposals about the action the learners should take to remedy the problem identified in their performance. Thus, feedback is an integral part of the diagnostic chain that comprises the identification of a problem, some understanding of its nature and possible causes, generation of feedback, and action to address the problem. We have exemplified different types of feedback that can potentially be given in the context of reading in an SFL and classified them in terms of the levels they focus on. Furthermore, we have reported on studies that cover particular issues with feedback; we have provided a more extensive treatment of research on DIALANG feedback because it sheds light on how learners react to radically different types and levels of feedback and because it also gives diagnostic feedback on reading in an SFL.

An analysis of existing types of feedback shows that, in principle, it is possible to provide a truly wide range of different types of feedback that cover all the levels postulated in, for example, the Hattie and Timperley model. It is likely that teachers and tests differ in the type, timing and amount of feedback that they can provide. Giving varied feedback is potentially easier for teachers because they interact with learners often for quite a long time and have many opportunities to observe, provide feedback, and guide learners to appropriate activities. The amount of feedback teachers provide to learners is obviously mediated by both such practical factors as the time available and the size of the groups and by more general, educational factors like teachers' training, experience, views of what types of feedback are effective (see Tarnanen & Huhta, 2011, and Chapter Nine in this book) and the traditions and characteristics of the educational system in which they work. Some researchers (Edelenbos & Kubanek-German, 2004) have proposed that teachers differ in terms of their diagnostic competence, which likely means that their ability to provide useful and different types of feedback also varies.

In contrast to what is possible in classrooms, most language tests provide a fairly limited range of feedback since it is very time-consuming and expensive to provide detailed feedback from paper-based tests. Moreover, the mandate of many tests does not require more than the reporting of an overall score. Thus, the typical test feedback is limited to an overall test score, which is problematic according to research we reviewed in this chapter, but it is the most heeded by users. Tests used by teachers in classrooms are the most flexible in this respect, as teachers often give the tests back to their students so that they can see how they did on the test overall and on each item. However, they, too, should not focus only on the task level, but try to expand feedback to cover strategy use.

Computer-based tests have obvious advantages in giving learners immediate and varied feedback (Alderson, 2005) and, indeed, some relatively new testing systems have been quite innovative when it comes to the feedback. DIALANG is the best-known example of this as it provides learners with a wide range of feedback that covers a range of theoretically important feedback levels. Research on DIALANG is thus interesting because it sheds light on how learners view different types of feedback provided by a computerized language testing system. The main conclusions of such studies are (1) that most learners regarded traditional test scores and task/item results as the most interesting and useful types of feedback, and (2) that feedback aimed at improving learners' metacognitive strategies (e.g., self-assessment feedback and advice for further learning) was considered somewhat useful. However, learners' opinions on these more innovative forms of feedback were divided; in addition, many learners appeared to be unsure what to think about such novel feedback. It is probably safe to conclude that feedback that goes beyond the task level is new to most language learners, and they would need practice and guidance in how to use such feedback. In fact, such feedback is likely novel to many language teachers, too, and some of them may tend to think that test scores are the most important type of feedback (Tang & Harrison, 2011). Ideally, feedback from a system like DIALANG is used under the guidance of the teacher and integrated into the everyday activities in the classroom.

There are, however, major gaps in our understanding of how diagnostic feedback from diagnostic assessments works in general and in reading in an SFL in particular. Research on diagnostic tests such as DIALANG has been limited to learners' perceptions of the usefulness of the feedback. While it is encouraging to find out that learners tend to believe diagnostic feedback is useful, we still lack empirical evidence about which types of feedback are effective in improving reading in an SFL, for example. Many users of DIALANG reported that the feedback they received increased their awareness of their own language skills and the nature of language proficiency in general. It may be that such awareness raising is one of the most notable effects of varied diagnostic feedback. Irrespective of the effects on learning outcomes that diagnostic feedback may have, it thus seems to improve at least some learner's understanding of themselves as language learners, which in itself is often an important goal in language education. One aspect of this still quite unknown territory is the effect on learning of feedback that focuses on the use of social and affective strategies. It appears clear from the large number of studies reviewed by Hattie (1999) and Hattie and Timperley (2007) that feedback focusing on metacognitive and cognitive strategies improves learning significantly. How these other types of strategies might improve learning, if they were focused on in feedback, needs more research.

Another gap in our understanding of the diagnosis of reading in an SFL concerns classrooms where most diagnostic assessment takes place and where most feedback is given. Alderson (2007) argues that we may improve our diagnostic procedures by studying what language teachers do when they gather information about their students' SFL reading skills and how they give students feedback. The next chapter will discuss classroom assessment to see what we might learn from that for diagnostic assessment.

9

DIAGNOSIS FROM THE PERSPECTIVE OF THE LANGUAGE CLASSROOM

It is fairly normal to assume that teachers are best placed to know what their learners are struggling with and what they are not having problems with. In fact, diagnosing learners' problems is generally said to be the responsibility of class teachers. Teacher Ingrid, responding to interviews described in Chapter Two, claimed that "we probably diagnose all day every day within the classroom context." Another teacher, Judith, claimed that her basic role as a class teacher was to diagnose if her students needed help with comprehension problems, whereupon she then referred the learners to a specialist teacher for remediation.

However, despite the fact that there is increasing interest in when and how teachers diagnose their learners' strengths and weaknesses in a second or foreign language (SFL) setting, there is little empirical evidence available in the literature as to exactly what teachers do or how they do it. There is even less information on how teachers diagnose problems specifically in reading in a second or foreign language. Furthermore, the role that learners themselves have in this kind of assessment is another little known aspect of diagnosis in the classroom.

The aim of this chapter is to present ideas and insights from previous work on diagnosing SFL reading, even if solid empirical research is rather scarce. We present examples of studies of classroom assessment that may be relevant for diagnosis even if the studies have not been labeled as 'diagnostic' by the researchers who carried them out. Studies of formative and dynamic assessment, in particular, appear to shed light on how language skills can be diagnosed in practice in the classroom. We discuss in some detail an example from the L1 reading literature (the Reading Recovery program by Clay, 1979) of what teachers of English as L1 do and how this can help teachers help learners in reading. The implications of this for teacher-based diagnosis of SFL reading are then discussed. We complement this review with an account of a sub-study in the

DIALUKI project, in which we interviewed a number of language teachers on how they go about diagnosing their students' SFL reading skills.

Toward the end of this chapter, we discuss a range of factors that are likely to affect how well teachers can diagnose their students' SFL reading skills, such as experience, knowing ones' students, class size, and the diagnostic assessment techniques used. We conclude the chapter by discussing how teachers' abilities to diagnose learners' SFL reading skills could be developed.

Previous Research on Classroom Assessment and Diagnosis by Teachers

Although this book focuses on diagnostic testing of reading and diagnostic reading tests, it is important to remember that tests are just one form of assessment and that assessment which takes place in classrooms by teachers (and also by the learners themselves) can yield diagnostically useful information. As we stated above, such assessment may not be called diagnostic but rather 'formative' or 'dynamic.' We discuss this next and then present examples and findings from studies that are relevant to the diagnosis of SFL reading.

General Characteristics of Assessment in the Classroom

As Pellegrino, Chudowsky, and Glaser (2001) note, classroom assessment is often understood as something done by the teacher for summative grading purposes, for example, in mid-term or end-of-course exams. However, exams represent only a fraction of the whole assessment process that goes on in classrooms. Classroom dialogue, questioning, seatwork and homework assignments, formal tests, less formal quizzes, projects, and portfolios are all examples of ways in which teachers observe student understanding and performance (Pellegrino et al., 2001; see also Davison & Leung, 2009).

Classroom assessment is often associated with formative assessment, which is contrasted with summative assessment for grading purposes. As is the case with so many other concepts in applied linguistics, formative assessment does not have one, fixed meaning. Usually, formative assessment is characterized as informal and fairly frequent assessment that takes place while learning and teaching are still happening. In addition, the results from these assessments are typically used by students to improve their learning (Davison & Leung, 2009). Formative assessment produces detailed information about their learners that helps teachers to direct their teaching (e.g., by working on the apparent gaps in learners' knowledge, ability, and skills). It also produces information for the learners that helps them to make progress. The above description of formative assessment sounds very familiar to those working on diagnostic assessment. The two have in fact often been used interchangeably in the assessment literature (e.g., Nitko, 1993; see Huhta, 2008, for a review) and the relationship between the two remains somewhat unclear to this day.

How much time do teachers spend on assessing their students? This probably depends on the teacher and the subject matter. What is considered as assessment also has an effect on estimates of the time spent on assessment in the classroom. Edelenbos and Kubanek-German (2004) report two studies in the Netherlands in which 49 English lessons in 20 primary schools were observed, which aimed at finding out about the teachers' assessment practices and the time they devoted to such activities. Teachers' behaviors were coded into categories including diagnostic and corrective behaviors. In this study, diagnostic behavior was defined very broadly: it included both formal tests (for both formative and summative purposes) and informal assessment activities such as checking understanding and homework, questioning, informal observation of both individuals and the whole class, assistance in interpreting feedback, and monitoring systematic errors (Edelenbos & Kubanek-German, 2004). Overall, diagnostic behaviors constituted over 11% of all behaviors, whereas correction accounted for about 6%. Diagnostic behaviors took place in four major contexts: during formal testing (administering and returning tests), during the repetition and discussion of previous lesson content, during exercises, and during summaries of new content.

A review of classroom assessment practices across subjects, mainly in science and mathematics, in mainstream primary and secondary education by Black and Wiliam (1998) revealed several weaknesses in teachers' assessment practices such as the dominance of summative assessment for grading purposes. Similar results were found by Rea-Dickins (2004) and Rea-Dickins and Gardner (2000). When teachers were asked about classroom assessment, they tended to stress the formal assessment mechanisms and understate observation-driven assessment. The findings do not mean that these teachers did not do any informal assessment; rather, they may have been accustomed to consider formative assessment as teaching, and therefore focused on summative assessment when asked specifically about assessment.

Teachers' Assessment Competence

Teachers clearly have a key role in assessing learners, although the exact nature of this role varies depending on a country's assessment culture. However, even in countries with frequent external testing, teachers assess their students for formative purposes, both informally and formally with tests. Thus, teachers' ability to assess must be an important factor in successful assessment for whatever purposes. Indeed, one of the conclusions of Rea-Dickins and Gardner's (2000) study of assessment of English as an additional language (EAL) in British primary schools was that "the knowledge that a teacher has about individual pupils, and about EAL development in general" is very important (p. 231). Much of this 'teacher knowledge,' as they call it, appears to be informal, undocumented information that teachers have about their pupils. Edelenbos and Kubanek-German (2004) refer to this type of knowledge as teachers' 'diagnostic competence.'

A diagnostically competent teacher is said to be able to interpret students' foreign language growth, skillfully dealing with assessment material and providing students with the help that they need in response to this diagnosis (Edelenbos & Kubanek-German, 2004). Another definition of a teacher's diagnostic competence comes from Doe (2011) who claims that it relates to "the teacher's competence using the diagnostic test and articulation of next steps for course planning" (p. 69).

Reading Assessment Procedures

Let us now move from a description of the general characteristics of classroom assessment to examine such assessments in more detail. What do teachers actually do when trying to find out about learners' reading skills? What tools or procedures do they use? How could such (potentially) diagnostic assessment be improved? The studies that we review below that shed light on these questions come from both L1 and SFL contexts.

Pijl (1992) studied 24 regular and 26 special education teachers in the Netherlands, focusing on the initial stages of reading development during the first years of primary education. The study described how teachers evaluate their students' progress in L1 reading tasks, how they register evaluation results and what implications for instruction are based on their evaluation data. The data were collected with the help of structured logbooks that the teachers kept for several weeks in which they described their evaluation procedures and instructional decisions.

Informal evaluation techniques such as 'accidental observations' and 'observations during task performance' were used most frequently, and often these two techniques were used together (Pijl, 1992). The combined use of different techniques was, on the whole, very common: On average, each reading task was assessed with two different techniques. Most teachers reported using more formal techniques such as 'giving a turn,' 'correcting exercises,' and 'applying a test' together with the above-mentioned informal ways of evaluating students' reading performance.

Only about a quarter of the evaluation results were recorded in the teachers' own files, although making notes in the worksheets or in the students' workbooks was also used (Pijl, 1992). On the whole, most of the tasks evaluated (54%) did not lead to any (written) records. The special education teachers differed from the regular teachers in that they used formal assessment instruments (i.e., tests) more often and also recorded students' performance in their files more regularly, which the researcher thought was a result of the training that the special education teachers had received.

The implications of the assessments for instruction were different for below average (i.e., students with difficulties in reading) and average students (Pijl, 1992). What happened with the average students was that the teacher simply let them go on to the next reading task and possibly gave them encouragement. The below average students were given encouragement more often than average students but they, too, were often simply given the next task. However, they were also significantly more often either given the same task to complete again, given re-instruction or more exercises to do. Hardly ever was either type of student given a task at a higher level (more demanding) as a result of an evaluation of their performance, not even the high-performing students, which the researcher interpreted to be due to the teachers' desire to prevent too much differentiation in how quickly different students made progress.

In the light of this study, Pijl (1992) finds it alarming that evaluation procedures do not lead to adjustments to instruction to meet the needs of the students. This may be because most informal evaluations, such as observations, go unrecorded, and only a minority of them (mostly tests and correction of homework or exercises) get recorded in the teacher's files. Therefore, as Pijl concludes, "the consequences [of evaluations] stay within the range of the teachers' 'normal' program" (p. 130). The researcher furthermore concludes that both regular and special education teachers in the primary schools

> try to gather an amount of information about student performance that enables them to correct difficulties or misconceptions and to go on with the teaching program. Making a detailed diagnosis and/or remedial plans is not the teacher's primary goal in evaluation. . . . In the perspective of the instruction of students with learning problems this is an alarming conclusion: evaluation procedures are not set up to serve as a basis for decisions on adjusting instruction to the needs of these students.
>
> (Pijl, 1992, p. 129)

Pijl speculates that this apparent lack of attention to diagnosis and remediation in (L1) reading could be due to the lack of useful tests or teachers' limited possibilities or capacities to individualize teaching.

In a more recent study, Bailey and Drummond (2006) were interested in how kindergarten and first-grade teachers in the United States identify students who struggle with literacy problems. They focused on 'a nascent risk group,' that is, those students who may be low achieving but who are not the ones with the most obvious difficulties in the class. Their rationale for choosing this group was that "the subtle complexities and inconsistencies in the performance profiles of these children may make the real roots of their problems difficult for teachers to diagnose" (Bailey & Drummond, 2006, p. 151). The study also aimed to find out whether language and literacy skills checklists can make teachers' perceptions become more evidence based.

The study included three measures (Bailey & Drummond, 2006). The teachers were first asked to pick one to four students whom they thought were falling behind the majority of the class. The teachers then had to give reasons for having identified the students by completing student nomination forms and answering the question "Please explain why this child was selected for inclusion in intervention (be as specific as possible)."

In order to find out about the teachers' orientation toward reading and their understanding of early literacy, Bailey and Drummond used concept maps. The teachers were asked to create maps indicating what they thought were the components and skills of early literacy and how these related to each other. To illustrate what a concept map might be like, they were given a map from another domain of child development (e.g., nutrition), showing its components (e.g., food, vitamins) and relationships between these components (e.g., causes). Some teachers also completed a comprehensive literacy checklist on their selected students by indicating whether the students were strong or weak on 47 statements describing skills, knowledge, or circumstances across seven domains, which varied from basic reading and cognitive skills to social interaction and motivation.

Bailey and Drummond's (2006) results show that the teachers identified at-risk students based on a mix of academic and social reasons, such as basic reading and writing skills, oral language abilities, and student shyness and quietness. When articulating their initial reasoning, few teachers relied on any documented sources and typically gave relatively vague reasons based on informal observation of the students. The use of detailed literacy checklists turned out to only slightly improve teachers' skill in analyzing reading problems.

Bailey and Drummond (2006) came to very similar conclusions about the teachers' diagnostic abilities as Pijl (1992). According to them,

> teachers may be having trouble diagnosing the exact nature of students' difficulties. In other words, they sense that something is wrong, but cannot pinpoint the particular problem. This finding may be a reflection of the degree of teacher knowledge of literacy processes.
>
> (Bailey & Drummond, 2006, p. 171)

Leung and Mohan (2004) also report a study that explored formative assessment practices using classroom observation. The research focused on fourth-grade classrooms in two multi-ethnic schools in England which included a mixture of English L1 and L2 speakers. The researchers used systemic functional linguistics to analyse teachers' and learners' talk during group activities completing reading comprehension tasks. Interestingly, Leung and Mohan show how skillful teachers can manage the discussion about texts in a way that is very likely to be beneficial not only for understanding the texts, but also for learning from them (see also Gibbons, 2003). When the texts were discussed in class, the teachers encouraged students to decide on their answers rather than guessing, and to provide reasons for their replies. Whenever necessary, the teachers repeated and clarified the criteria for deciding on answers. They also scaffolded the discussion about the texts with questions and comments, which led the learners to evaluate the correctness of their answers and to think about reasons for their decisions. Thus, the teachers often treated learners' answers as provisional rather than final, and the learners were encouraged to revise them if they were not exactly what was expected. The teachers observed in Leung and Mohan's study were in fact involved in a rather similar mediation process to the one that takes place in dynamic assessment (see Chapter Three).

Flynn and Rahbar's (1998) study sheds light on how different methods that teachers use to gather information about their students' language skills can complement each other. The researchers studied the prediction of English as L1 reading problems of kindergarten children in the United States and found that the combination of formal screening tests and assessment by the teachers resulted in a better prediction of reading problems than either of them alone. Some researchers (e.g., Johnston, 1987), however, argue that the teacher's role in the assessment (provided the teacher has enough expertise in what he or she is evaluating) is more important when compared to external tests because seeing the learner performing a task is likely to influence the instructional interactions that occur. "If the information is secondhand, no matter how detailed, it is much less likely to influence the automatic instructional interactions" (Johnston, 1987, p. 747).

Dynamic Assessment in the Classroom

The following examples illustrate how dynamic assessment (DA, discussed in more detail in Chapter Three) has been applied in the SFL classroom. Poehner (2009) offers examples of two kinds of group-based dynamic assessments that he calls concurrent and cumulative DA. In both the teacher conducts mediation not with one student but with several. The main difference between the two approaches appears to be that the cumulative group DA is more systematic in its attempt to push the whole group toward mastery of a problem.

Group DA is in fact very much like whole class instruction, as Poehner (2009) admits, but he argues that its "contribution to L2 education is that it renders classroom interactions more systematic and more attuned to learners' emergent abilities" (p. 488). Poehner and Lantolf (2005) consider the systematic nature of dynamic assessment to be one of its strengths compared to formative assessment, which they claim to be "a hit-or-miss process that varies from teacher to teacher and presumably even for the same teacher from episode to episode" (p. 254).

Davin (2013) studied how a combination of dynamic assessment and common instructional conversation could improve assessment by making it more systematic. The context was a combined fourth- and fifth-grade primary school Spanish foreign language classroom in the United States. Typical of interventionist dynamic assessment (see Chapter Three for details), the Spanish teacher used a hierarchical set of pre-planned prompts that increased in explicitness if the learner failed to provide an acceptable answer:

- pause with a questioning look;
- repetition of the entire phrase with emphasis on the source of error;

- repetition of the specific location of the error;
- provision of two or more options for the learner to choose from; and
- provision of an acceptable response and an explanation (Davin, 2013, p. 310).

The learner was given an opportunity to give the correct answer after each prompt. An important part of the assessment process was the systematic record-keeping by the teacher of the amount of mediation (prompts) that each student needed at different points in time and of the likely source of the error at each time. This allowed the teacher to keep track of students' progress and to provide them with systematized feedback during the mediation/assessment process.

Face-to-face dynamic assessment is usually an individual process with only the teacher and the student as participants. Davin extended the approach by utilizing practices typical of regular instructional conversation by having the teacher open the assessment to the entire class if the teacher considered that there was an opportunity for the others to learn from the mediation process carried out with an individual student. Thus, as a by-product, other students had an opportunity to benefit from the dynamic assessment of a single student.

Davin's (2013) examples mostly concern the productive skills, but they can conceivably be applied to the dynamic assessment of reading and to the combination of private and group-level mediation illustrated in that study.

Interestingly, it is the L1 reading literature and particularly the literature on learning to read in English as one's first language that detailed accounts are presented of what teachers do and how this can help them help learners in reading. This is particularly the case in the Reading Recovery programs developed to help children to learn to read in their first language, as described by Alderson (2005).

Reading Recovery Program Approach

One example of a Reading Recovery program comes from Clay (1979, 1985), who developed an approach to the early detection and treatment of reading difficulties in New Zealand in the late 1970s. The approach consists of two main phases: (1) administration of a Diagnostic Survey toward the end of the children's first year at school to all children who are not obviously making good progress in reading, and (2) administration of the actual Reading Recovery program activities to children identified as struggling readers in the Diagnostic Survey. (For a more recent example of developments in teaching reading in the L1, see the Reading and Writing Project at Teachers College, Columbia University, in the United States; http://readingandwritingproject.com/)

The Diagnostic Survey was developed by observing and describing reading behaviors in children with marked difficulties in beginning reading, and by observing teachers teaching reading so that teaching responses to learners' reading behavior during individual reading tuition sessions with those children could be described. Procedures for dealing with these difficulties were developed by observing teachers; by piloting, discussing, and modifying a large number of techniques; and by linking those techniques and teacher and pupil behaviors with theories about reading. Teachers were asked, for example, to explain why they used a certain technique or book, which factors influenced their decisions, and why they thought their pupils reacted in the way they did. Clay found that children's reading difficulties were very diverse. She also noted that teachers had difficulties in explaining or justifying their teaching and sometimes felt uncomfortable or embarrassed about articulating the basis of teaching decisions.

The procedures in the Diagnostic Survey were retained only if they had the potential to result in useful teaching procedures. Clay stresses the importance of using many observational tasks, since "no one technique is satisfactory on its own" (Clay, 1985, p. 16). The Diagnostic Survey is particularly concerned with recording the way the child deals with text, words and letters, rather than with test scores per se. The Survey includes a number of techniques, some of which are in fact tests of reading-related behaviors or contents: a Record of Reading Behavior on Books, Letter Identification, Concepts about Print, a Word Test using lists of words from the reading materials being used in class, a Writing Vocabulary Test, a Dictation, and Writing Samples.

The Record of Reading Behavior on Books technique involves a 'running record' of the child's text reading. This technique allows for the assessment of a child's reading performance as he or she reads aloud materials at three levels of difficulty. The reading takes about 10 minutes to complete, and the analysis involves marking every word read correctly, identifying every error made, and making notes about the child's self-corrections and their use of clues.

The Letter Identification technique aims to find out what ways of identifying letters a child uses (whether he or she uses the name of a letter, a sound that is acceptable for the letter, or responses such as "it begins like . . ."). The observer also records which letters the child confuses and which letters appear to be unknown.

The Concepts about Print test is a 5 to10 minutes task consisting of 24 items with detailed instructions for their administration that aims to explore the child's understanding of important features of printed language. These features include concepts like what is the front of a book, what is a letter or a word, what is the first letter in a word, what is the difference between upper case and lower case letters, what is the function of spaces and punctuation, and so forth.

The Word Test is a compilation of the 45 most frequent words of a specific Ready to Read book series. The test score indicates the extent to which a child masters the reading vocabulary in that book series.

In addition to the above techniques and tests, teachers are also advised to examine their pupil's writing behaviors by collecting examples of their writing (Writing Samples). This is justified by Clay (1979), since "a poor writing vocabulary may indicate that, despite all his efforts to read, a child is in fact taking very little notice of visual differences in print" (p. 22). Writing performances can tell the teacher, for example, whether the child has good letter formation, and how many letter forms he or she has acquired. In addition to collecting samples of learners' writing, the teacher administers other writing-related tests as part of the Diagnostic Survey. In the Writing Vocabulary Test, the child is asked to write down all the words he or she knows how to write. In the Dictation test, the child writes down simple sentences such as 'I have a big dog at home'; he or she is then given credit for every sound written correctly. Clay (1979) argues that "the scores give some indication of the child's ability to analyze the words s/he hears or says and to find some way of recording the sounds s/he hears as letters" (p. 24).

We are not aware of any such detailed advice to, or procedures for the use of, teachers of reading in an SFL. Therefore, the aim of the research to be reported below is to begin to understand how SFL reading teachers go about diagnosing their learners' strengths and problems.

An Interview Study of Diagnosing SFL Reading

As part of the DIALUKI study on diagnosing SFL reading and writing, 16 teachers of English as a foreign language from 12 different Finnish primary (Grades 1–6) and lower secondary schools (Grades 7–9) were interviewed. The purpose was to investigate what these language teachers say about diagnosis, and in what ways they practice diagnosis in their teaching routines and classroom activities. We aimed to find out how teachers actually identify or clarify the strengths and weaknesses of their pupils' SFL reading, how they treat these in order to achieve good learning results, and what they perceive to be the most effective approaches for providing challenges for pupils with good skills and helping those with weaker skills.

The interviews covered the following topics:

- Background of the teacher
- How texts are used in the classroom and how they are worked on
- What kind of texts are used
- Diagnosing reading and writing (observing the strengths and weaknesses of pupils, how pupils are assessed)
- The help available to those with difficulties in reading and writing.

The extracts translated (from the original Finnish) from the interview transcripts' areas covered are (a) Teachers' perceptions and methods of teaching reading, (b) challenges in teaching and assessing reading, and (c) diagnosis and treatment of reading skills. Table 9.1 gives the names and some background information of the five teachers whose interviews are quoted in this chapter.

TABLE 9.1 Background information of the teachers involved in the DIALUKI project and quoted in this chapter

Teacher	Years of experience	Current position and grades and subjects she has taught
Anna (F)	16 years	English teacher in a primary school, has taught also in lower and upper secondary school and adults
Tanja (F)	16 years	English teacher in a primary school
Laura (F)	6 years	English teacher in a lower secondary school, has also taught in primary school
Emma (F)	20 years	English and Swedish teacher in a lower secondary school
Kristiina (F)	15 years	English teacher in a lower secondary school, has also taught in primary and upper secondary school and adults

Note: F = female, M = male. Finnish primary school covers Grades 1 through 6 and school begins at the age of 7. From primary schools the pupils move on to lower secondary school at age 12 or 13 to begin Grade 7. Lower secondary school includes Grades 7–9.

Teachers' Perceptions and Methods of Teaching Reading

One of the most interesting points of the teacher interviews related to the different perceptions that the teachers had about teaching reading. For some, teaching reading was not at all easy, and many teachers were not easily able to describe their method of teaching reading. Several teachers answered this question by mentioning reading comprehension and translating English texts into Finnish.

In the following excerpt, teacher Kristiina talks about how she encouraged her pupils to search for main themes while reading, browsing rather than translating word for word. Kristiina describes reading as a *by-product*:

Kristiina on how she teaches reading in English:

> Interviewer: What kind of experiences do you have of teaching reading in English or what do you think about it?
>
> Kristiina: I have not really thought about it that way, it sort of comes like as a by-product, you sort of like read. I suppose you would have to think about it in some way, like how you do it. I have tried to teach pupils different kinds of texts so that—this we read intensively and this extensively. I have tried to encourage them by saying that if you do not understand everything that's okay, don't get stuck on it . . . I don't really have any training in how to teach, um, reading, because I am not a class teacher . . . teaching studies are very theoretical, I mean you learn while practicing it.

The teacher interviews suggested that reading in English is often an activity that is done as homework rather than in the classroom, where the focus is often on communication through speaking activities. Because reading exercises are so often done at home, some teachers felt that it is hard to check this aspect of language learning, as they could not be sure if the pupils had done their reading homework. They also reported that it was sometimes difficult to know if some pupils were participating when reading aloud was done as a group activity in the classroom.

Reliance on textbooks was very often seen in teachers' descriptions of their use of study materials. This is in line with an earlier questionnaire-based survey of foreign language teachers in lower secondary education in Finland; practically every one of the over 300 teachers surveyed reported the text and exercise books to be very important for their lesson plans (Luukka et al., 2008). The teachers involved in our interview study reported that the reading exercises they used came mostly from the textbook, especially in the primary school, and some teachers said that they follow very strictly (even 'slavishly') the outline of the book and its texts.

Why do language teachers in Finland rely on the textbook so much? One reason may be the fact that modern textbooks offer a variety of texts for different purposes. Especially those teachers who have been teaching for a long time said that English textbooks have changed—texts nowadays are more interesting, challenging, and appealing to pupils, and they offer a variety of texts for pupils with different skills. As one teacher said, the texts in textbooks "have a plot and they are inspiring and fun." Another thought that pupils are the ones who depend on textbooks, not necessarily the teacher.

Although reliance on textbooks came up in many interviews, there were a few teachers who seemed to have adopted a routine to use texts outside the textbook. For example, one teacher used extra texts (and gave extra credit points to those who read the texts) to motivate students and to provide them with more challenges.

The teacher interviews showed how vague the teachers' understanding of reading is. Most teachers did not seem to have a very clear idea of the construct of SFL reading, which is similar to the findings of Clay (1979) during the development of her Diagnostic Survey approach to L1 reading. One teacher's idea of learning to read in English simply by repeating English words after the teacher's model seems to suggest that some teachers at least consider reading in English rather unproblematic. The dominant role of the textbook in the FL classroom implies that textbooks can play an important role in the teachers' efforts to diagnose learners' reading skills and also in individualizing reading practice after whatever diagnosis has taken place.

Challenges in Teaching and Assessing Reading

The second issue arising in the teacher interviews with obvious relevance to diagnosis was the challenges that the teachers encountered when teaching and assessing reading in English. These were quite varied; especially among teachers working in lower secondary schools. Motivating the students in general and finding interesting texts appeared to be major issues at that level.

Teacher Emma on the challenges of teaching reading to 14- and -15-year-old teenagers:

> Emma: the most challenging thing is to get them to make an effort, that they would bother so much as to look at the word list [which is in a different part of the textbook than the text] when they get the text in front of them many are like "no, not this long," "I'm too tired." Then of course some pupils have difficulties in . . . putting together the main ideas, they cannot see what is the important point and they get stuck on the first. If they don't understand the first two sentences then it's game over, and that sort of [lack of] belief in your own abilities, but there are some brilliant characters who can do it fluently and can look up [the answer] right away . . . so I think that the real challenge in lower secondary classes is [that the pupils are not] making an effort . . . with the text.

Several teachers mentioned large group sizes and lack of time to get to know the learners as obstacles to finding out about the learners' strengths and weaknesses. This was particularly true for language teachers who moved between different schools and had up to 10 different classes to teach. Getting to know one's students takes time, and the larger the groups, the more time is required. One of the teachers very aptly referred to a new, unknown group of pupils as 'a faceless mass' that the teachers can only start to differentiate as time passes.

One challenge for the teachers seems to be the huge individual differences in students' English skills; several teachers reported that there is no 'average class,' but many have either very good or very poor skills in English.

Teacher Anna on challenges in teaching reading in English:

> Anna: There are substantial differences between pupils in fifth grade, it is unbelievable, those differences, at which levels some of them are . . . usually you have to differentiate teaching downward [for weaker students] in every class but now we have pupils with such strong skills that they require differentiation upward.

The challenges that the interviewed teachers mentioned also included motivating teenage learners, and getting to know individual students' strengths and weaknesses if the total number of students that the teacher had to teach was big and heterogeneous. Lack of motivation for reading or for studying the language in general is a very different problem from lack of vocabulary and grammatical knowledge when it comes to diagnosing reading in an SFL. The problem of teaching large groups underlines one of the most important features of effective diagnosis in the classroom: getting to know the students' skills and knowledge means that the teacher has to spend enough time with each student in order to know them well enough. Fleeting encounters and chance observations that go unrecorded do not lead to a detailed understanding of each student's strengths and weaknesses. The heterogeneity of the students poses a further, more practical challenge for the teacher: how to find ways and the time to individualize teaching.

Diagnosis and Treatment of Reading Skills

Teachers were also asked how they try to identify the strengths or weaknesses of their pupils. Most of them felt that the ability to diagnose comes through knowing the pupils over the course of time. Some said that noticing pupils' strengths and weaknesses is 'instinctive.' Diagnosing reading was something that they practiced by listening to pupils read aloud or by following their progress in classroom activities.

Teacher Tanja on how she finds out about students' strengths and weaknesses in reading in English:

> Tanja: Well, I don't know if I have really tried to consciously clarify those [strengths and weaknesses], except in the tests you have to, of course, in order to give grades to them, but it comes in the course of time; I mean when you have the same class for 1 year or 2 or 3 years then you just know it—you see and remember the pupil's face, you are like, oh, that's it, he was the one who was good at that and he was good at something else . . . it just comes in the course of time.

Some teachers with considerable teaching experience felt confident in their ability to find out how good their pupils were, but what they reported to us suggested that they were talking more about summative rather than formative/ diagnostic assessment, as they referred to students' level or used other such general terms about learners' proficiency. However, some teachers were able to specify in some detail the problems their students had in reading.

Teacher Anna on her students' reading problems:

> Well, I guess there are so many words that they don't understand and they are struggling to find the right one.

Teacher Laura on her students' reading difficulties:

> You do see in that foreign language too that if you don't read anything in Finnish it's terribly difficult . . . the longer the sentence . . . when you start that sentence well you get to the end, it's that understanding, that sentence understanding . . . that there's the beginning and the end . . . they in a way cannot join them so it doesn't make sense . . . even if you understand the beginning and you understand the end but you can't

construct a whole from it so that the reason behind that is that they don't have the habit of reading.

Teacher Laura on how she notices if new pupils in Grade 7 have reading problems in English:

> But you do notice it right away that a pupil . . . they mix those letters . . . and then it's terribly slow . . . it's precisely that comprehension of texts, it's so . . . well they don't understand those texts where it's the clearest is when a pupil can manage those vocabulary exercises and such and those simplest and easiest sentences, but when there are more difficult sentences and more difficult grammatical structures then they are somehow difficult.

Laura added that the explanations and translations of the more difficult words and structures of the text provided by the textbook were particularly helpful for such struggling pupils.

One teacher said that some learners' reading problems were probably due to them not knowing many of the words in the text, which prevented them from locating the place in the text needed for answering particular comprehension questions in a test situation. Another referred to problems with concentration and memory. Yet another teacher mentioned long, grammatically complex sentences as a particular problem in reading.

As far as the approaches to gathering information about learners' strengths and weaknesses is concerned, several teachers reported using a combination of tests and more informal approaches to gathering information about the learners' language skills, such as checking homework and observing classroom activities. Some teachers had developed very personalized approaches to identifying problems in reading. For example, one teacher had learned to notice how learners with problems in reading aloud texts in English tried to hide that fact when it was their turn to read.

Activities singled out as useful for identifying reading problems included translation of the text or parts of it, asking questions about the text (orally or in writing), and reading aloud. Silence during classroom activities was considered by some teachers to signify that a learner may have problems. Teachers sometimes reported being 'surprised' when a different source of information, such as a test or homework, provided them with new insights into the strengths or weaknesses that they had not been able to observe in the classroom.

The teachers who were able to describe in some detail their students' problems in reading in English mentioned students' lack of vocabulary knowledge and their problems in making sense of the meaning at sentence level (connecting the beginning and end of sentences in a meaningful way, especially in longer and more complex sentences). The fact that the teachers were mostly in favor of using both tests and informal observation of reading performance is similar to the approach adopted in the L1 Reading Recovery program reported in Clay (1979, 1985).

Typically, the interviewed DIALUKI teachers specializing in English in the primary school reported discussing the pupils with their class teacher and the special education teacher, especially when those pupils appeared to struggle, in order to find out how they were doing in L1 and other subjects and if they had been diagnosed as having any learning problems. In the teachers' experience, pupils with problems in L1 tended to have problems in English, too. Some modified this by saying that this was not always automatically so, and one even reported a pupil who turned out to have a specific problem in learning a foreign language although the special education teacher had initially dismissed her diagnosis.

Discussion and Conclusions

We will first summarize the main challenges that language teachers face when attempting to diagnose their learners' problems in reading in an SFL. After that we will discuss a range of factors that can have an effect on how easy or difficult it is to diagnose reading. We will then briefly discuss selected techniques that can, in addition to those mentioned in the reviews of research, help teachers to gather diagnostic information from their students. Finally, we will revisit the notion of a language teacher's diagnostic competence.

Perhaps the main challenge for diagnostic assessment in the classroom that emerges from the studies reviewed here is teachers' limited understanding of what reading involves. This was reported by Clay (1979) and by Bailey and Drummond (2006), and it was also very clear in the DIALUKI interviews. Some teachers did not think that they consciously taught reading, although, when prompted, they could describe in some detail how they instructed their students to work with texts. It is likely that many SFL teachers do not consider themselves specifically as teachers of reading because that is seen as the task of the mother-tongue teacher. The focus of foreign language teaching in primary and lower secondary education in Finland is on the development of oral skills, according to the National Core Curriculum (National Board of Education, 2004), which is also likely to contribute to the lack of emphasis on reading among the teachers interviewed.

Because Finnish is an extremely regular language in the correspondence between letters and sounds, most children learn to read in Finnish during the first few months at school. Lack of apparent reading problems in L1 may lead SFL teachers to believe that reading in another language is merely a matter of learning new words and grammatical rules, and of learning to pronounce the words in a comprehensible way.

It was clear in the interviews that the teachers were quite capable of describing the procedures by which they tried to find out about the strengths and weaknesses of their students. They were usually less able to articulate which aspects of reading they paid attention to when doing this. There were some exceptions to this general lack of a more detailed analysis of learners' reading performance, which may indicate that some teachers had made progress in developing their 'diagnostic competence' (see Edelenbos & Kubanek-German, 2004).

A somewhat different challenge to diagnostic assessment emerged in the DIALUKI interviews that seems to relate to the finding by, for example, Black and Wiliam (1998), that summative assessment often dominates teachers' thinking of all kinds of assessment. The DIALUKI interviews suggest that teachers operate at several different levels when they assess their pupils and that the broader levels in fact referred to summative rather than formative/diagnostic assessment. At the broadest level, the teachers had a clear idea of how good or poor whole groups of students were and thus whether they could do certain exercises with them or not. This had obviously to do with students' age and grade level (older students being better), but it is also possible that groups or classes at the same grade level might differ clearly from each other. Within the class level, teachers developed an understanding of which learners were good or poor in English (Black & Wiliam, 1998, also noted that teachers are usually good at comparing students, but may struggle with criterion-referenced interpretation of their skills). At the level of the macro-skills or areas of language, the teachers seemed to be able to discern how individual learners' skill profiles might differ. For example, students with good oral skills might have problems in writing. Or students who might be unwilling (and possibly unable) to speak much during the lessons may have a rather good command of the written language. Teachers referred to such cases as 'surprises,' which suggests that the default expectation may be that learners have a fairly even skill profiles.

All the above levels (group, individual, macro-skill) are very relevant to summative assessment for grading purposes. They are useful for formative or diagnostic purposes only in rather limited ways. It obviously makes sense to be aware of individual learners' and entire groups' overall level of proficiency when deciding which activities are relevant to them. And it is good to know about individuals' strengths and weaknesses in, for example, speaking versus writing to select for them exercises that focus on their weaker skills. However, we argue that a more effective diagnosis needs to get at a more detailed level than those described above as that would enable the setting of sufficiently concrete goals that are achievable in a relatively short period of time (see Chapter Eight on the importance of such goals). It would also enable the design of tasks that are relevant to the specific aspects of, for example, reading that are problematic for the learner.

Factors That Can Affect Diagnostic Assessment by Teachers

The following points summarize the factors that can affect the diagnosis by language teachers based on both the DIALUKI teacher interviews and the studies reviewed in this chapter.

Experience can matter. More experienced teachers interviewed in the DIALUKI study mentioned having noticed that their ability to spot problems had improved over time. This was often referred to as an 'instinct,' which appeared to be a rather unanalyzed and unanalyzable skill, although the teachers were usually able to describe that in some more detail when prompted to do so. We should caution, however, against assuming that experience alone is the answer. Johnston (1987), discussing assessment and diagnosis of L1 reading in the classroom, points out that expertise in evaluating reading is complex and does not come simply with years of classroom experience, but requires effort and familiarity with what happens in reading and in learning to read.

Getting to know your students matters: Learning to know students' abilities and characteristics at anything more than a very superficial level takes considerable time, and this simple fact was mentioned in various ways by practically all DIALUKI teachers. In the Finnish primary school, the class teacher typically takes his or her own class from grade one to the end of primary school in grade six. Also, the English teacher spends at least 4 years with the pupils, as in most schools the first foreign language (English in over 90% of schools) starts in Grade 3. In the lower secondary school, teachers can spend 3 years with the same students (from Grade 7 to Grade 9). Thus, teachers have plenty of time to get to know the learners. Getting to know the students and, thus, having time to diagnose them, is only a temporary problem if the same teacher continues teaching the same students. It is, however, a serious impediment for teachers who only or mostly work as temporary replacement teachers substituting teachers who are away on sick or maternity leave.

Class size/number of learners may matter. Large class size is obviously an obstacle that slows down the process of learning and remembering individual learners' strengths and weaknesses. However, the issue may be modified by other factors. This is clearly a challenge in the first term when the teacher starts working with new students; over time, the teacher is certain to get to know the students better. This is probably an issue that affects some teachers more than others depending on how their work is organized. Some foreign language teachers at primary level work in only one or two big schools, others have to teach in several different schools in the region and, thus, lack a permanent 'home base' with regular contacts to pupils or other teachers outside the lessons.

Systematicity and careful recording matter. Systematic gathering of data on student performance, with a range of techniques, increases the reliability and representativeness of the information on which to base diagnosis (Clay, 1985; Bailey & Drummond, 2006). It is also important that the teacher records the gathered information for him- or herself, as it has been found that unrecorded observations lead to action less often than information that the teacher has written down in some form.

Use of multiple techniques and sources of information matters: Previous research (Clay, 1985; Flynn & Rahbar, 1998) cautions against reliance on any one source of information about learners' strengths and weaknesses. The teachers interviewed in the DIALUKI study also reported using a variety of sources of information. Although some of them preferred either formal tests or informal observations, most reported making use of both types of assessment. Indeed, one of the questions that need further research is what specific information teachers can obtain about learners' strengths and especially weaknesses during classroom activities and how such information might best be gathered. What information should be gathered with the help of tests? Monitoring performance and progress during lessons is challenging, if the groups are big, as was mentioned by several teachers. The fact that the test results produced surprises for some teachers who had been observing the students in question in the classroom also suggests there are limitations to what can be learned about pupils during the lessons. Some teachers seem clearly to prefer tests as sources of information; is this because tests are better instruments for gathering detailed diagnostic information, or is it because some teachers cannot or do not want to do systematic monitoring of learners' classroom performance for diagnostic purposes?

The method of gathering diagnostic information may matter when it comes to acting on that information. Some research (e.g., Pijl, 1992) suggests that teachers may place greater value on data from sources that they considered more reliable and objective (e.g., tests) than their informal observations. Importantly, the most common consequence of informal observation of learners performing tasks was not a change in the instruction, but simply a decision to move to the next task. In contrast, the correction of tests and homework was more likely to result in the teacher taking corrective action.

Consultation with other teachers matters: Language teachers should not forget that they are not alone, and that they can usually discuss their students' problems with colleagues who teach the same students. It is also often possible to consult a specialist such as a special education teacher or a psychologist if the teacher suspects that a student has a learning problem and possibly needs remedial action. This was indeed what several teachers interviewed in the DIALUKI study reported doing.

It is often difficult to distinguish between language problems, learning problems, lack of motivation, neglect of homework, problems at home, and low self-esteem. A similar mixture of linguistic and socio-economic reasons was also found by Bailey and Drummond (2006) to be among the key factors that L1 teachers in their study used to explain reading problems. It appears that a consideration of the above factors is one of the first steps foreign language teachers take in order to understand why a student struggles with the language. It is at this stage that they presumably consult the classroom teacher and the special education teacher (e.g., to rule out more general learning problems or dyslexia). If the learner does not appear to have such problems, the teacher has to decide how to tackle the combination of low achievement, low motivation and neglect of homework that are probably reciprocally linked. Is there a way to increase the learner's motivation to learn the language? If the teacher can identify particular strengths and weaknesses in the learner's language skills, would it be better to work on their strengths or on their weaknesses to boost their motivation and self-esteem?

Techniques for Obtaining Diagnostic Information About Reading

One of the main themes that we have discussed in this chapter has been the variety of approaches that language teachers typically use to obtain information that is potentially diagnostically useful. These range from formal tests for summative and formative purposes to different informal techniques such as observing classroom activities, analyzing learners' homework, and listening to how learners read aloud. We conclude this chapter by presenting a few additional approaches to the assessment of reading that may be particularly useful for gathering diagnostic information about SFL learners' reading skills in the classroom, but that have been referred to only indirectly in the previous discussion, if at all. These approaches are taken from Hedgcock and Ferris (2009) and are summarized below:

- *Talking about reading*: Conversations between the teacher and the student or between students about reading in general and about particular texts they have just read and the problems encountered in them is a very straightforward approach suitable for assessment in the classroom (see Alderson, 2000, p. 336). Such interaction about reading has the added benefit that it engages the students themselves in the diagnostic process and may make them more aware of their reading and increase their ability to self-regulate their reading (this last point is also the aim of certain types of feedback; see Chapter Eight on feedback). It is entirely possible that sometimes teachers engage in such discussions with their students as a result of observing their reading behavior in the classroom—so some instances of 'observing reading activities' reported in the research literature and reviewed in this chapter may be about 'talking about reading.' It should be noted here that the teacher asking questions about the text can also be useful but it can also be very different from actually discussing the text, if the teacher answers his or her own questions almost immediately without giving the learners enough time to respond.
- *Using a reading journal*: This is an informal journal/notebook in which the students write their notes, thoughts, questions, summaries, reviews, and so forth, of the texts they have read. Such journals can be used by learners to monitor their comprehension and to make comprehension visible, among other things (see also Aebersold & Field, 1997).
- *Using a literacy portfolio*: Similar to other portfolios, a literacy portfolio can take many forms and can include both formal examples of reading such as tests and informal student products (e.g., selected entries from a reading journal) and also self-assessment by the student.

• *Learner self-assessment:* Self-assessment of strengths and weaknesses in reading is an activity that can enhance learners' awareness of their reading; it is also a way for the learners to generate feedback for themselves to complement information that comes mainly from the teacher and from the tests taken in the classroom. Discussing L1 readers, Johnston (1987) claims that failure of the learner to self-correct, because of lack of self-assessment skills, is "probably the clearest indicator of reading difficulties" (p. 746).

Toward Teachers' Diagnostic Competence

Language teachers develop knowledge about testing and assessment as part of their training and in their work with students in the classroom. The most prominent function of assessment for most teachers is summative assessment, in order to give grades, and they often worry considerably about the quality and fairness of their summative assessments. We argue that it is equally important that teachers become experts in formative and diagnostic assessment and that they develop their 'diagnostic competence.'

A key component of an SFL teacher's diagnostic competence, according to Edelenbos and Kubanek-German (2004) is an ability to interpret students' foreign language growth. In the context of reading in an SFL, this means an understanding of the construct of reading and its development. Thus, knowledge about different techniques to obtain diagnostic information as described above, while obviously important, is not enough for teachers. They also need to learn about the construct itself, about the reading process and factors that are related to it and can affect it (see also Clay, 1985).

It was apparent, for example, in the teacher interviews carried out in the DIA-LUKI project that teachers varied considerably in how far they reported going beyond the unspecified reading skill when they try to find out about the learners' strengths and weaknesses. Only rarely did the teachers talk about the learners' reading ability by referring to the skills and concepts that theories of reading use, such as distinguishing main ideas from details or the role of memory in reading. This suggests that these theories were not familiar to the teachers or, at least, were not made use of when they attempted to diagnose their students' reading.

However, teachers should develop an understanding of what is involved in reading in both L1 and SFL or, as Johnston (1987) argues, they should be helped to become experts in evaluating the process of literacy development. As far as reading specifically in English as L1 is concerned, Moats (2001, quoted in Bailey & Drummond, 2006) claims that teachers should develop, for example, their ability to differentiate phonemic awareness, phonological processing, and phonics before they can recognize students' difficulties and give them accurate feedback related to those aspects of reading.

Becoming an expert in reading in an SFL is thus a cornerstone of a teacher's diagnostic competence. There is, however, more to skillful diagnosis than knowledge about the construct being assessed. Johnston (1987) summarizes the expertise that a good L1 (English) reading teacher needs in the following way:

> Aside from the ability to see and hear patterns in the development of reading and writing processes, experts have procedural knowledge. In the case of classroom evaluation experts, this involves, for example, how to set a context so that certain behaviors are most likely to occur, how to record those behaviors, file and update the records, and prevent some children from being missed.
>
> (p. 745)

Johnston's definition reminds us of the importance of the entire process of diagnosis, and of the need to be systematic in one's elicitation of data and performances from the learners on which to base a diagnosis, and also to be systematic in recording one's observations so that they can be acted on. In order for the diagnosis to be of any use, all the steps from identifying that something is a problem in a learner's reading to implementing activities that aim at addressing the problem should be taken.

In the next and final chapter of this book we will discuss the entire diagnostic chain that needs to be in place for diagnosis to have an effect on reading in an SFL. We will focus on describing how research on diagnosing SFL proficiency and its development could be carried out and on what appear to be the main points and issues in diagnosing reading in an SFL, and therefore, which suggest areas in which more research needs to be done.

10

STATE OF THE ART OF THE DIAGNOSIS OF SFL READING AND THE CHALLENGES AHEAD

In this final chapter we will first summarize the key points of the previous chapters by focusing on the main ideas that appear particularly important for improving our understanding of how reading in a second or foreign language (SFL) might be diagnosed. We will then discuss the whole diagnostic process because we believe that it is useful to see diagnosis as one step in a process that, hopefully, leads to some action that addresses the problems identified through diagnosis. In the remainder of the chapter we will address a range of issues and topics that need to be studied further that arise from the review of research presented in this book.

Chapter Summaries

Chapter One began this book with the observation that the diagnostic testing of second or foreign language ability is an undeveloped field, as we currently have no theory of how SFL diagnosis should be carried out. Nor is it clear what principles and procedures diagnosis should follow and how practitioners should go about doing diagnosis.

Chapter Two explored how diagnosis is theorized and carried out in a diverse range of professions with a view to finding commonalities, which can be applied to language assessment and which could be developed into a set of hypothesized features and principles, if not yet a theory. One aim of the chapter was to set an agenda and a direction for how such a theory might be realized.

Ten informants were interviewed ranging from a car mechanic and a computer systems support manager to medical experts, psychologists, and teachers specializing in literacy and reading difficulties.

The main conclusions for SFL reading drawn from the interviews can be summarized as follows:

- Diagnosis begins with a comparison with normal behavior or norms.
- Diagnosis requires that there are theoretically grounded methods, procedures, tasks, techniques, tests, and guidelines for the identification and categorization of problems.
- Technology plays an increasingly important role in diagnosis.
- Knowledge of the area to be diagnosed is crucial and so is experience in doing diagnosis.
- Treatment or action needs to complement diagnosis.
- Self-report and self-assessment are often an important part of diagnosis.
- Diagnosis is often multi-disciplinary (the diagnostician seeks help from other experts).
- Development of a knowledge base of problems and causes of difficulties in SFL reading is essential.
- There is a need for the training of SFL teachers in the diagnosis of strengths and weaknesses, especially but not only in SFL reading.

Chapter Three set out to develop a framework for SFL diagnosis by examining the literature on diagnosis. A number of hypothetical features are proposed that diagnostic SFL tests are likely to display, as diagnostic tests are more likely to focus on discrete language skills than on integrated higher-order skills. A number of recent SFL tests were introduced that aim to be diagnostic (DIALANG, DELNA, and DELTA), which we illustrated in more depth in subsequent chapters.

These 'diagnostic' SFL reading tests contain items that aim at tapping different aspects of reading such as understanding the main idea, understanding details or making inferences. This, however, cannot be a distinguishing feature of a diagnostic test because more general reading tests, such as the PISA or TOEFL tests, also use items tapping various components of reading. The provision of detailed, immediate feedback to individual learners on the different aspects of reading and its underlying processes is likely one key characteristic that differentiates diagnostic reading tests from proficiency and achievement tests that, at best, only report a total score for reading.

Dynamic assessment (DA) seeks to establish what learners can do independently and what they can do individually in face-to-face interaction between a learner and a teacher. However, computerized group tests could be designed that implement DA principles and provide item-level feedback to test takers.

Cognitive diagnostic assessment (CDA) involves content analyses of the skills, sub-skills, and processes engaged by SFL reading tests. Item-level test results are analyzed by statistical modeling to identify individuals' ability to engage in such processes. What is needed is the application of CDA, not to proficiency tests but to tests that are designed specifically for diagnosis. Obviously, meaningful diagnosis involves well-grounded understanding of relevant constructs so that test items can be meaningfully related to different aspects of the constructs.

Chapter Four addressed the construct of reading in a second or foreign language; we reviewed what both L1 and SFL reading research have to say about reading. There are numerous theories of reading, but some themes appear to be common and can thus serve as the basis for constructing and evaluating the validity of diagnostic reading tests.

One of the key characteristics of diagnostic assessment presented in the literature is that diagnosis involves a detailed analysis of performance. Reading has many components and many different levels. Therefore, diagnostic reading tests that attempt to measure different components of reading are, in principle, on the right track, although whether they have managed to select the diagnostically most useful components and operationalize them properly is still unclear.

Reading consists of at least two kinds of processes, commonly called lower-level and higher-level processes. Both levels are relevant to diagnostic testing. Lower-level processes include recognizing the sounds of a language through print, word recognition, syntactic parsing, and encoding meaning as propositions. Working memory, which we address in Chapter Six, has a key role in both these processes. Higher-level processes involve skills and resources (e.g., background, topical, and cultural knowledge), strategies, inferences, and monitoring of comprehension. In higher-level processes, a distinction is made between the ability to extract the meaning that the writer has attempted to convey (where the reader builds a text model of comprehension) and the interpretation that the reader makes, which is affected both by the reader's knowledge and his/her purpose in reading (this is known as the reader's situation model of the text). It is assumed that many weaker SFL readers rely too much on a situation model of comprehension, based on what little they manage to understand of the text, which can lead them astray when they try to build a text model (i.e., when trying to understand the writer's intended meaning).

Reading researchers commonly distinguish between reading product and reading process. Diagnosticians want to know both what a reader has understood or misunderstood, and why. The product of reading is typically what one has understood, demonstrated through one's answers to comprehension questions or summaries. The process of reading, however, is normally silent, invisible, internal to the reader, and rarely externalized. The problem in diagnosing the products of reading is that *what* one has understood may well be influenced by *how* the researcher has elicited the (mis)understanding. Therefore, the reading task and its demands affect the picture that the diagnostician gets of learners' strengths and weaknesses in reading.

Metacognitive awareness plays a role in comprehension because weaker readers are less likely to plan for, monitor, and evaluate their (in)comprehension effectively and accurately. All readers experience difficulty at some point: the problem for diagnosis is to know when difficulties are due to wider problems with text processing, with underlying skills, with linguistic, cognitive, or strategic competences, or with something completely different, such as lack of motivation.

In the second half of this chapter, we described in much more detail the nature of the reading tests used in recent diagnostic SFL tests, and considered how well they could be said to be diagnostic.

DIALUKI is an ongoing research project that aims to explore the diagnostic potential of a wide range of linguistic, cognitive, affective, and background variables. The outcomes of this research may well lead to the development of more sensitive diagnostic tools than currently exist for SFL reading. Therefore, Chapters Five to Nine presented more information both about the results from DIALUKI, and the various non-reading measures used in DIALUKI.

Chapter Five began the process of discussing in greater detail research that sheds light on factors that have been found to correlate with performance on L1 and SFL reading tests. This discussion began with addressing in this chapter the linguistic basis of SFL reading, in particular the role of vocabulary and grammatical knowledge in SFL reading.

The research reviewed indicated that while vocabulary knowledge seems to be more important in SFL reading than grammatical knowledge, there are circumstances when grammatical knowledge may be more crucial. However, clearly both types of knowledge are needed in most reading tasks. The role of vocabulary knowledge compared with grammar knowledge may vary according to the purpose of reading, the type of text and task, or even learner characteristics. Recent thinking (Purpura, 2004a, 2014a; Alderson & Kremmel, 2013) suggests that the distinction between the two is probably a false dichotomy and it makes more sense to consider both aspects to lie on a continuum of lexicogrammar.

The DIALUKI study found a close relationship between SFL reading and performance on a simple segmentation task in L1 or SFL. Furthermore, the learners' L1 is likely to influence which linguistic measures are most strongly related to reading performance, and thus potentially most diagnostically useful. This clearly has relevance to the design of diagnostic tests and test items.

We presented concrete examples of diagnostic vocabulary and grammar tests. While many vocabulary and grammatical tasks are somewhat limited, there are some interesting possibilities that add new, nontraditional dimensions to linguistic knowledge (e.g., the segmentation tasks mentioned above and tests of formulaic sequences). We also explored how diagnostic testing might be enhanced by automated analysis of the characteristics of texts.

Chapter Six focused on the cognitive demands of the reading process and on how the process leads to the reading product (i.e., comprehension). We examined the role in SFL reading of the basic cognitive skills in both lower- and higher-level reading processes. Learners' ability to perform on the more basic cognitive tasks that reflect the effectiveness of their working memory, phonological processing, or access to vocabulary in memory can be used to predict L1 reading difficulties. DIALUKI therefore explored the role of such tasks in SFL reading, where the cognitive processes were tested in both the learners' L1 and in their SFL. DIALUKI findings to date from cross-sectional and longitudinal studies show that although cognitive measures in the learners' first language do predict a degree of variance in their SFL reading performance, much stronger predictions are achieved when the same measures are couched in the target SFL language.

Because problems in these basic skills may result in problems in higher-level reading abilities, such basic skills have diagnostic potential. The fact that different languages use different writing systems makes the role of sound-symbol mapping in reading problems quite different across writing systems. Thus, diagnosis of reading may well need to be language specific, at least to some extent.

To become a more fluent reader, one must also be efficient in recognizing words. Fast word recognition depends partly on vocabulary size, so vocabulary size tests are frequently used in diagnosis. It is also important that the recognition of most words in a text becomes automatic, as this frees up resources for fluent reading and comprehension of the text.

Working memory is also crucial in reading. Low working memory capacity impedes comprehension because a reader has insufficient resources to make inferences or connect one's background knowledge to what is read. It may also make deficient phonological processing even worse by causing the reader to forget the beginning of the sentence by the time they reach the end of the sentence.

Chapter Seven discussed how reading might be related to language learners' background characteristics and motivation to learn and use the second or foreign language. Background factors that have a relationship with reading performance include where learners live (country or region, urban or rural), family socioeconomic status, and the characteristics of the school that they attend. Also, the better educated the parents, the better the child's reading skills.

DIALUKI explored several potential indicators in learners' backgrounds of problems in L1 or SFL reading, such as attendance in special education classes, and occurrence of reading difficulties in the child's family. Even one indicator of potential problems was enough to 'predict' that the learner belonged to the weaker group of readers.

Learners' background may be interesting, but it is in most cases not very useful for diagnostic purposes, because it is not usually possible to do anything about learners' backgrounds, such as the education or socioeconomic status of the parents.

This chapter also examined learners' motivation to learn and use an SFL. Motivation is particularly interesting from the diagnostic point of view because it is a factor that is arguably more amenable to change. Affecting a learner's motivation may not be easy but it is an issue that the language teaching profession is used to addressing, by trying to ensure that, for example, the materials, the approach to teaching, and the learning environment in general are as interesting and relevant as possible.

The DIALUKI study found that the learners' SFL self-concept, anxiety, motivational intensity, and self-regulation were related, to varying degrees, depending on the group studied, to learners' SFL reading performance. However, it is difficult to say if low SFL self-concept and high anxiety are somehow 'causing' poor SFL reading performance. More likely it is the case, at least with some learners, that poor results, poor SFL self-concept and higher anxiety form a vicious circle where these different factors reinforce each other. The learners' ability to regulate their learning (e.g., "I try to find opportunities to practice my English") is particularly interesting. Inability to regulate (i.e., to plan, monitor, and modify) one's SFL learning and use can conceivably be acted on and improved.

Chapter Eight addressed the role of feedback in the diagnostic process. Feedback is a key component in diagnostic assessment because it conveys the results and interpretations of the diagnosis to those who are in a position to do something with that information, such as take action to address an identified weakness. Usually, the provider of the feedback is the teacher, but feedback may be built into a computerized system that presents it directly to the learner, or both to the learner and the teacher.

Feedback could improve learners' use of different kinds of learning and reading strategies that help them to understand a particular text they are reading and, more generally, to take action that improves their reading in the longer run (e.g., strategies for selecting suitable texts to read in the future).

Combining feedback about learners' performance on a particular reading task with feedback that tries to improve learners' reading process (e.g., monitoring of comprehension) and regulation of their learning (e.g., setting own goals for reading) is characteristic of recent thinking about diagnostic feedback. In addition, diagnostic feedback may also contain hints or explicit proposals about the action the learners should take to remedy the problem identified in their performance, which echoes what is done in dynamic assessment. Furthermore, diagnostic feedback need not be limited to external sources, but may be generated by the learners themselves. This obviously involves an ability to self-assess, which is a feature of diagnosis often identified in other areas than language education (see the interviews in Chapter Two with medical doctors, psychologists, and diagnosticians). The hidden nature of reading processes further argues for a considerably bigger role for self-assessment in the diagnosis of SFL reading.

Chapter Nine discussed how language teachers might be best placed to know what their learners' SFL reading problems are. However, we lack evidence as to exactly what or how teachers diagnose their students' SFL reading.

The detailed advice that teachers give in Reading Recovery programs for L1 reading may be relevant for the development of similar procedures for SFL reading. Such advice originated in a diagnostic survey which observed and described L1 reading behaviors in children with marked difficulties in beginning L1 reading and by observing teachers teaching reading to those children. Based on the observations, procedures for dealing with reading difficulties were developed and linked with theories about L1 reading. Such a survey of the teaching of SFL reading could be very useful.

Teacher interviews in the DIALUKI project shed light on how SFL reading teachers go about diagnosing their learners' reading problems. The research suggested that teachers' experience in teaching reading is important. Teachers can develop an intuitive understanding of what a particular learner's problems might be and how to address them, but this requires the teacher to spend enough time with the learner during a sufficiently long period of time. Systematic recording of potentially diagnostic evidence is important. It is also important for teachers to consult other experts, such as teachers of learning disabled pupils and school psychologists, to establish the possible causes of the perceived weaknesses in the learner's SFL reading.

It is, however, often difficult to distinguish between language problems, learning problems, lack of motivation, neglect of homework, problems at home, and low self-esteem. Consultation both with school colleagues and the child's parents or guardians can significantly help in narrowing down the likely reasons for the child's SFL reading problems.

It was clear from the teacher interviews that, apart from the practical problem of knowing each pupil in a large class well enough to identify the causes of their problems, the main challenges for diagnostic assessment in the classroom are teachers' limited understanding of what reading involves and a lack of appropriate tools for diagnosing learners' SFL reading skills. Therefore, the key ingredients in improving diagnostic assessment in classrooms are, first, an increase in teachers' diagnostic competence, and second, the development of similar tools and procedures for diagnosing SFL reading as have been developed for diagnosing L1 reading problems.

Diagnosis as a Single Event vs. Diagnosis as a Chain of Action

Having summarized the key points of the previous chapters in this volume, we will next discuss the whole diagnostic process: of what does it consist? The diagnosis of reading in SFL can be seen as being limited to the identification of a particular problem in a learner's reading skills. However, it is also possible to take a broader view and consider what precedes and what follows such a diagnosis, and look at the entire diagnostic process.

As has been argued before (Alderson, 2005, 2007; Alderson & Huhta, 2011), a sufficiently detailed understanding of the constructs that are of interest and of their development is a necessary prerequisite for useful diagnosis. Construct definitions then need to be operationalized as diagnostic tests and other diagnostic assessment procedures. Only after these steps have been accomplished successfully can we diagnose learners' strengths and weaknesses. The results of the diagnostic procedures must be interpreted properly and communicated to the interested parties, such as the teacher and the learner. That is, the main stakeholders should get feedback in a form that is understandable to them. And then some action (e.g., treatment, remediation, intervention) should take place that leads to an improvement in the weaknesses that were identified.

As we reported in Chapter Two, and in the beginning of the above summaries, the relationship between diagnosis and treatment is viewed differently depending on the field, such as computer science or medicine. In some fields, the two are considered to be distinct acts that follow each other in a linear fashion, whereas in other fields they often intertwine and take place simultaneously in an iterative fashion. However, it is important to be aware of the fact that the usefulness of the diagnosis of SFL reading depends on the success of the entire process. An elaborated understanding of constructs and the successful identification of a problem in a learner's skills are of no use if there is a failure to communicate that finding in an understandable fashion to learners and/or their teachers, or if they fail to take appropriate action based on that feedback. The entire diagnostic chain must be followed through for diagnosis to have the desired effect.

An example of how the diagnostic process can be broken was mentioned in Chapter Three, where it was reported that the information produced by a diagnostic testing project described by Shohamy (1992) was ignored by some of the collaborating schools. While we do not know why this was the case in that particular context, it is a good example of a broader obstacle that diagnostic testing has to tackle: For diagnosis to be of any use, some action must take place based on the diagnosis. One of the reasons that the diagnostic process may be broken is the fact that diagnosis takes time and so does turning that information into useful diagnostic feedback and action. As Ebel and Frisbie (1991) put it, one of the reasons for the lack of success of diagnosis in educational contexts is that "effective diagnosis and remediation take a great deal more time than most teachers have or most students would be willing to devote" (p. 309).

Another reason why diagnostic information may not be acted on—or sought after in the first place—could be the more important role given to summative testing in many contexts, as discussed in Chapter Nine on diagnosis in the classroom. In Pijl's (1992) words, "making a detailed diagnosis and/or remedial plans is not the teachers' primary goal in evaluation" (p. 129).

How and whether diagnostic information is used, is crucial. Research suggests that formative assessment can improve learning, but only if instruction is reorganized to make use of the assessments (see Black & Wiliam, 1998). The same applies to diagnostic testing: diagnostic information should be integrated meaningfully into teaching and learning for it to have a positive impact (Huhta, 2008).

Diagnostic testing can also be viewed as one stage in a series of tests whose purposes differ but which follow each other in a logical sequence. In some contexts at least, a proficiency test might be administered first as part of a gate-keeping exercise, followed by a placement test once the students have been admitted, to see what course or level to place them in, and then a diagnostic test, possibly administered on an individual basis, to probe more deeply into areas of weakness identified by the placement test. This in fact resembles what the DELNA test appears to do (see Chapter Three) although the last component in DELNA is a group test.

Research on Diagnosing Reading in an SFL—What Should Be Studied?

We will next discuss topics and issues that have arisen when conducting our study on diagnosing reading in SFL and when reviewing previous research in the area. We feel these issues are sufficiently important and of such general interest that they deserve to be among the focal areas for future research.

Reading Strategies and Reading Skills

Bernhardt's (2005) summary of the results of her SFL reading research (cited in Hedgcock & Ferris, 2009) appears to show that while L1 reading skill accounts for 14% to 21% of the variance in reading measures, and SFL linguistic knowledge accounts for 30% of the variance, that still leaves 50% of the variance unaccounted for. It is possible that a range of variables that have not been explored in previous research might contribute towards much of the remaining 50% of the variance. These might include variables explored in DIALUKI, such as motivation, but comprehension strategies, reader engagement (Guthrie & Wigfield, 1997), as well as knowledge of the topic of the texts, would also be worth including in future research.

In particular, strategies for reading have been the focus of much recent research into reading instruction and they might well prove to have value for the diagnosis of reading strengths and weaknesses. A useful list of such strategies, adapted from Grabe and Stoller (2002), is presented in Hedgcock and Ferris (2009, p. 41) and reproduced in Figure 10.1.

Although such strategies may not provide useful diagnostic information, it is entirely possible that exploring in depth with learners the reasons for failure or inadequate application of such strategies might well reveal insights that could lead to diagnoses and treatment. Certainly, strategy research with a view to gathering such diagnostic insights would be worth conducting. Indeed, Hedgcock and Ferris (2009) make helpful observations on the value of strategy instruction and research. However, it is also worth noting the reservations of Macaro (2006) about the lack of evidence for the effectiveness of strategy training in foreign language education.

An area which has frequently been the focus of reading research in both L1 and SFL is that of so-called reading skills, yet in DIALUKI, for example, we

Specify a purpose for reading
Plan a reading process
Preview the text
Predict text contents
Verify text conditions
Generate questions about the text
Locate answers to questions
Compare text to existing schemata
Summarize textual information
Generate inferences
Notice and analyze text structure
Re-read
Use discourse markers to understand textual relationships
Check comprehension accuracy
Track reading difficulties
Repair comprehension failures
Critique a text or point of view
Reflect on and discuss what has been learned

FIGURE 10.1 Sample reading strategies

decided to prioritize less conventional areas of SFL research, such as the cognitive measures we reported in Chapter Six. However, there is certainly a case for investigating to what extent mastery or awareness of reading sub-skills might have diagnostic value (see Chapter One). Unfortunately, there are almost as many taxonomies of reading sub-skills as there are reading researchers, and it is far from certain that individual sub-skills can be shown to be necessary to complete a reading task successfully. It is more likely that a combination of such sub-skills might lead to success than possessing or not possessing any individual sub-skill. Nevertheless, there could be value in further exploration of strong and weak readers' use of reading sub-skills, especially using qualitative research techniques such as think-aloud verbal protocols, stimulated recalls, and eye-tracking in combination with retrospective interviews, in order to identify either the use, non-use, or misuse of such sub-skills, or reasons for misinterpretation of textual information that have their origin in less skillful reading.

Reading speed is another possibly useful indicator of problems with reading in an SFL. It is well known that SFL readers, however good their comprehension, usually read more slowly than equivalent L1 readers, which can be a source of considerable frustration. However, the reading comprehension of advanced SFL readers may equal that of L1 readers despite the difference in reading speed. Carver's (1997, 2000) research shows that as the speed of reading changes, the reader's level of understanding varies. Speeds may range from around 100 words per minute (wpm) to 500 or 600 wpm or even higher, and this variation relates to the reader's purpose, the nature of the information they seek or are required to understand, as well as the nature of the texts themselves. Reading speed is often seen as a component of reading fluency. The relationship between reading fluency and reading comprehension is well established and clear in L1, but rather unknown for SFL (e.g., Jenkins et al., 2003; Grabe, 2010). In L1 reading aloud, fluency measures are useful for diagnostic purposes, indicating potential difficulties in reading comprehension (e.g., Rasinski, 2003). In DIALUKI, we have not explored the diagnostic value of reading speed in its relation to comprehension, but it could be worth exploring this in future research.

Reading aloud is also a common technique used by classroom teachers which we have not explored in DIALUKI for its diagnostic value, although it was used as an outcome measure in an extensive reading and vocabulary intervention study. Some teachers we interviewed reported using it as a way to learn about their students' reading more generally. Furthermore, the Reading Recovery teachers looking at L1 reading use reading aloud regularly as a diagnostic technique. However, its value in SFL reading diagnosis is less clear, since there are bound to be problems with pronunciation, which are not necessarily due to reading problems per se. Nevertheless, the use of reading aloud is frequently advocated as having potential for diagnosis, which it would be worth exploring. It has, after all, been used in the past in order to conduct miscue analysis on the results (see Rigg, 1977). Weaver (2002) has developed a system for conducting oral reading sessions and for analyzing miscues that might be worth adapting for SFL diagnosis purposes.

As regards what teachers could do in the classroom to teach SFL reading in general, it is worth remembering Grabe's (2004) 10 implications from research for the teaching of reading in SFL:

1. Ensure word recognition fluency.
2. Emphasize vocabulary learning and create a vocabulary-rich environment.
3. Activate background (schematic) knowledge in appropriate ways.
4. Ensure effective language knowledge and general comprehension skills.
5. Teach text structure and discourse organization.
6. Promote the strategic reader rather than teach individual strategies.
7. Build reading fluency and reading rate: aim for reading efficiency.
8. Promote extensive reading.
9. Develop readers' intrinsic motivation for reading.
10. Plan and implement a coherent curriculum for student learning. (p. 46)

Doubtless many teachers of SFL reading have heeded this research-based advice. However, we are unaware of any synthesis of the results of implementing such advice, and we suggest, first, that it might be worth unpacking why such advice is thought to be useful, and, second, what insights may be gained from exploring where and why such advice might have proved to be unhelpful or ineffective. In other words, we are suggesting turning on its head the relation between research and the implementation of advice from the results, and instead trying to understand why such advice might not succeed and what insights any lack of success might give us into reading difficulties, reading failure, and readers' weaknesses as well as their causes.

Role of Technical Reading Skills in SFL Reading Comprehension and the Language in Which the Instruments Are Administered

Focusing on technical reading skills and their related components as a way to diagnose and possibly also treat problems in reading comprehension in SFL is an interesting possibility. We know from L1 reading research that problems in the basic mechanics of reading (decoding of letters, letter combinations, and whole words, rapid access to words in memory, sense of basic syntactic patterns) often indicate dyslexia or other such problems in reading or in language more generally. To what extent should a diagnostic toolkit for SFL reading include tasks that require the learner to demonstrate the mastery of these technical aspects of reading? What should the tasks that address problems in such skills look like? Approaches to treating L1 dyslexia indicate that exercises that train certain basic components underlying fluent reading can be quite successful with many struggling young learners when administered in a game-like environment that also adapts to the learners' performance level. This is what happens, for example, in the computer game Ekapeli for Finnish or Graphogame for English (www.graphogame.com; Lyytinen et al., 2009; Kyle et al., 2013). Recent research also suggests that computerized exercises of auditory language processing can improve the decoding and reading-related skills (e.g., reading fluency, segmenting words into syllables and phonemes, and constructing words from phonemes and syllables) of English FL learners whose reading skills are poor in both L1 and FL (Björn & Leppänen, 2013). Improvements in technical reading skills are likely to lead to improvements in comprehension, which is why training of the technical skills is potentially beneficial to all other reading skills.

The study reported in Chapter Six on the extent to which technical reading skills and other such cognitive skills predict reading comprehension outcomes in L1 and SFL showed that the skills needed for the basic technical aspects of reading do indeed play a role in comprehension, especially when a second or foreign language is concerned. However, the study also demonstrated that in interpreting the results of cognitive tasks one must be cautious for several reasons, all connected to language. To be able to use the results for diagnostic purposes, a standardized test with suitable norms should be used. The Finnish tests that we used came from the Jyväskylä Longitudinal Study of Dyslexia, where they were used to diagnose dyslexia in L1. It is obvious that the standard scores for monolingual Finnish children cannot be used with bilingual or immigrant children even if their strongest language is Finnish. What is a normal or average score for monolingual children on a task administered in L1 may be beyond the reach of a normal or average immigrant or bilingual child, and lead to wrong decisions concerning the need for special education or other support.

As the study showed, similar tests function differently in different language populations. In monolinguals there is, for example, a clear difference in how the cognitive tasks predict reading in L1 and SFL, whereas bilinguals do not show such a clear distinction and the predictions are in general stronger than in monolinguals. Creating norms that would be suitable for all bilinguals or all immigrant groups would be very difficult because test takers' backgrounds vary so greatly in terms of how long they have been exposed to different languages; in what situations they use each language; what languages they use at home; how long they have lived in the country as immigrants; whether they are immigrants themselves or children of immigrants; whether they go to L1 classes; what their attitudes are towards L1 and the SFL, and so on.

Another challenge in using cognitive tests in diagnosing is that the tasks administered in the language of reading seem to predict more strongly the reading outcome than tasks administered in the L1. Thus, not only do the test taker's languages play a role but the test language is also important. Guidelines on the use of cognitive tasks usually recommend that L1 be used when administering the tasks, but with bilinguals or immigrants it is not always clear what their L1 is and, more importantly, whether the L1 is still their strongest language. Our results suggest that testing in one language is not necessarily enough and that this is especially true in the case of multilingual children.

An exploratory study such as the one described in Chapter Six gives us valuable information about the role of cognitive skills in reading comprehension in SFL. However, there is still a long way to go from such a study to reliable diagnostic tests focusing on cognitive skills relevant for reading in different linguistic populations.

Given the results of DIALUKI, where it appears that cognitive tests from L1 Finnish delivered in English have greater predictive power for the SFL than the Finnish equivalents predict either L1 or SFL reading, perhaps it would be worth taking more L1 cognitive tests used for English L1 speakers (not Finnish L1 speakers) and seeing how they compare with the tests we have already used. Perhaps also using interventions intended for English L1 literacy classes could be used with EFL learners to see if children grasp more easily the link between sounds and symbols when they are ordered in such a way as to convey the regularities of English spelling, as taught to young English L1 beginning readers. In general, very little is known about the contribution of different phonological memory, decoding, and other technical aspects of reading to SFL reading comprehension. Therefore, almost any studies in this area are likely to be highly useful for understanding the diagnosis of SFL reading.

The question of using the L1 or SFL in research instruments also applies to the language(s) through which learners can convey their understanding of texts, because the language of the reading tasks (e.g., in multiple-choice questions) and of the responses (in constructed responses in general and in constructed summary tasks in particular) may have an effect on the information we get on learners'

SFL reading skills. In particular, this issue concerns beginning learners where the challenge for item writers (in international examinations in particular) has always been to phrase the instructions and tasks/items in a way that is not more difficult than the text to be understood. Instructions and tasks should be comprehensible to the learners whose reading skills we wish to understand. In principle, diagnostic tests face the same challenge: how to ensure that the learners are not impeded from demonstrating their reading (or other) skills when they cannot use their L1 for that purpose.

Challenges of Diagnosis in the Real World

We will next address some of the challenges faced by those who want to diagnose SFL skills, and reading in particular, as part of their work.

Diagnosis by Teachers and the Role of Teaching Materials

The teacher interviews in the DIALUKI study reported in Chapter Nine raised a number of questions about the limitations and possibilities for teachers to diagnose their students' strengths and weaknesses in SFL reading. Perhaps the biggest concern was the variable understandings and approaches to teaching reading in FL English and the role of reading in the FL curriculum. Given how reading researchers struggle to conceptualize the highly complex phenomenon of reading, this is perhaps not a surprise. However, it exemplifies perfectly the challenges faced by attempts to diagnose something in the absence of clear construct definitions.

Despite this major hurdle, the teachers felt that they were able to identify their students' strengths and weaknesses, sometimes in some detail, if they could follow the students for sufficient time and gather different kinds of information both through observation of classroom behavior and homework and through analyzing the results of various kinds of quizzes and tests. Primary school teachers differ from lower secondary teachers in that they typically know their pupils very well and have more opportunities to follow their development, whereas in lower secondary schools the same teacher teaches such a large number of pupils that it is impossible to focus on individual pupils' weaknesses.

One of the potentially important contributions to diagnosis might be via teaching materials. Teaching materials probably play an important role in most educational cultures. This is certainly true for a country such as Finland, as we know both from previous studies (Luukka et al., 2008) and from our teacher interviews. Some teachers felt they were almost 'slaves' to the textbook. Thus, the textbook matters very much even if the choice of textbooks is made locally by the teachers and/or the school.

The significance of the above for the process of diagnosing and addressing weaknesses in SFL reading and proficiency in general is that a textbook package with diagnostic exercises and tests included is potentially a very important factor in the success of classroom-based diagnosis. A diagnostically oriented textbook series would contain tasks that manage to tease out information about both the product and the process of reading, at different levels of detail. At least some of the tasks should be computerized, as explained later in this chapter. The tasks should provide the teacher and the learner with feedback that targets all the levels of feedback defined in models, such as the one by Hattie and Timperley (2007): the levels of product, process, and self-regulation, as well as the level of one's self whenever the latter is deemed useful for reasons of encouragement and motivation. The textbook should also offer enough materials for individualized teaching; this was a feature valued by several teachers interviewed in our study. Interestingly, the teachers used the non-core materials in the textbooks as extra tasks for the more able students. Nobody mentioned using extra texts and tasks to diversify teaching for the benefit of struggling learners. Apparently, the less able readers mostly stick with the core texts and exercises that everybody else also goes through before possibly moving to additional materials. It may be that typical textbooks have few if any tasks specifically targeting struggling SFL learners.

In order to understand the diagnosis of SFL reading by teachers and how they make use of tests, textbooks, and other materials, we need studies that combine interviews of both teachers and students with classroom observations and analyses of the tests and other materials as well as homework. Ideally, such studies should be longitudinal. Given the great influence of textbooks in many educational systems, studies that combine analyses of textbooks with interviews of textbook writers are needed: how might the writers try to incorporate formative/diagnostic assessment in the materials and exercises and how do they design formative/diagnostic tests that are sometimes included in the teacher's guide that comes with the textbook series? A further question that needs examination is the relationship between the diagnostic information that teachers can obtain about learners' strengths and weaknesses by informally observing classroom activities and the information that they gather by using formal (diagnostic and other) tests. How exactly can the two types of information best complement each other?

Motivation in Diagnosis

As we have seen in previous chapters, learners' (lack of) motivation to read in an SFL is often a contributor to weaknesses in reading, and so diagnoses of SFL reading problems should include an investigation of learners' motivation. Indeed, motivating students to read in an SFL or to study the language in the first place came up as an important everyday problem in the interviews of the language teachers of teenaged learners.

However, motivation relates to all kinds of diagnostic tests. A recent study by Tsang (2013) shows that a low-stakes diagnostic test (in her case the DELTA, described in Chapters Three and Four) may not motivate students to demonstrate how well they can perform in the language. Students' motivation was measured by the *Student Opinion Scale* (Sundre & Moore, 2002). Tsang's informants said that they were not motivated to prepare for the test, nor to respond to the tasks very seriously, because there were no obvious consequences for failing or doing well on the test. Interestingly, some informants said that the information was quite interesting, although they were unsure what they could do about it, which echoes the findings from studies of learners' perception of feedback from DIALANG reported in Chapter Eight. In the future, therefore, the relationship between the stakes of the diagnostic assessments and the quality of the diagnostic information obtained should receive more attention in language testing research.

Given the fact that the teacher can have a major effect on learners' motivation (see Dörnyei, 2001, and the discussion at the end of Chapter Seven), it is surprising that no measures seem to have been developed in L2 motivation research to examine the effect on motivation of the teacher. In contrast, such measures exist for parental and peer influences. Examining the teacher's role in learner motivation, and the design of instruments needed in such research, would therefore seem to be an area worth exploring in order to understand how it might contribute to the diagnosis of SFL skills.

Feedback in Diagnosis

Providing feedback to learners is an everyday phenomenon in the classroom, and language tests can also be used as a source of information about learners' strengths and weaknesses. Designing appropriate feedback and deciding on what feedback to give, how and when, are serious challenges and success in this is crucial for the diagnosis to have the intended effect. Given the opaque nature of reading in L1 or SFL, we face even greater challenges in deciding how to find out about learners' reading problems and how to best provide learners—and their teachers—with feedback. Chapter Eight argued for the importance of ensuring that feedback is varied enough and that an overemphasis on the correctness of the responses (task-level feedback) should be avoided. While such feedback can be effective for learning, it is nevertheless one-sided and may not help the learner to perform better on other and/or more difficult tasks than the one on which the feedback was given.

Feedback also needs to be intelligible to its users (see, e.g., Jang, 2009a). Use of the learners' first language or a language they know well enough is one way to try to ensure intelligibility. A particular challenge for automated feedback is the extent to which learners can interpret and act on it without a teacher's assistance. Research on DIALANG feedback reviewed in Chapter Eight suggests that unaided language learners can find it difficult to know how to make use of feedback that goes beyond the test or item score and addresses their self-regulation abilities. For most learners, interpreting and benefiting from such feedback may require their teacher's help. This may also depend on the amount of feedback. Many learners probably find it difficult to prioritize feedback and actions that should follow from it if much feedback is available. Advances in automated analysis of learner language, in particular, make it possible to provide a wealth of feedback to SFL learners. It may even be tempting to give learners as much feedback as possible through such systems. This has the danger of swamping the learner with too much information. Learners obviously need awareness and also guidance in selecting and focusing on the most relevant feedback for their current state of learning.

Because the diagnostic assessment of SFL reading is such a novel area, it is difficult to judge to what extent the feedback studies carried out on other SFL skills and in entirely different areas of education inform us about the best ways to provide feedback on SFL reading. For example, it would be important to increase our understanding of how to design feedback that focuses on the SFL reading processes and that increases the learner's self-regulation skills, as well as to study under what circumstances such feedback might be more effective than the straightforward feedback on task performance.

Finally, it should be noted that learners' motivation, goal orientation, self-regulation and metalinguistic knowledge vary and all can have an effect on how they receive and make use of feedback based on a diagnosis of their skills. Not all learners might welcome feedback on their weaknesses, as was noted in Chapter Eight. Sometimes work needs to done first to improve the learners' current level of motivation or metacognitive awareness, or to try to help them realize its usefulness for their achieving at least some goals. Studies, preferably longitudinal, that attempt to look at the interactions and combined effects on the usefulness of feedback of a range of factors such as those listed above are needed for a broader understanding of how diagnosis and feedback fit into the entire learning and teaching process.

Minimum Amount of Diagnostic Evidence

The issue of a minimum amount of evidence concerns the amount of required information within one diagnostic dimension, such as a particular grammatical category. How many items or tasks do we need as a minimum to administer to a learner to find out if he or she has problems in that dimension? Or how many times should a teacher observe a particular problem in a learner's performance? A response to a single multiple-choice item yields too little information for most diagnostic purposes. But how many items or observations do we need? This is not an easy question to answer as the decision depends on several considerations. One consideration may be the dimension or category of the skill measured: If the dimension consists of a large number of possibly somewhat heterogeneous components, a greater number of items is probably required in order to get even a reasonably accurate picture of how well the learner masters that dimension.

However, a smaller, more uniform category may require only a small number of items for diagnosis.

Another consideration is the consequences of the diagnosis. Alderson (2005) argues that diagnostic tests are typically low stakes or even no stakes. The consequences of different diagnostic tests may nevertheless vary to some extent, for example, with regard to the ease with which erroneous diagnoses can be corrected. Therefore, if it is easy to correct a wrong conclusion about a learner's proficiency, even a minimal amount of diagnostic information may be useful. This may be the case in many classrooms where the teacher is responsible for both diagnosing and acting on the diagnostic information. But if the decisions based on the diagnosis are difficult to implement—such as placement into a different program or possibly into a different school—then it is better to base the diagnosis on sufficient evidence. In such situations, the designers of diagnostic assessment should probably consult guidelines for constructing more high-stakes tests where the number of items is determined largely on psychometric considerations. Certain analytical approaches, such as Cognitive Diagnostic Assessment (see Chapter Three), require that each cognitive attribute of interest is covered by a certain number of items.

A related issue concerns the grain size of the diagnostic categories. The optimal, most useful grain size of diagnostic information may differ depending on the exact purpose of diagnosis but this is still a rather poorly understood aspect of diagnosis. When is a total score from a vocabulary or grammar test useful and when is information about different aspects of vocabulary or grammar needed? Does the optimal grain size for diagnostic information depend on such factors as the purpose of reading? The more fine grained the information required, the more likely it is that an individual rather than a group-based diagnosis is needed.

An important area in the future would, therefore, be to develop a better conceptual understanding of how different degrees of detail in diagnosis relate to different uses of (diagnostic) testing, so that designers of diagnostic assessments would have a clearer idea of how to design their diagnostic system with regard to the number and detail of diagnostic categories. Such an analytical framework would probably also be useful in validating diagnostic assessments.

Advances and Promising Openings in Diagnostic Assessment

Technological Advances—Promises and Challenges

Changes in information and communication technologies (ICT) are changing teaching, learning, and using second and foreign languages. They are also changing assessment and testing, including for diagnostic purposes. Remember that DIALANG, the first large-scale language test specifically designed to be diagnostic, is an online, computer-based system. ICT has the potential to increase the use and efficiency of diagnostic assessment and testing (Alderson, 2005) both in the classroom and, more generally, as stand-alone diagnostic systems available to everybody.

The teacher interviews reported in Chapter Nine suggest that the introduction of different new technologies in the classroom can change the way reading is practiced. The emergence of computers in schools may have had only a minor effect, especially if the classroom has only one or two computers, enabling only one or two learners at a time to work on computerized exercises—and possibly miss whatever the teacher is working on with the whole class at the same time. Only if the lesson takes place in a computer lab can everybody have equal access to individualized exercises. In the future, this may change, however, if more groups of learners are equipped with tablets or smart phones, and if they start to be used on a regular basis in instruction.

Another trend taking place in some countries is the introduction of smartboards to the classroom. This can expand and change the way the teacher presents content matter to the entire class and how the students as a group interact with the teaching material. The smartboard may help the weak or slow readers in particular, as the teachers interviewed in the DIALUKI study reported.

However, a smartboard or any other new technology alone is unlikely to change teaching. A smartboard used by a teacher who is willing to learn to use the new device efficiently and properly is more likely to do the trick. One of the teachers interviewed who had just received a smartboard in his classroom was quite frustrated because the new device was difficult to use and took too much attention away from teaching and learning. Of course, the situation might change after the teacher and the students become more familiar with the new devices.

Computerization of diagnosis in general will increase in the future because of the many benefits it offers (Alderson, 2005). Unlike the teacher, it never tires, it provides feedback to all students (immediately or in a delayed fashion, depending on the design), and it can present each learner with activities that suit their skills based on an analysis of the learners' responses during previous exercises or test tasks.

Three lines of development in computer-based diagnosis seem particularly interesting. The first one is based on the principles of dynamic assessment described in Chapter Three, and involves the provision of adaptive feedback, for example, progressively revealed hints and clues about the correct answer, which could be interpreted diagnostically or used as diagnosis (see Güthke, 1982; Grigorenko, Sternberg, & Ehrman, 2000). Recent small-scale research on the use of adaptive feedback with teenage learners of English showed positive reactions to this kind of feedback by both learners and their teacher and also illustrated in some detail how the learners interacted with the feedback and even how such feedback promotes the learning of the particular language points studied (Leontjev, submitted).

The second is the analysis of the process of reading and responding to reading tasks recorded by eye-trackers (see Bax, 2013; McCray, 2014), which would allow the provision of process level feedback, which is nowadays very rarely done on any language task (see Chapter Eight on the levels of feedback). In particular, any information about the time and distribution of time spent on items, tasks, and texts might tell us something about the reading processes that resulted in particular correct or incorrect responses.

The third kind of development relates to advances in the automated analysis of learner language, both spoken and written. New computerized language examinations, such as the *TOEFL iBT* and the *Pearson Test of English Academic*, employ scoring algorithms that can analyze and evaluate a wide range of specific features in test-takers' written and/or spoken productions. Feeding information about the results of these kinds of analyses back to the students and their teachers has considerable diagnostic potential. Using automated analysis of language is obviously somewhat limited when it comes to reading in SFL. However, the analysis of the characteristics of responses to task types that require production of language (in writing, usually) might yield some diagnostically useful information. Furthermore, automated analysis of the language of the test texts may also have diagnostic potential.

Future research on diagnosing reading in SFL could make use of certain new developments in research methods and analytical approaches developed in other disciplines. Using eye-tracking while completing reading tasks can yield rich information about the process of reading that is otherwise so difficult to analyze for diagnosis and feedback. Combining eye-tracking with brain research could provide us with even deeper understanding of what takes place while reading. Examples of developments in the statistical approaches include the procedures used in Cognitive Diagnostic Assessment described in Chapter Three, and the profile analysis of test items implemented in the Profile-G program (see www.ealta.eu.org/resources.htm), developed by Verhelst at CITO in the Netherlands.

Conclusions

We conclude this chapter by making a few general points about the diagnosis of SFL reading based on the research reviewed in this book and by making use of the tentative principles for diagnostic SFL assessment proposed by Alderson et al. (2014). In addition, we will introduce a topic of research which is rather common in other areas of language testing, but which has hitherto been ignored almost completely in diagnostic language testing, namely test washback and impact.

First, we repeat the point made at the beginning of Chapter One, namely the importance of not forgetting that weaknesses in reading, or any other language skill, may be due to a number of different factors or their interaction. Trying to find out if a learner's reading problems stem from a disability or from something else is probably a necessary starting point for a diagnosis. The constructs related to different causes of weaknesses (e.g., disability vs. lack of a particular skill vs. motivation vs. teaching) are bound to differ. Identifying the reasons for weaknesses is obviously very challenging since many language teachers may not be trained to identify and tackle a wide variety of different issues in learning. However, the teacher should not be seen as the only person responsible for correctly diagnosing SFL reading or anything else in the learners. We saw earlier how the language teachers interviewed in our study regularly consulted other teachers. Taking different stakeholders' views into account is also one of the principles for diagnostic assessment recommended by Alderson et al. (2014). Some of the learners' problems are probably such that the teacher can do very little about them (e.g., problems related to the learners' background), which is analogous to a medical doctor diagnosing an untreatable condition in a patient (see Chapter Two). However, it is important for teachers to be aware of all the possible issues, even if they can tackle only some of them in their teaching.

Second, ensuring that the entire chain from diagnosis to feedback to action or intervention is not broken is very important. Diagnosis without proper feedback and subsequent action that addresses the problems identified is not really very useful, as it does not lead to an improvement in the learner's current state (see also the principles for diagnostic assessment in Alderson et al., 2014). This is partly a question of money and politics, as was found in DIALUKI. Many interviewed teachers complained how few resources are provided for helping those learners who obviously have difficulties. Very often the extra support does not address a particular problem, but simply involves doing the same exercises in a smaller group or giving extra time for doing the same exercises. It is, thus, not necessarily tailored to the student's diagnosed needs.

Third, a characteristic of successful diagnostic assessment is that it is regular and systematic. The studies reviewed in this book indicate that if the observations made during assessment are not systematically recorded by the teacher they are unlikely to lead to appropriate action (Pijl, 1992) and that making assessment and feedback more planned and systematic is a factor that improves the usefulness of assessment (Black & Wiliam, 1998; Davin, 2013).

Fourth, since language learning is a longitudinal process, diagnosis should also be longitudinal. One reason why a diagnosis carried out longitudinally is probably more useful than a one-shot diagnostic test is the coverage of a diagnostic test in terms of dimensions or categories. Hughes (1989) claimed that a comprehensive diagnostic test of grammatical ability would have to be vast (see Chapter Three). Although we do not yet know how extensive a diagnostic test should be (Alderson, 2005), it is likely that a comprehensive diagnostic test of SFL reading consists of several dimensions and is therefore unlikely to be very short. Splitting such a test into several parts and administering them over a period of time is obviously more practical and allows a wider coverage of diagnostic dimensions of knowledge and skills.

Fifth, teachers and tests complement each other in diagnosis. Alderson et al. (2014) elaborate on this point in one of their principles for diagnostic assessment by arguing that diagnostic assessment should ideally start by the teacher observing the learners and making an initial assessment of them, followed by the use of specifically designed diagnostic tools and/or expert help. This would then lead to making decisions about how best to treat the problems identified.

Tests provide a systematic and often valid and researched means of diagnosis. They can be used to obtain information from all the learners even in large classes and they can, if so designed, cover a relatively wide range of skills and domains. Unfortunately, validated and user-friendly diagnostic tools that target specific areas of SFL reading do not exist yet, and therefore, their development should be one of the priorities of research into SFL diagnosis in the future. Teachers, for their part, usually have a longitudinal perspective on their learners' skills after having observed them on numerous tasks. They can help learners to interpret results and feedback from diagnostic tests, and, importantly, they can provide them with individualized guidance for appropriate action after diagnosis. However, as has been frequently pointed out, language teachers need more training in understanding how SFL reading develops and what the problems in such development might be, given the target language and the characteristics of the learners (e.g., age and level of proficiency).

An extension of the previous point, based on the research reviewed in this book, is that we often need a range of different kinds of measures and procedures to understand what learners' weaknesses are and what the likely reasons for these weaknesses are, since the reasons can be so varied. This was in fact our assumption when we started building the battery of research instruments for DIALUKI Study One and the results, overall, tend to confirm this assumption, as a wide range of different measures appear to predict SFL reading.

Finally, we wish to introduce a topic that has received particularly scant attention in the field of diagnostic assessment (which is itself relatively new), namely, the impact of diagnostic tests. Washback from language tests or their impact more generally is an important and rather popular topic in language testing research. A rare exception to the lack of studies of washback in diagnostic assessment is a study of the impact of the Hong Kong-based DELTA system on learners and teachers (Wong & Raquel, 2013). Since the purpose of diagnostic testing is to identify learners' strengths and weaknesses and to help address those weaknesses, it could be argued that the test should have a positive effect on teaching and learning of the language in question. Indeed, Jang (2012) argues that "[u]nlike high-stakes proficiency tests, pedagogical changes through a systematic diagnostic feedback loop are part of *the intended effects* in diagnostic assessment" (p. 124). If the effect of a diagnostic test is 'neutral,' that is, it does not have any effect at all, we might have grounds to say that the test has failed its primary purpose, and it may have serious validity issues (or alternatively, the diagnostic chain has been broken at some point; see the beginning of this chapter). Tsang's (2013) study on students' motivation to take the diagnostic DELTA test suggests a further issue with the validity of diagnostic tests. As reported earlier, most of the students studied were not very motivated to take the test seriously because they considered it to have no consequences for them. A possible remedy, the researcher suggested, could be to increase the stakes of the test, thus making the students take it more seriously.

Jang (2012) warns that diagnostic tests can have negative consequences for teaching and learning in certain contexts. It has been claimed, for example, that the fine-grained construct definitions needed in diagnostic testing might narrow what will be taught. The danger of such negative impact may increase if diagnosis becomes a major purpose of nationwide, and thus important, tests. Jang argues that the stakes of diagnostic tests are not automatically low, but that they are different in kind compared with so-called high-stakes tests. If diagnosis focuses on problems in learners' skills it might have serious negative consequences for learners' self-esteem. A similar point about the mismatch between the possible negative connotations of diagnosis and an approach to language teaching that emphasizes the potential in the learners was made by Spolsky (1992) a long time ago. Recently, Alderson et al. (2014) warned against misinterpreting the typical discourse in diagnostic assessment about weaknesses and treatments; language learning difficulties should not be pathologized. Therefore, it may be important not to focus exclusively on the weaknesses but cover both strengths and weaknesses in learners' performance and report on both.

We hope that the various proposals we have made throughout this chapter for more comprehensive studies of diagnosis that take into account a wide range of factors, including and expanding on those studied in DIALUKI, in addition to aspects of learners' reading strategies, their reading skills, their background knowledge, and so on, will inspire and inform further research into the strengths and weaknesses that learners have when reading in an SFL. We also hope we have succeeded in contributing to an increase in understanding of diagnostic testing in general and of diagnosing SFL reading in particular.

Above all, we hope that the reader has gained a better overview of the application of research results to the teaching and diagnosis of SFL reading which will eventually lead to a better understanding of diagnosis, as well as to the improvement of procedures for diagnosing learners' strengths and weaknesses in SFL reading. Perhaps in the future this can then contribute to improvements in the diagnosis of SFL listening, SFL speaking, and writing and, ultimately, SFL communication abilities more generally.

REFERENCES

Ableeva, R. (2010). *Dynamic assessment of listening comprehension in second language learning* (Unpublished doctoral dissertation). The Pennsylvania State University, USA.

Aebersold, J. A., & Field, M. L. (1997). *From reader to reading teacher.* Cambridge: Cambridge University Press.

Alderson, J. C. (1984). Reading in a foreign language: A reading problem or a language problem? In J. C. Alderson & A. H. Urquhart (Eds.), *Reading in a Foreign language* (pp. 1–24). London: Longman.

Alderson, J. C. (1993). The relationship between grammar and reading in an English for academic purposes test battery. In D. Douglas & C. Chapelle (Eds.), *A new decade of language testing research: Selected papers from the 1990 Language Testing Research Colloquium* (pp. 203–219). Alexandria, VA: TESOL.

Alderson, J. C. (2000). *Assessing reading.* Cambridge: Cambridge University Press.

Alderson, J. C. (2005). *Diagnosing foreign language proficiency: The interface between learning and assessment.* New York, NY: Continuum.

Alderson, J. C. (2007). The challenge of (diagnostic) testing: Do we know what we are measuring? In J. Fox, M. M. Wesche, D. Bayliss, L. Cheng, C. E. Turner, & C. Doe (Eds.), *Language testing reconsidered* (pp. 21–39). Ottawa, ON: University of Ottawa Press.

Alderson, J. C. (2010). Cognitive diagnosis and Q-matrices in language assessment: A commentary. *Language Assessment Quarterly, 7*(1), 96–103. doi:10.1080/15434300903426748

Alderson, J. C. (2012). Diagnosing foreign language reading proficiency for learners of different age groups. In H. Pillay (Ed.), *Teaching language to learners of different age groups. Proceedings of the 46th RELC International Seminar* (pp. 29–46). Singapore: Regional Language Centre.

Alderson, J. C., & Bachman, L. (2004). Series editor's preface to Assessing Grammar. In J. E. Purpura, *Assessing grammar* (ix–x). Cambridge: Cambridge University Press.

Alderson, J. C., Brunfaut, T., & Harding, L. (2014). Towards a theory of diagnosis in second and foreign language assessment: Insights from professional practice across diverse fields. *Applied Linguistics, 1–25.* doi:10.1093/applin/amt046

Alderson, J. C., Clapham, C., & Wall, D. (1995). *Language test construction and evaluation.* Cambridge: Cambridge University Press.

Alderson, J.C., & Cseresznyés, M. (2003). Reading and use of English. In J. C. Alderson (Series Ed.), *Into Europe: Prepare for modern English exams.* Retrieved December 31, 2013, from www.lancaster.ac.uk/fass/projects/examreform/into_europe/Reading_and_Use_of_English.pdf

Alderson, J. C., Figueras, N., Kuijper, H., Nold, G., Takala, S., & Tardieu, C. (2004). *The development of specifications for item development and classification within The Common European Framework of Reference for Languages: Learning, teaching, assessment. Reading and listening.* Final Report of the Dutch CEFR Construct Project. Unpublished manuscript.

Alderson, J. C., Figueras, N., Kuijper, H., Nold, G., Takala, S., & Tardieu, C. (2006). Analysing tests of reading and listening in relation to the Common European Framework of Reference for Languages: The experience of The Dutch CEFR Construct Project. *Language Assessment Quarterly, 3*(1), 3–30. doi:10.1207/s15434311laq0301_2

Alderson, J. C., & Huhta, A. (2005). The development of a suite of computer-based diagnostic tests based on the Common European Framework. *Language Testing, 22*(3), 301–320. doi:10.1191/0265532205lt310oa

Alderson, J. C., & Huhta, A. (2011). Can research into the diagnostic testing of reading in a second or foreign language contribute to SLA research? In L. Roberts, G. Pallotti, & C. Bettoni (Eds.), *EUROSLA Yearbook: Annual conference of the European Second Language Association* (Vol. 11, pp. 30–52). Amsterdam, The Netherlands: John Benjamins.

Alderson, J. C., Huhta, A., Nieminen, L., Ullakonoja, R., & Haapakangas, E.-L. (2012, April). *Characteristics of weak readers of English as a foreign language.* Paper Presented at 34th Language Testing Research Colloquium, Princeton, USA.

Alderson, J. C., & Kremmel, B. (2013). Re-examining the content validity of a grammar test: The (im)possibility of distinguishing vocabulary and structural knowledge. *Language Testing, 34*(4) 535–556. doi:10.1177/0265532213489568

Aljaafreh, A., & Lantolf, J.P. (1994, Winter). Negative feedback as regulation and second language learning in the Zone of Proximal Development. *The Modern Language Journal, 78*(4), 465–483.

ALTE (Association of Language Testers in Europe). (1998). *Multilingual glossary of language testing terms.* Cambridge: Cambridge University Press.

Bachman, L.F. (1990). *Fundamental considerations in language testing.* Oxford: Oxford University Press.

Bachman, L. F., & Palmer, A.S. (1996). *Language testing in practice.* Oxford: Oxford University Press.

Bachman, L. F., & Purpura, J.E. (2008). Language assessments: Gatekeepers or door openers? In B. Spolsky & F. M. Hult (Eds.), *The handbook of educational linguistics* (pp. 456–468). Oxford: Blackwell Publishing.

Baddeley, A. (2003). Working memory: Looking back and looking forward. *Nature Reviews Neuroscience, 4,* 829–839. doi:10.1038/nrn1201

BADT (Birmingham Assessment and Diagnostic Test). (n.d.). *Assessment and Diagnostic Test—Answer Sheet and Questionnaire.* Birmingham University, UK.

Bailey, A. L., & Drummond, K. V. (2006). Who is at risk and why? Teachers' reasons for concern and their understanding and assessment of early literacy. *Educational Assessment, 11*(3/4), 149–178. doi:10.1080/10627197.2006.9652988

Balzer, W., Doherty, M., & O'Conner, R. (1989). Effects of cognitive feedback in performance. *Psychological Bulletin, 106*(3), 410–433. doi:10.1037/0033-2909.106.3.410

Bax, S. (2013). The cognitive processing of candidates during reading tests. Evidence from eye-tracking. *Language Testing, 30*(4), 441–465. doi:10.1177/0265532212473244

Bejar, I. (1984). Educational diagnostic assessment. *Journal of Educational Measurement, 21*(2), 175–189. doi:10.1111/j.1745-3984.1984.tb00228.x

Bernhardt, E. B. (2005). Progress and procrastination in second language reading. *Annual Review of Applied Linguistics*, 25, 133–150. doi:10.1017/S0267190505000073

Björn, P., & Leppänen, P. (2013). Accelerating decoding-related skills in poor readers learning a foreign language: A computer-based intervention. *Educational Psychology: An International Journal of Experimental Educational Psychology*. doi:10.1080/01443410.2013.797336

Black, P., & Wiliam, D. (1998). Assessment and classroom learning. *Assessment in Education, 5*(1), 7–74. doi:10.1080/0969595980050102

Bong, M., & Skaalvik, E. M. (2003). Academic self-concept and self-efficacy: How different are they really? *Educational Psychology Review, 15*(1), 1–40.

Bookbinder, G. E., Vincent, D., & Crumpler, M. (2002). *Salford Sentence Reading Test: Teacher's Manual*. London: Hodder Education.

Bowey, J. A. (2005). Predicting individual differences in learning to read. In M. J. Snowling & C. Hulme (Eds.), *The science of reading: A handbook* (pp. 155–172). Malden, MA: Blackwell.

Bransford, J., Stein, B., & Shelton, T. (1984). Learning from the perspective of the comprehender? In J. C. Alderson & A. H. Urquhart (Eds.), *Reading in a foreign language* (pp. 28–44). London: Longman.

Buck, G., & Tatsuoka, K. (1998). Application of the rule-space procedure to language testing: Examining attributes of a free response listening test. *Language Testing, 15*(2), 119–157. doi:10.1177/026553229801500201

Buck, G., Tatsuoka, K., & Kostin, I. (1997). The subskills of reading: Rule-space analysis of a multiple-choice test of second language reading comprehension. *Language Learning, 47*(3), 423–466. doi:10.1111/0023-8333.00016

Buck, G., Tatsuoka, K., Kostin, I., & Phelps, M. (1997). The sub-skills of listening: Rule-space analysis of a multiple-choice test of second language listening comprehension. In V. Kohonen, A. Huhta, L. Kurki-Suonio, & S. Luoma (Eds.), *Current developments and alternatives in language assessment: Proceedings of LTRC 96* (pp. 589–624). Jyväskylä, Finland: University of Jyväskylä and University of Tampere.

Butler, A., Godbole, N., & Marsh, E. (2013). Explanation feedback is better than correct answer feedback for promoting transfer of learning. *Journal of Educational Psychology, 105*(2), 290–298. doi:10.1037/a0031026

Butler, D., & Winne, P. (1995). Feedback and self-regulated learning: A theoretical synthesis. *Review of Educational Research, 65*(3), 245–281. doi:10.3102/00346543065003245

Carver, C., & Scheier, M. (1990). Origins and function of positive and negative affect: A control-process view. *Psychological Review, 97*(1), 19–35. doi:10.1037/0033-295X.97.1.19

Carver, R. P. (1997). Reading for one second, one minute or one year from the perspective of rauding theory. *Scientific Studies of Reading, 1*, 3–43. doi:10.1207/s1532799xssr0101_2

Carver, R. P. (2000). *The cause of high and low reading achievement*. Mahwah, NJ: Erlbaum.

Cheung, H., & Lin, A.M.Y. (2005). Differentiating between automatic and strategic control processes: Toward a model of cognitive mobilization in bilingual reading. *Psychologia, 48*, 39–53. doi:10.2117/psysoc.2005.39

Chiu, M., & Khoo, L. (2005). Effects of resources, inequality, and privilege bias on achievement: Country, school, and student level analyses. *American Educational Research Journal, 42*(4), 575–603.

Cizek, G. J., & Bunch, M. B. (2007). *Standard setting.* Thousand Oaks, CA: Sage.

Clariana, R. B., Wagner, D., & Roher Murphy, L. C. (2000). Applying a connectionist description of feedback timing. *Educational Technology Research and Development, 48*(3), 5–22. doi:10.1007/BF02319855

Clarke, M. (1980). The short-circuit hypothesis of ESL reading: Or when language competence interferes with reading performance. *The Modern Language Journal, 64*(2), 203–209. doi:10.1111/j.1540-4781.1980.tb05186.x

Clay, M. (1979). *Reading: The patterning of complex behavior* (2nd ed.). Portsmouth, NH: Heinemann.

Clay, M. (1985). *Reading: The patterning of complex behavior* (3rd ed.). Portsmouth, NH: Heinemann.

Council of Europe. (2001). *Common European framework of reference for languages: Learning, teaching and assessment.* Cambridge: Cambridge University Press.

Coxhead, A. (2000). A new academic word list. *TESOL Quarterly, 34*(2), 213–238. doi:10.2307/3587951

Criterion. (n.d.). Retrieved December 31, 2013, from www.ets.org/criterion

Csizér, K., & Dörnyei, Z. (2005). Language learners' motivational profiles and their motivated learning behavior. *Language Learning, 55*(4), 613–659. doi:10.1111/j.0023-8333.2005.00319.x

Csizér, K., & Kormos, J. (2009). Motivation, language identity and the L2 self. In Z. Dörnyei & E. Ushioda (Eds.), *Motivation, language identity and the L2 self* (pp. 98–119). Bristol: Multilingual Matters.

Csizér, K., Kormos, J., & Sarkadi A. (2010). The dynamics of language learning attitudes and motivation: Lessons from an interview study of dyslexic language learners. *The Modern Language Journal, 94*(3), 470–487. doi:10.1111/j.1540-4781.2010.01054.x

Daneman, M., & Carpenter, P. A. (1980). Individual differences in working memory and reading. *Journal of Verbal Learning and Verbal Behavior, 19*(4), 450–466.

Davies, A., Brown, A., Elder, C., Hill, K., Lumley, T., & McNamara, T. (1999). *Dictionary of language testing.* Cambridge: Cambridge University Press.

Davin, K. (2013). Integration of dynamic assessment and instructional conversations to promote development and improve assessment in the language classroom. *Language Teaching Research, 17*(3), 303–322. doi:10.1177/1362168813482934

Davis, F. B. (1968). Research in comprehension in reading. *Reading Research Quarterly 3*(4), 499–545. Retrieved July 15, 2014, from www.jstor.org/stable/747153

Davison, C., & Leung, C. (2009). Current issues in English language teacher-based assessment. *TESOL Quarterly, 43*(3), 393–415. doi:10.1002/j.1545-7249.2009.tb00242.x

DELNA *(Diagnostic English Language Needs Assessment).* Retrieved December 31, 2013, from www.delna.auckland.ac.nz/uoa/

DELNA Handbook. *Handbook for candidates at the University of Auckland.* Retrieved December 31, 2013, from www.delna.auckland.ac.nz/webdav/site/delna/shared/delna/documents/delna-handbook.pdf

DELTA (Diagnostic English Language Tracking Assessment). Retrieved December 31, 2013 from http://gslpa.polyu.edu.hk/eng/delta_web/

Denckla, M. B., & Rudel, R. (1974). Rapid 'automatized' naming of pictured objects, colors, letters and numbers by normal children. *Cortex, 10*(2), 186–202.

Diagnosis. (1987). In *Collins COBUILD English language dictionary*. London: HarperCollins.

Diagnosis. (2013). In *The Merriam-Webster Online Dictionary*. Retrieved December 31, 2013, from www.merriam-webster.com/dictionary/diagnosis

DIALANG. Retrieved December 31, 2013, from www.lancaster.ac.uk/researchenterprise/dialang/about.htm/

DIALUKI (Toisen tai vieraan kielen lukemisen ja kirjoittamisen diagnosointi (Diagnosing reading and writing in a second or foreign language). Retrieved December 31, 2013, from www.jyu.fi/dialuki

DiBello, L. V., Roussos, L. A., & Stout, W. (2007). Review of cognitively diagnostic assessment and a summary of psychometric models. In C. R. Rao & S. Sinharay (Eds.), *Handbook of statistics* (Vol. 26, pp. 1–52). doi:10.1016/S0169-7161(06)26031-0

Doe, C. (2011). The integration of diagnostic assessment into classroom instruction. In D. Tsagari & I. Csépes (Eds.), *Classroom-based language assessment* (pp. 63–76). Frankfurt am Main: Peter Lang GmbH, Internationaler Verlag der Wissenschaften.

Dörnyei, Z. (2001). *Motivational strategies in the language classroom*. Cambridge: Cambridge University Press.

Dörnyei, Z. (2005). *The psychology of the language learner: Individual differences in second language acquisition*. London: Longman Pearson.

Dörnyei, Z., & Ottó, I. (1998). Motivation in action: A process model of L2 motivation. *Working Papers in Applied Linguistics, 4*, 43–69.

Dörnyei, Z., & Ushioda, E. (2011). *Teaching and researching motivation*. Harlow, England: Pearson Education.

Droop, M., & Verhoeven, L. (2003). Language proficiency and reading ability in first- and second language learners. *Reading Research Quarterly, 38*(1), 78–103. doi:10.1598/RRQ.38.1.4

Earley, P., & Kanfer, R. (1985). The influence of component participation and role models on goal acceptance, goal satisfaction, and performance. *Organizational Behavior & Human Decision Processes, 36*(3), 378–390. doi:10.1016/0749-5978(85)90006-8

Ebel, R., & Frisbie, D. (1991). *Essentials of educational measurement*. Englewood Cliffs, NJ: Prentice Hall.

Edelenbos, P., & Kubanek-German, A. (2004). Teacher assessment: The concept of 'diagnostic competence.' *Language Testing, 21*(3), 259–283. doi:10.1191/0265532204lt284oa

Ehri, L. C., & Snowling, M. J. (2004). Developmental variation in word recognition. In C. A. Stone, E. R. Silliman, B. J. Ehren, & K. Apel (Eds.), *Handbook of language and literacy: Development and disorders* (pp. 433–460). New York: Guilford Press.

Elder, C., & Randow, J. (2008). Exploring the utility of a web-based English language screening tool. *Language Assessment Quarterly, 5*(3), 173–194. doi:10.1080/15434300802229334

English Year 1 Phonics Screening Check. (2012). *Assessment framework for the development of the Year 1 phonics screening check*. Standards and Testing Agency, UK. Retrieved December 31, 2013, from www.gov.uk/government/uploads/system/uploads/attachment_data/file/230810/Phonics_assessment_framework.PDF

e-rater. Retrieved December 31, 2013, from www.ets.org/erater/about

European Commission. (2012). *First European survey on language competences. Final Report*. Retrieved July 15, 2014, from http://ec.europa.eu/languages/policy/strategic-framework/documents/language-survey-final-report_en.pdf

Everatt, J., Smythe, I., Adams, E., & Ocampo, D. (2000). Dyslexia screening measures and bilingualism. *Dyslexia: An International Journal of Research and Practice, 6*(1), 42–56. doi:10.1002/(SICI)1099-0909(200001/03)6:1<42::AID-DYS157>3.0.CO;2-0

Floropoulou, C. (2002). *Foreign language learners' attitudes to self-assessment and DIALANG: A comparison between Greek and Chinese learners of English* (Unpublished master's thesis). Lancaster University, UK.

Flynn, J. M., & Rahbar, M. H. (1998). Improving teacher prediction of children at risk for reading failure. *Psychology in the Schools, 35*(2), 163–172. doi:10.1002/(SICI)1520-6807(199804)35:2<163::AID-PITS8>3.0.CO;2-Q

Foy, P., & Kennedy, A. M. (2008). *Progress in International Reading Literacy Study (PIRLS): PIRLS 2006 User Guides.* Retrieved July 15, 2014, from http://timss.bc.edu/pirls2006/user_guide.html

Fransson, A. (1984). Cramming or understanding: Effects of intrinsic and extrinsic motivation on approach to learning and test performance. In J. C. Alderson & A. H. Urquhart (Eds.), *Reading in a foreign language* (pp. 86–121). London: Longman.

Frederickson, N., & Frith, U. (1998). Identifying dyslexia in bilingual children: A phonological approach with inner London Sylheti speakers. *Dyslexia: An International Journal of Research and Practice, 4*(3), 119–131. doi:10.1002/(SICI)1099-0909(199809)4:3<119::AID-DYS112>3.0.CO;2-8

Frost, R. (2005). Orthographic systems and skilled word recognition processes in reading. In M. J. Snowling & C. Hulme (Eds.), *The science of reading: A handbook* (pp. 272–295). Malden, MA: Blackwell.

Gao, X. (2010). *Strategic language learning: The roles of agency and context.* Bristol: Multilingual Matters.

Gardner, R. C. (1985). *Social psychology and second language learning: The role of attitudes and motivation.* London: Arnold.

Gardner, R. C., & Lambert, W. E. (1959). Motivational variables in second language acquisition. *Canadian Journal of Psychology, 13,* 266–272.

Gardner, R. C., & Lambert, W. E. (1972). *Motivational variables in second-language acquisition.* Rowley, MA: Newsbury House.

Gardner, R. C., Masgoret, A.-M., Tennant, J., & Mihic, L. (2004). Integrative motivation: Changes during a year-long intermediate-level language course. *Language Learning, 54*(1), 1–34. doi:10.1111/j.1467-9922.2004.00247.x

Gathercole, S. E. (2006). Nonword repetition and word learning: The nature of the relationship. *Applied Psycholinguistics, 27*(4), 513–543. doi:10.1017.S0142716406060383

Geva, E. (2000). Issues in the assessment of reading disabilities in L2 children—beliefs and research evidence. *Dyslexia: An International Journal of Research and Practice, 6*(1), 13–28. doi:10.1002/(SICI)1099-0909(200001/03)6:1<13::AID-DYS155>3.0.CO;2-6

Gibbons, P. (2003). Mediating language learning: Teacher interactions with ESL students in a content-based classroom. *TESOL Quarterly, 37*(2), 247–273. doi:10.2307/3588504

Goodman, K. (1969). Analysis of oral reading miscues: Applied psycholinguistics. *Reading Research Quarterly, 5*(1), 9–30. Retrieved July 15, 2014, from www.jstor.org/stable/747158

Grabe, W. (1991). Current developments in second language reading research. *TESOL Quarterly, 25*(3), 375–406. doi:10.2307/3586977

Grabe, W. (2004). Research on teaching reading. *Annual Review of Applied Linguistics, 2,* 44–69. doi:10.1017/S0267190504000030

Grabe, W. (2009). *Reading in a second language: Moving from theory to practice.* Cambridge: Cambridge University Press.

Grabe, W. (2010). Fluency in reading—thirty-five years later. *Reading in a Foreign Language, 22*(1), 71–83. Retrieved December 31, 2013, from http://nflrc.hawaii.edu/rfl/April2010/articles/grabe.pdf

Grabe, W., & Stoller, F. L. (2002). *Teaching and researching reading.* Harlow, England: Long-man/Pearson Education.

Grigorenko, E., & Sternberg, R. (1998). Dynamic testing. *Psychological Bulletin, 124*(1), 75–111.

Grigorenko, E., Sternberg, R., & Ehrman, M. (2000). A theory-based approach to the measurement of foreign language learning ability: The Canal-F theory and test. *The Modern Language Journal, 84*(3), 390–405. doi:10.1111/0026-7902.00076

Gupta, P. Lipinski, J. Abbs, B., & Lin, P.-H. (2005). Serial position effects in nonword repetition. *Journal of Memory and Language, 53*(1), 141–162. doi:10.1016/j.jml.2004.12.002

Güthke, J. (1982). The Learning Test concept: An alternative to the traditional static intelligence test. *The German Journal of Psychology, 6*(4), 306–324.

Güthke, J., & Beckmann, J. F. (2000). The learning test concept and its applications in practice. In C.S. Lidz & J.G. Elliott (Eds.), *Dynamic assessment: Prevailing models and applications* (pp. 17–69). Amsterdam, The Netherlands: Elsevier.

Guthrie, J.T., & Wigfield, A. (Eds.). (1997). *Reading engagement: Motivating readers through integrated instruction.* Newark, NJ: International Reading Association.

Halliday, M.A.K. (1973). *Explorations in the functions of language.* London: Edward Arnold.

Hattie, J. A. (1999). *Influences on student learning* (Inaugural professorial address, University of Auckland, New Zealand). Retrieved December 31, 2013, from www.education.auckland.ac.nz/webdav/site/education/shared/hattie/docs/influences-on-student-learning.pdf

Hattie, J., & Timperley, H. (2007). The power of feedback. *Review of Educational Research, 77*(1), 81–112. doi:10.3102/003465430298487

Häyrinen, T., Serenius-Sirve, S., & Korkman, M. (1999). *Lukilasse. Lukemisen, kirjoittamisen ja laskemisen seulontatestistö peruskoulun ala-asteen luokille 1–6.* [Lukilasse. Screening battery for reading, writing, and arithmetic in primary school grades 1–6]. Helsinki: Psykologien kustannus Oy.

Haywood, H., & Lidz, C. (2007). *Dynamic assessment in practice: Clinical and educational applications.* Cambridge: Cambridge University Press.

Hedgcock, J. S., & Ferris, D. R. (2009). *Teaching readers of English: Students, texts, and contexts.* New York: Routledge

Henning, G. (1975). Measuring foreign language reading comprehension. *Language Learning, 25*(1), 109–114. doi:10.1111/j.1467-1770.1975.tb00111.x

Hoover, W.A., & Gough, P.B. (1990). The simple view of reading. *Reading and Writing: An Interdisciplinary Journal, 2*(2), 127–160.

Horwitz, E. K. (1986). Preliminary evidence for the reliability and validity of a foreign language anxiety scale. *TESOL Quarterly, 20*(3), 559–562. doi:10.2307/3586302

Horwitz, E. K., Horwitz, M. B., & Cope, J. (1986). Foreign language classroom anxiety. *The Modern Language Journal, 70*(2), 125–132. doi:10.1111/j.1540-4781.1986.tb05256.x

Hughes, A. (1989). *Testing for language teachers.* Cambridge: Cambridge University Press.

Hughes, A. (2003). *Testing for language teachers* (2nd ed.). Cambridge: Cambridge University Press.

Huhta, A. (2008). Diagnostic and formative assessment. In B. Spolsky F. & Hult (Eds.), *Handbook of educational linguistics* (pp. 469–482). Malden, MA: Blackwell.

Huhta, A. (2010). *Innovations in diagnostic assessment and feedback: An analysis of the usefulness of the DIALANG language assessment system.* (Unpublished doctoral dissertation). University of Jyväskylä, Finland.

Huibregtse, I., Admiraal, W., & Meara, P. (2002). Scores on a yes-no vocabulary test: Correction for guessing and response style. *Language Testing, 19*(3), 227–245. doi:10.1191/0265532202lt229oa

Iwaniec, J. (2014a). *Motivation of pupils from southern Poland to learn English. System: An International Journal of Educational Technology and Applied Linguistics.* 45, 67–78. doi: 10.1016/j.system.2014.05.003a

Iwaniec, J. (Iwaniec). The Ideal L2 Self, English self-concept and self-efficacy beliefs: What role do they play in language learning motivation? In K. Csizér & M. Magid (Eds.), *The impact of self-concept on second language learning* (pp. 189–205). Bristol: Multilingual Matters.

Jacobs, E. L. (2001). The effects of adding dynamic assessment components to a computerized preschool language screening test. *Communication Disorders Quarterly, 22*(4), 217–226.

Jang, E. E. (2009a). Cognitive diagnostic assessment of L2 reading comprehension ability: Validity arguments for Fusion Model application to *LanguEdge* assessment. *Language Testing, 26*(1), 31–73. doi:10.1177/0265532208097336

Jang, E. E. (2009b). Demystifying a Q-matrix for making diagnostic inferences about L2 reading skills. *Language Assessment Quarterly, 6*(3):210–238. doi:10.1080/15434300903071817

Jang, E. E. (2012). Diagnostic assessment in classrooms. In G. Fulcher & F. Davidson (Eds.), *The Routledge handbook of language testing in a nutshell* (pp. 120–134). Abingdon, England: Routledge.

Jang, E. E., & Wagner, M. (2014). Diagnostic feedback in language classroom. In A. Kunnan (Ed.), *Companion to language assessment.* Oxford: Wiley-Blackwell.

Jenkins, J. R., Fuchs, L. S., van den Broek, P., Espin, C., & Deno, S. L. (2003). Sources of individual differences in reading comprehension and reading fluency. *Journal of Educational Psychology, 95*(4), 719–729.

Johns, T. (n.d.). *Birmingham Assessment and Diagnostic Test.* Undated manuscript. Birmingham University, UK.

Johns, T. (1976). *Why diagnose?* Memorandum dated July 18, 1976. Birmingham, UK: Department of English, University of Birmingham.

Johnston, P. (1987). Teachers as evaluation experts. *The Reading Teacher, 40*(8), 744–748.

Jongejan, W., Verhoeven, L., & Siegel, L. S. (2007). Predictors of reading and spelling abilities in first- and second-language learners. *Journal of Educational Psychology, 99*(4), 835–851. doi:10.1037/0022-0663.99.4.835

Karabenick, S., & Knapp, J. (1991). Relationship of academic help-seeking to the use of learning strategies and other instrumental achievement behavior in college students. *Journal of Educational Psychology, 83*(2), 221–230. doi:10.1037/0022-0663.83.2.221

Kieffer, M. J., & Lesaux, N. K. (2012). Direct and indirect roles of morphological awareness in the English reading comprehension of native Spanish, Filipino, Vietnamese, and English speakers. *Language Learning, 62*(4), 1170–1204. doi:10.1111/j.1467-9922.2012.00722.x

Kintsch, W. (1998). *Comprehension: A framework for cognition.* New York, NY: Cambridge University Press.

Kintsch, W., & Rawson, K. A. (2005). Comprehension. In M. J. Snowling & C. Hulme (Eds.), *The science of reading: A handbook* (pp. 209–226). Malden, MA: Blackwell.

Kirby, J. R., Parrila, R. K., & Pfeiffer, S. L. (2003). Naming speed and phonological awareness as predictors of reading development. *Journal of Educational Psychology, 95*(3), 453–464. doi:10.1037/0022-0663.95.3.453

Kissau, S. (2006). Gender differences in second language motivation: An investigation of micro- and macro-level influences. *Canadian Journal of Applied Linguistics, 9*(1), 73–96.

Kluger, A. N., & DeNisi, A. (1996). The effects of feedback interventions on performance: A historical review, a meta-analysis, and a preliminary feedback intervention theory. *Psychological Bulletin, 119*(2), 254–284. doi:10.1037/0033-2909.119.2.254

Kluger, A. N., & DeNisi, A. (1998). Feedback interventions: Towards the understanding of a double-edge sword. *Current Directions in Psychological Science, 7*(3), 67–72.

Koda, K. (1989). The effects of transferred vocabulary knowledge on the development of L2 reading proficiency. *Foreign Language Annals, 22*(6), 529–540. doi:10.1111/j.1944-9720.1989.tb02780.x

Koda, K.(2005). *Insights into second language reading.* Cambridge: Cambridge University Press.

Koda, K. (2008). Impacts of prior literacy experience on second language learning to read. In K. Koda & A. M. Zehler (Eds.), *Learning to read across languages: Cross-linguistic relationships in first- and second language literacy development* (pp. 68–96). New York: Routledge.

Kormos, J., & Csizér, K. (2008). Age-related differences in the motivation of learning English as a foreign language: Attitudes, selves and motivated learning behavior. *Language Learning, 58*(2), 327–355. doi:10.1111/j.1467-9922.2008.00443.x

Kormos, J., Kiddle, T., & Csizér, K. (2011). Systems of goals, attitudes, and self-related beliefs in second-language learning motivation. *Applied Linguistics, 32*(5), 495–516. doi:10.1093/applin/amr019

Kremmel, B. (2012). *Explaining variance in reading test performance through linguistic knowledge: The relative significance of vocabulary, syntactic and phraseological knowledge in predicting second language reading comprehension* (Unpublished master's thesis). Lancaster University, UK.

Krosnick, J., Holbrook, A., Berent, M., Carson, R., Hanemann, W. M., Kopp, . . . Conaway, M. (2002). The impact of "no opinion" response options on data quality: Non-attitude reduction or an invitation to satisfice? *Public Opinion Quarterly, 66*(3), 371–403. doi:10.1086/341394

Kulhavy, R. W. (1977). Feedback in written instruction. *Review of Educational Research, 47*(2), 211–232. doi:10.3102/00346543047002211

Kulhavy, R. W., & Stock, W. A. (1989). Feedback in written instruction: The place of response certitude. *Educational Psychology Review, 1*(4), 279–308. doi:10.1007/BF01320096

Kulhavy, R. W., White, M., Topp, B., Chan, A., & Adams, J. (1985). Feedback complexity and corrective efficiency. *Contemporary Educational Psychology, 10*(3), 285–291.

Kunnan, A., & Jang, E. (2009). Diagnostic feedback in language testing. In M. Long & C. Doughty (Eds.), *The handbook of language teaching* (pp. 610–625). Oxford, UK: Blackwell.

Kuo, L.-J., & Anderson, R. C. (2006). Morphological awareness and learning to read. A cross-language perspective. *Educational Psychologist, 41*(3), 161–180. doi:10.1207/s15326985ep4103_3

Kuo, L.-J., & Anderson R.C. (2008). Conceptual and methodological issues in comparing metalinguistic awareness across languages. In K. Koda & A.M. Zehler (Eds.), *Learning to read across languages: Cross-linguistic relationships in first- and second language literacy development* (pp. 39–67). New York, NY: Routledge.

Kupari, P., Sulkunen, S., Vettenranta, J., & Nissinen, K. (2012). *Enemmän iloa oppimiseen. Neljännen luokan oppilaiden lukutaito sekä matematiikan ja luonnontieteiden osaaminen. Kansainväliset PIRLS- ja TIMSS-tutkimukset Suomessa* [More joy in learning. Fourth graders' skills in reading, mathematics and natural sciences. International PIRLS- and TIMSS-studies in Finland]. Jyväskylä: Koulutuksen tutkimuslaitos.

Kyle, F., Kujala, J., Richardson, U., Lyytinen, H., & Goswami, U. (2013). Assessing the effectiveness of two theoretically motivated computer-assisted reading interventions in the United Kingdom: GG Rime and GG Phoneme. *Reading Research Quarterly, 48*(1), 61–76. doi:10.1002/rrq.038

Laine, E., & Pihko, M.-L. (1991). *Kieliminä ja sen mittaaminen* [Language identity and its measurement]. Kasvatustieteiden tutkimuslaitoksen julkaisusarja A. Tutkimuksia 47. Jyväskylä: Kasvatustieteiden tutkimuslaitos.

Lantolf, J., & Poehner, M. (2004). Dynamic assessment of L2 development: Bringing the past into the future. *Journal of Applied Linguistics, 1*(2), 49–72. doi:10.1558/japl.1.1.49.55872

Larsen-Freeman, D. (1991). Teaching grammar. *Teaching English as a Second or Foreign Language, 2,* 279–295.

Lau, I. C., Yeung, A., S., Jin, P., & Low, R. (1999). Toward a hierarchical, multidimensional English self-concept. *Journal of Educational Psychology, 91*(4), 747–755.

Lee, Y-W., & Sawaki, Y. (2009a). Application of three cognitive diagnosis models to ESL reading and listening assessments. *Language Assessment Quarterly, 6*(3):239–263. doi:10.1080/15434300903079562

Lee, Y-W., & Sawaki, Y. (2009b). Cognitive diagnosis approaches to language assessment. An overview. *Language Assessment Quarterly, 6*(3), 172–189. doi:10.1080/15434300902985108

Leong, C., Ho, M., Chang, J., & Hau, K. (2013). Differential importance of language components in determining secondary school students' Chinese reading literacy performance. *Language Testing, 30*(4), 419–439. doi:10.1177/0265532212469178

Leontjev, D. (submitted). *Exploring learners' and teachers' perspectives on automated adaptive corrective feedback.* Manuscript submitted for publication.

Leung, C., & Mohan, B. (2004). Teacher formative assessment and talk in classroom contexts: Assessment as discourse and assessment of discourse. *Language Testing, 21*(3), 335–359. doi:10.1191/0265532204lt287oa

Lezak, M. D., Howieson, D. B., Loring, D. W., Hannay, H. J., & Fischer, J. S. (2004). *Neuropsychological assessment* (4th ed.). Oxford: Oxford University Press.

Li, H. (2011). A cognitive diagnostic analysis of the MELAB reading test. *Spaan Fellow Working Papers in Second or Foreign Language Assessment* (Vol. 9, pp. 17–46). Ann Arbor: University of Michigan.

Li, S. (2010). The effectiveness of corrective feedback in SLA: A meta-analysis. *Language Learning, 60*(2), 309–365. doi:10.1111/j.1467-9922.2010.00561.x

Liao, Y-F. (2009). *A construct validation study of the GEPT reading and listening sections: Re-examining the models of L2 reading and listening abilities and their relations to lexico-grammatical knowledge.* (Unpublished doctoral dissertation). Teachers College, Columbia University, USA.

Lindeman, J. (2005). *Ala-asteen Lukutesti: Käyttäjän käsikirja* [Reading test for primary school, 3rd ed.]. Turku: Oppimistutkimuksen keskus.

Lunzer, E., Waite, M., & Dolan, T. (1979). Comprehension and comprehension tests. In E. Lunzer & K. Gardner (Eds.), *The effective use of reading* (pp. 37–71). London: Heinemann Educational.

Lupker, S. J. (2005). Visual word recognition: Theories and findings. In M. Snowling & C. Hulme (Eds.), *The science of reading: A handbook* (pp. 39–60). Malden, MA: Blackwell.

Luukka, M-R., Pöyhönen, S., Huhta, A., Taalas, P., Tarnanen, M., & Keränen, A. (2008). *Maailma muuttuu—mitä tekee koulu? Äidinkielen ja vieraiden kielten tekstikäytänteet koulussa ja vapaa-ajalla* [The world changes—how does the school respond? Mother tongue and foreign language literacy practices at school and in free-time.] University of Jyväskylä: Centre for Applied Language Studies.

Lyytinen, H., Erskine, J., Kujala, J., Ojanen, E., & Richardson, U. (2009). In search of a science-based application: A learning tool for reading acquisition. *Scandinavian Journal of Psychology, 50*(6), 668–675. doi:10.1111/j.1467-9450.2009.00791.x

Lyytinen, H., Leinonen, S., Nikula, M., & Leiwo, M. (1995). In search of the core features of dyslexia: Observations concerning dyslexia in the highly orthographically regular

Finnish language. In V. W. Berninger (Ed.), *The varieties of orthographic knowledge II: Relationship to phonology, reading, and writing* (pp. 177–204). Dordrecht, The Netherlands: Kluwer Academic Publishers.

Lyster, R., & Ranta, L. (1997). Corrective feedback and learner uptake: Negotiation of form in communicative classrooms. *Studies in Second Language Acquisition, 19*(1), 37–66.

Lyster, R., Saito, K., & Sato, M. (2013). Oral corrective feedback in second language classrooms. *Language Teaching, 46*(01), 1–40. doi:10.1017/S0261444812000365

Macaro, E. (2006). Strategies for language learning and language use: Revising the theoretical framework. *The Modern Language Journal, 90*(3), 320–337. doi:10.1111/j.1540-4781.2006.00425.x

Malin, A., Sulkunen, S., & Laine, K. (2013). *PIAAC 2012. Kansainvälisen aikuistutkimuksen ensituloksia* [PIAAC 2012. First results from the international adult survey]. Opetus- ja kulttuuriministeriön julkaisuja 2013:19. Opetus- ja kulttuuriministeriö.

Manning, W. H. (1987). *Development of cloze-elide tests of English as a second language* (TOEFL Research Report 23). Princeton, NJ: Educational Testing Service.

Marsh, H. W. (1990). The structure of academic self-concept: The Marsh/Shavelson model. *Journal of Educational Psychology, 82*(4), 623–626. doi:10.1037/0022-0663.82.4.623

Martin, D., & Miller, C. (2003). *Speech and language difficulties in the classroom.* Abingdon, UK: David Fulton.

Martinez, R. (2011). *The development of a corpus-informed list of formulaic sequences for language pedagogy* (Unpublished doctoral dissertation). University of Nottingham, UK. Retrieved December 31, 2013, from http://etheses.nottingham.ac.uk/2963/1/555398.pdf

Martinez, R., & Schmitt, N. (2012). A phrasal expressions list. *Applied Linguistics, 33*(3), 299–320. doi:10.1093/applin/ams010

McCray, G. (2014). *Statistical modelling of cognitive processing in reading comprehension in the context of language testing* (Unpublished doctoral dissertation). Lancaster University, UK.

Meara, P., & Buxton, B. (1987). An alternative to multiple-choice vocabulary tests. *Language Testing, 4*(2), 142–151. London: Macmillan. doi:10.1177/026553228700400202

MELAB (Michigan English Language Assessment Battery). Retrieved December 31, 2013, from www.cambridgemichigan.org/melab

Milner, B. (1971). Interhemispheric differences in the localization of psychological processes in man. *British Medical Bulletin, 27*(3), 272–277.

Montrul, S. (2008). *Incomplete acquisition in bilingualism: Re-examining the age factor.* Amsterdam, The Netherlands: John Benjamins.

Montrul, S. (2012). Is the heritage language like a second language? In L. Roberts, C. Lindqvist, C. Bardel & N. Abrahamsson (Eds.), *EUROSLA Yearbook* (Vol. 12, pp. 1–29). Amsterdam, The Netherlands: John Benjamins. doi:10.1075/eurosla.12.03mon

Mory, E. (1996). Feedback research. In D. H. Jonassen (Ed.), *Handbook of research for educational communications and technology* (pp. 919–956). New York: Simon & Schuster Macmillan.

Mory, E. (2004). Feedback research revisited. In D. H. Jonassen (Ed.), *Handbook of research on educational communications and technology* (2nd ed., pp. 745–784). Mahwah, NJ: Erlbaum.

Moussavi, S. A. (2002). *An encyclopedic dictionary of language testing* (3rd ed.). Taipei: Tung Hua Book Company.

Mullis, I., Martin, M., Foy, P., & Drucker, K. (2012). *PIRLS 2011 International Results in Reading.* Amsterdam, The Netherlands: TIMSS & PIRLS International Study Center & IEA. Retrieved December 31, 2013, from http://timssandpirls.bc.edu/pirls2011/international-results-pirls.html

Munby, J. (1978). *Communicative syllabus design*. Cambridge: Cambridge University Press.

Murphey, T. (2010). Creating languaging agencing. *The Language Teacher, 34*(4) 8–11. Retrieved December 31, 2013, from http://jalt-publications.org/files/pdf/the_language_teacher/04_2010tlt.pdf

MY access. Retrieved December 31, 2013, from www.vantagelearning.com/products/my-access-school-edition/

Nation, I.S.P. (2001). *Learning vocabulary in another language*. Cambridge: Cambridge University Press.

National Board of Education. (2004). *National core curriculum for basic education 2004*. Helsinki: Author. Retrieved December 31, 2013, from www.oph.fi/english/curricula_and_qualifications/basic_education

Nelson, J., Perfetti, C., Liben, D., & Liben, M. (2011). *Measures of text difficulty: Testing their predictive value for grade levels and student performance. Technical report to the Gates Foundation.* Retrieved July 15, 2014, from www.ccsso.org/Documents/2012/Measures%20ofText%20Difficulty_final.2012.pdf

Netten, A., Droop, M., & Verhoeven L. (2011). Predictors of reading literacy for first and second language learners. *Reading and Writing, 24*(4), 413–425. doi:10.1007/s11145-010-9234-2

Nieminen, L., Huhta, A., Ullakonoja, R., Haapakangas, E.-L., & Alderson J. C. (2012, March). *Can language learners' background predict reading in SFL?* Paper presented at GURT 2012 conference, Washington, DC, USA.

Nitko, A. (1993). Designing tests that are integrated with instruction. In R. Linn (Ed.), *Educational measurement* (pp. 447–474). Phoenix, AZ: Oryx Press.

Noels, K.A. (2001). Learning Spanish as a second language: Learners' orientations and perceptions of their teachers' communication style. *Language Learning, 51*(1), 107–144.

OECD. (2009). *PISA 2009 framework: Key competencies in reading, mathematics and science*. Paris: Author.

OECD. (2010). *PISA 2009 results: What students know and can do: Student performance in reading, mathematics and science* (Vol. 1). Paris: Author.

OECD. (2013). *OECD skills outlook 2013: First results from the Survey of Adult Skills*. Paris: Author.

OOPT (Oxford On-line Placement Test). Retrieved October 13, 2011, from http://fds.oup.com/www.oup.com/elt/oet/ift/oopt_measure.pdf

Oxford, R.L. (2011). *Teaching and researching language learning strategies*. London: Pearson.

Paris, S.P., & Hamilton, E.E. (2009). The development of children's reading comprehension. In S.E. Israel & G.G. Duffy (Eds.), *Handbook of research in reading comprehension* (pp. 32–53). New York, NY: Routledge.

Pellegrino, J. W., Chudowsky, N., & Glaser, R. (2001). *Knowing what students know: The science and design of educational assessment*. Washington, DC: National Academies Press.

Perfetti, C.A., & Dunlap, S. (2008). Learning to read: General principles and writing system variations. In K. Koda & A.M. Zehler (Eds.), *Learning to read across languages: Cross-linguistic relationships in first- and second-language literacy development* (pp. 13–38). New York, NY: Routledge.

Perfetti, C.A., Landi, N., & Oakhill, J. (2005). Acquisition of reading comprehension skills. In M. Snowling & C. Hulme (Eds.), *The science of reading: A handbook* (pp. 227–247). Malden, MA: Blackwell.

Pigada, M., & Schmitt, N. (2006). Vocabulary acquisition from extensive reading: A case study. *Reading in a Foreign Language, 18*(1), 1–28. Retrieved December 31, 2013, from http://nflrc.hawaii.edu/rfl/April2006/pigada/pigada.pdf

Pijl, S. J. (1992). Practices in monitoring student progress. *International Review of Education, 38*(2), 117–131. doi:10.1007/BF01098509

Poehner, M. E. (2009). Group dynamic assessment: Mediation for the L2 classroom. *TESOL Quarterly, 43*(3), 471–491. doi:10.1002/j.1545-7249.2009.tb00245

Poehner, M. E., & Lantolf, J. (2005). Dynamic assessment in the language classroom. *Language Teaching Research, 9*(3), 233–265. doi:10.1191/1362168805lr166oa

Poehner, M. E., & Lantolf, J. P. (2013). Bringing the ZPD into the equation: Capturing L2 development during Computerized Dynamic Assessment (C-DA). *Language Teaching Research, 17*(3), 323–342.

Purpura, J. E. (1997). An analysis of the relationships between test takers' cognitive and metacognitive strategy use and second language test performance. *Language Learning, 47*(3), 289–325.

Purpura, J. E. (1998). Investigating the effects of strategy use and second language test performance with high- and low-ability test takers: A structural equation modelling approach. *Language Testing, 15*(3), 333–379. doi:10.1177/026553229801500303

Purpura, J. E. (2004a). *Assessing grammar.* Cambridge: Cambridge University Press.

Purpura, J. E. (2004b). Validating questionnaires to examine personal factors in L2 test performance. In M. Milanovich & C. Weir (Eds.), *European language testing in a global context: Proceedings of the Association of Language Testers of Europe (ALTE) conference of Barcelona* (pp. 93–115). Cambridge: Cambridge University Press.

Purpura, J. E. (2012). Assessment of grammar. In C. Chapelle (Ed.), *The encyclopedia of applied linguistics.* New York, NY: John Wiley and Sons.

Purpura, J. E. (2014a). Assessing grammar. In A. J. Kunnan, (Ed.), *The companion to language assessment.* Boston, MA: John Wiley & Sons.

Purpura, J. E. (2014b). Cognition and language assessment. In A. J. Kunnan (Ed.), *The companion to language assessment.* Boston, MA: John Wiley & Sons.

Purpura, J. E. (2014c). Language learner strategies and styles. In M. Celce-Murcia, D. Brinton, & A. Snow (Eds.), *Teaching English as a second or foreign language* (4th ed.). Boston, MA: Heinle Cengage Learning.

Qian, D. (2002). Investigating the relationship between vocabulary knowledge and academic reading performance: An assessment perspective. *Language Learning, 52*(3), 513–536. doi:10.1111/1467-9922.00193

Ramirez, G., Chen, X., Geva, E., & Kiefer, H. (2010). Morphological awareness in Spanish-speaking English language learners: Within and cross-language effects on word reading. *Reading and Writing, 23*(3/4), 337–358. doi:10.1007/s11145-009-9203-9

Rasinski, T. V. (2003). *The fluent reader: Oral reading strategies for building word recognition, fluency and comprehension.* New York, NY: Scholastic Professional Books.

Rea-Dickins, P. (1991). What makes a grammar test communicative? In J. C. Alderson & B. North (Eds.), *Language testing in the 1990s: The communicative legacy* (pp. 112–131). New York, NY: HarperCollins.

Rea-Dickins, P. (2004). Understanding teachers as agents of assessment. *Language Testing, 21*(3), 249–258. doi:10.1191/0265532204lt283ed

Rea-Dickins, P. (2008). Classroom-based language assessment. In E. Shohamy & N. H. Hornberger (Eds.), *Encyclopedia of language and education* (2nd ed., Vol. 7: Language testing and assessment, pp. 257–271). Heidelberg, Germany: Springer.

Rea-Dickins, P., & Gardner, S. (2000). Snares and silver bullets: Disentangling the construct of formative assessment. *Language Testing, 17*(2), 215–243. doi:10.1177/ 026553220001700206

Read, J. (2000). *Assessing vocabulary.* Cambridge: Cambridge University Press.

Reid, G. (2007). *Motivating learners in the classroom: Ideas and strategies.* London: Paul Chapman.

Rigg, P. (1977). The miscue ESL project. In H. D. Brown, C. A. Yorio, & R. H. Crymes (Eds.), *Teaching and learning ESL: Trends in research and practice: On TESOL '77* (pp. 106–118). Washington, DC: TESOL.

Robinson, P. (2005). Aptitude and second language acquisition. *Annual Review of Applied Linguistics, 25,* 45–73. doi:10.1017/S0267190505000036

Roth, F. P. (2004). Word recognition assessment frameworks. In C. A. Stone, E. R. Silliman, B. J, Ehren & K. Apel (Eds.), *Handbook of language and literacy: Development and disorders* (pp. 461–480). New York, NY: Guilford Press.

Römer, U. (2009). The inseparability of lexis and grammar: Corpus linguistic perspectives. *Annual Review of Cognitive Linguistics, 7,* 141–163. doi:10.1075/arcl.7.06rom

Ryan, S. (2008). *The ideal L2 selves of Japanese learners of English* (Doctoral dissertation). Nottingham University. Retrieved December 31, 2013, from http://etheses.nottingham. ac.uk/550/1/ryan-2008.pdf

Sadler, R. (1989). Formative assessment and the design of instructional systems. *Instructional Science, 18,* 119–144.

Sawaki, Y., Kim, H.-J., & Gentile, G. (2009). Q-matrix construction: Defining the link between constructs and test items in large-scale reading and listening comprehension assessments. *Language Assessment Quarterly, 6*(3), 190–209. doi:10.1080/15434300902801917

Schellings, G., van Hout-Wolters, B., Veenman, M., & Meijer, J. (2013). Assessing metacognitive activities: The in-depth comparison of a task-specific questionnaire with think-aloud protocols. *European Journal of Psychology of Education, 28*(3), 963–990.

Schiff, R., & Califf, S. (2007). Role of phonological and morphological awareness in L2 oral word reading. *Language Learning, 57*(2), 271–298. doi:10.1111/j.1467-9922.2007.00409.x

Schmitt, N., Jiang, X., & Grabe, W. (2011). The percentage of words known in a text and reading comprehension. *The Modern Language Journal, 95*(1), 26–43. doi:10.1111/j.1540-4781.2011.01146.x

Schmitt, N., Schmitt, D., & Clapham, C. (2001). Developing and exploring the behaviour of two new versions of the Vocabulary Levels Test. *Language Testing, 18*(1), 55–88. doi:10.1177/026553220101800103

Schonell, F. J., & Goodacre, E. (1971). *Psychology and teaching of reading* (5th ed.). London: Oliver & Boyd.

Schoonen, R., Hulstijn, J., & Bossers, B. (1998). Metacognitive and language-specific knowledge in native and foreign language reading comprehension: An empirical study among Dutch students in grades 6, 8 and 10. *Language Learning, 48*(1), 71–106. doi:10.1111/1467-9922.00033

Segalowitz, N. (2000). Automaticity and attentional skill in fluent performance. In H. Riggenbach (Ed.), *Perspectives on fluency* (pp. 200–210). Ann Arbor: University of Michigan Press.

Seymour, P. H. K., Aro, M., & Erskine, J. M. (2003). Foundation literacy acquisition in European orthographies. *British Journal of Psychology, 94*(2), 143–174.

Shiotsu, T. (2010). *Components of L2 reading: Linguistic and processing factors in the reading test performances of Japanese EFL learners.* Cambridge: Cambridge University Press.

Shiotsu, T., & Weir, C. J. (2007). The relative significance of syntactic knowledge and vocabulary breadth in the prediction of reading comprehension test performance. *Language Testing, 24*(1), 99–128. doi:10.1177/0265532207071513

Shohamy, E. (1992). Beyond proficiency testing: A diagnostic feedback testing model for assessing foreign language learning. *The Modern Language Journal, 76*(4), 513–521. doi:10.1111/j.1540-4781.1992.tb05402.x

Sinclair, J. (2004). *Trust the text: Language, corpus and discourse.* London: Routledge.

Sirin, S. (2005). Socioeconomic status and academic achievement: A meta-analytic review of research. *Review of Educational Research, 75*(3), 417–453. doi:10.3102/00346543075003417

Skehan, P. (1991). Individual differences in second language learning. *Studies in Second Language Acquisition, 13*(2), 275–298. doi:10.1017/S0272263100009979

Sparks, R. L., Paton, J., Ganschow, L., Humbach, N., & Javorsky, J. (2008). Early first-language reading and spelling skills predict later second-language reading and spelling skills. *Journal of Educational Psychology, 100*(1), 162–174. doi:10.1037/0022-0663.100.1.162

Spolsky, B. (1992). The gentle art of diagnostic testing revisited. In E. Shohamy & A. R. Walton (Eds.), *Language assessment for feedback: Testing and other strategies* (pp. 29–41). Dubuque, IA: Kendall/Hunt.

Stanovich, K. E. (1988). Explaining the differences between the dyslexic and the garden-variety poor reader: The phonological-core variable-difference model. *Journal of Learning Disabilities, 21*(10), 590–604. doi:10.1177/002221948802101003

Steffensen, M. S., Joag-Dev, C., & Anderson, R. C. (1979). A cross-cultural perspective on reading comprehension. *Reading Research Quarterly, 15*(1), 10–29. Retrieved July 15, 2014, from www.jstor.org/stable/747429

Sternberg, R. J. (1987). Most vocabulary is learned from context. In M. McKeown & M. Curtis (Eds.), *The nature of vocabulary acquisition* (pp. 89–103). Hillsdale, NJ: Erlbaum.

Sternberg, R. J., & Grigorenko, E. L. (2002). *Dynamic testing: The nature and measurement of learning potential.* Cambridge: Cambridge University Press.

Sulkunen, S., Välijärvi, J., Arffman, I., Harju-Luukkainen, H., Kupari, P., Nissinen, K., Puhakka, E., & Reinikainen, P. (2010). *PISA09. Ensituloksia* [PISA09. First results]. Opetus- ja kulttuuriministeriön julkaisuja 2010: 21. Helsinki: Opetus- ja kulttuuriministeriö.

Sundre, D., & Moore, D. (2002). The Student Opinion Scale: A measure of examinee motivation. *Assessment Update, 14*(1), 8–9. Retrieved December 31, 2013, from http://onlinelibrary.wiley.com/doi/10.1002/au.141/pdf

Taguchi, T., Magid, M., & Papi, M. (2009). The L2 motivational self system among Japanese, Chinese and Iranian learners of English: A comparative study. In Z. Dörnyei & E. Ushioda (Eds.), *Motivation, language identity and the L2 self* (pp. 66–97). Bristol, England: Multilingual Matters.

Tang, J., & Harrison, C. (2011). Investigating university tutor perceptions of assessment feedback: Three types of tutor beliefs. *Assessment & Evaluation in Higher Education, 36*(5), 583–604. doi:10.1080/02602931003632340

Tarnanen, M., & Huhta, A. (2011). Foreign language assessment and feedback practices in Finland. In D. Tsagari & I. Csépes (Eds.) *Classroom-based language assessment* (pp. 129–146). Frankfurt am Main: Peter Lang.

Tatsuoka, K. K. (1983). Rule space: An approach for dealing with misconceptions based on item response theory. *Journal of Educational Measurement, 20*(4), 345–354. doi:10.1111/j.1745-3984.1983.tb00212.x

Tatsuoka, K. K. (1990). Toward an integration of item-response theory and cognitive error diagnosis. In N. Fredericksen, R. Glaser, A. Lesgold, & M. G. Shafto (Eds.), *Diagnostic monitoring of skill and knowledge acquisition* (pp. 453–388). Hillsdale, NJ: Erlbaum.

Thompson, T. (1998). Metamemory accuracy: Effects of feedback and the stability of individual differences. *American Journal of Psychology, 111*(1), 33–42. Retrieved July 15, 2014, from www.jstor.org/stable/1423535

Toe-by-toe website. Retrieved December 31, 2013, from www.toe-by-toe.co.uk/

TOEFL iBT (Test of English as a Foreign Language Internet-based Test). Retrieved December 31, 2013, from www.ets.org/toefl/ibt/about

TORCH. (2003). *Test of Reading Comprehension* (2nd ed.). Melbourne: Australian Council for Educational Research (ACER) Press.

Tsang, H. K. (2013). *Student motivation on a diagnostic and tracking English language test in Hong Kong* (Doctoral dissertation). Institute of Education, University of London.

Tseng, W., Dörnyei, Z., & Schmitt, N. (2006). A new approach to assessing strategic learning: The case of self-regulation in vocabulary acquisition. *Applied Linguistics, 27*(1), 78–102. doi:10.1093/applin/ami046

Ullakonoja, R., Nieminen, L. & Huhta, A. (2013). Suomen kielen oppimismotivaatio, luetunymmärtäminen ja kirjoitustaito venäjää kotikielenään puhuvilla peruskoululaisilla [Motivation to learn Finnish, reading comprehension and writing ability among comprehensive school students with Russian as the home language]. *Kasvatus, 44*(5), 508–521.

Urmston, A. (2012, March 24–27). *Diagnostic testing of ESL reading skills: Relating test-taking strategies to reading abilities.* Presentation at the American Association of Applied Linguistics conference, Chicago, IL.

Urmston, A., Raquel, M., & Tsang, C. (2013). Diagnostic testing of Hong Kong tertiary students' English language proficiency: The development and validation of DELTA. *Hong Kong Journal of Applied Linguistics, 14*(2), 60–82.

Urquhart, A. H., & Weir, C. J. (1998). *Reading in a second language: Process, product and practice.* London: Longman.

Ushioda, E. (2011). Motivating learners to speak as themselves. In G. Murray, G. Xuesong, & T. Lamb (Eds.), *Identity, motivation and autonomy in language learning* (pp. 11–24). Bristol, England: Multilingual Matters.

van Compernolle, R., & Kinginger, C. (2013). Promoting metapragmatic development through assessment in the Zone of Proximal Development. *Language Teaching Research, 17*(3), 282–302. doi:10.1177/1362168813482917

Van Gelderen, A., Schoonen, R., de Glopper, K., Hulstijn, J., Simis, A., Snellings, P., & Stevenson, M. (2004). Linguistic knowledge, processing speed and metacognitive knowledge in first and second language reading comprehension: A componential analysis. *Journal of Educational Psychology, 96*(1), 19–30. doi:10.1037/0022-0663.96.1.19

Van Gelderen, A., Schoonen, R., de Glopper, K., Hulstijn, J., Snellings, P., Simis, A., & Stevenson, M. (2003). Roles of linguistic knowledge, metacognitive knowledge and processing speed in L3, L2 and L1 reading comprehension: A structural equation modeling approach. *International Journal of Bilingualism, 7*(7), 7–25. doi:10.1177/136 70069030070010201

Vellutino, F. R., Fletcher, J. M., Snowling, M. J., & Scanlon, D. M. (2004). Specific reading disability (dyslexia): What have we learned in the past four decades? *Journal of Child Psychology and Psychiatry, 45*(1), pp. 2–40. doi:10.1046/j.0021-9630.2003.00305.x

Vygotsky, L. (1978). *Mind in society: The development of higher psychological processes.* Cambridge, MA: Harvard University Press.

Walter, C. (2004). Transfer in reading comprehension skills to L2 is linked to mental representation of text and to L2 working memory. *Applied Linguistics, 25*(3), 315–339. doi:10.1093/applin/25.3.315

Wang, M., Cheng, C., & Chen, S. (2006). Contribution of morphological awareness to Chinese-English biliteracy acquisition. *Journal of Educational Psychology, 98*(3), 542–553. doi:10.1037/0022-0663.98.3.542

Weaver, C. (2002). *Reading process and practice: From socio-psycholinguistics to whole language* (3rd ed.). Portsmouth, NH: Heinemann.

Wechsler, D. (1987). *Manual for the Wechsler Memory Scale-Revised*. San Antonio, TX: The Psychological Corporation.

Wechsler D. (1997). *Wechsler Memory Scale–third edition manual*. San Antonio, TX: The Psychological Corporation.

Wechsler, D. A. (1945). Standardized memory scale for clinical use. *Journal of Psychology*, *19*, pp. 57–95.

Wilkins, D. (1972). *Linguistics in language teaching*. London: Edward Arnold.

Wolf, M. (1986). Rapid alternating stimulus (R.A.S.) naming: A longitudinal study in average and impaired readers. *Brain and Language*, *27*(2), 360–379.

Wolf, M., & Bowers, P. G. (1999). The double-deficit hypothesis for the developmental dyslexias. *Journal of Educational Psychology*, *91*(3), 415–438.

Wong, R., & Raquel, M. (2013, May). *Consequences of diagnostic assessment on teaching and learning*. Paper presented at the EALTA conference, Istanbul.

Woodcock, R. W., & Johnson, M. B. (1989). *Woodcock-Johnson Psycho-Educational Battery— Revised*. Itasca, IL: Riverside.

WHO (World Health Organization). (1992). *The ICD-10 classification of mental and behavioural disorders*. Geneva: Author. Retrieved December 31, 2013, from www.who.int/classifications/icd/en/bluebook.pdf.

WHO (World Health Organization). (2004). *WHO guide to mental and neurological health in primary care* (2nd ed.). Melbourne: The Royal Society of Medicine Press

WriteToLearn. Retrieved December 31, 2013, from www.writetolearn.net/

Yamashita, J. (1999). *Reading in a first and a foreign language: A study of reading comprehension in Japanese (the L1) and English (the L2)* (Unpublished doctoral dissertation). Lancaster University, UK.

Yang, R. (2003). *Investigating how test-takers use the DIALANG feedback* (Unpublished master's thesis). Lancaster University, UK.

Yashima, T. (2009). International posture and the ideal L2 self in the Japanese EFL context. In Z. Dörnyei & E. Ushioda, (Eds.), *Motivation, language identity and the L2 self* (pp. 144–163). Bristol, England: Multilingual Matters.

Ziegler, J. C., & Goswami, U. (2005). Reading acquisition, developmental dyslexia, and skilled reading across languages: A psycholinguistic grain size theory. *Psychological Bulletin*, *131*(1), 3–29. doi:10.1037/0033-2909.131.1.3

Zimmerman, B. J. (1989). Models of self-regulated learning and academic achievement. In B. J. Zimmerman & D. H. Schunk (Eds.), *Self-regulated learning and academic achievement: Theory, research, and practice* (pp. 1–25). New York, NY: Springer-Verlag.

INDEX